"This is a brilliant treatise on the current challenge[s facing university-]based initial teacher education. A thoughtful and w[ise analysis,] problematizing what is meant by quality in teacher e[ducation, teacher] knowledge, teacher educators and governance frames the cross-national research carried out by the author to illustrate each one of these challenges. The central question of what is involved in taking quality teacher education at scale is answered in the two chapters discussing the contexts of transformation through the architectures of practice and space. The last chapter on *Modelling ITE Practice* brings together the valuable lessons accumulated via this exciting and innovative research project. A clear message that emerges from this work is the importance of securing the sustainability of university-based teacher education for the common good. The book is a must for those interested in a thoughtful and critical analysis of how socioeconomic, cultural, and political contexts are shaping teacher education across different settings and how diverse institutions are managing to respond to these forces."

— *Maria Teresa Tatto*, Professor, Division of Educational Leadership and Innovation, Southwest Borderlands Professor of Comparative Education, Mary Lou Fulton Teachers College, Arizona State University

"This is a highly original and important study of large scale teacher education provision in five locations around the world. Drawing on her extensive fieldwork and on a wide range of literature, Clare Brooks brings the spatial perspective of a human geographer to explore a range of 'quality conundrums'. The book will stimulate critical debates in policy and practice in teacher education for many years to come."

— *Ian Menter*, Emeritus Professor of Teacher Education, Department of Education, University of Oxford. President of British Educational Research Association, 2013–2015

"Professor Brooks's background in geography shines through in this wonderfully nuanced account of the effects of global and local discourses on teacher education in five different countries. Based on rich in-depth case studies of five universities with large teacher education programmes, she skilfully explores how they navigate the 'quality conundrums' that both support and threaten the quality of teacher education in those (and other) locations. This is a must read for those working in the fields of teacher education and policy, along with all concerned about the relationship between teacher education quality *and* equity whilst facing intense reform and scrutiny internationally."

— *Martin Mills*, Professor of Education, Queensland University of Technology

INITIAL TEACHER EDUCATION AT SCALE

Debates about what constitutes quality in initial teacher education have resulted in a series of quality conundrums that have to be unravelled by teacher educators. Using the lens of scale and adopting a new approach to understanding quality, this book draws upon empirical research into five large-scale, high-quality university-based teacher education providers in Australia, Canada, England, New Zealand and the US. The resulting model of initial teacher education practice shows how ideological concepts and accountability structures around teacher education are in constant tension with operational realities. The book explores how successful large-scale providers have reconciled those tensions and conundrums to ensure their provision is consistently high quality. The accounts also present a robust defence for university-based teacher education.

The practice-based accounts of how tensions around quality and scale are being reconciled reveal the competing discourses around teacher professionalism, research and the role of the university in teacher education. The analysis presented promises to change the way we view high-quality teacher education across all providers and international contexts, not just those of large scale.

This book will be of great interest to teacher educators, policymakers and educational leaders.

Clare Brooks is Professor of Education and Pro-Director: Education at the UCL Institute of Education, United Kingdom.

INITIAL TEACHER EDUCATION AT SCALE

Quality Conundrums

Clare Brooks

LONDON AND NEW YORK

First published 2021
by Routledge
2 Park Square, Milton Park, Abingdon, Oxon OX14 4RN

and by Routledge
52 Vanderbilt Avenue, New York, NY 10017

Routledge is an imprint of the Taylor & Francis Group, an informa business

© 2021 Clare Brooks

The right of Clare Brooks to be identified as author of this work has been asserted by her in accordance with sections 77 and 78 of the Copyright, Designs and Patents Act 1988.

All rights reserved. No part of this book may be reprinted or reproduced or utilised in any form or by any electronic, mechanical, or other means, now known or hereafter invented, including photocopying and recording, or in any information storage or retrieval system, without permission in writing from the publishers.

Trademark notice: Product or corporate names may be trademarks or registered trademarks, and are used only for identification and explanation without intent to infringe.

British Library Cataloguing-in-Publication Data
A catalogue record for this book is available from the British Library

Library of Congress Cataloging-in-Publication Data
Names: Brooks, Clare, author.
Title: Initial teacher education at scale : quality conundrums / Clare Brooks.
Description: Abingdon, Oxon ; New York : Routledge, 2021. | Includes bibliographical references and index.
Identifiers: LCCN 2020047723 (print) | LCCN 2020047724 (ebook) | ISBN 9780367543020 (hardback) | ISBN 9780367543013 (paperback) | ISBN 9781003088608 (ebook)
Subjects: LCSH: Teachers—Training of. | Teachers colleges—Administration. | Educational leadership. | Teachers—Professional relationships.
Classification: LCC LB1707 .B78 2021 (print) | LCC LB1707 (ebook) | DDC 370.71/1—dc23
LC record available at https://lccn.loc.gov/2020047723
LC ebook record available at https://lccn.loc.gov/2020047724

ISBN: 978-0-367-54302-0 (hbk)
ISBN: 978-0-367-54301-3 (pbk)
ISBN: 978-1-003-08860-8 (ebk)

Typeset in Bembo
by codeMantra

CONTENTS

Acknowledgements   *ix*

1   Quality conundrums in initial teacher education   1

2   The practice quality conundrum   31

3   The research quality conundrum   60

4   The knowledge quality conundrum   85

5   The teacher educator quality conundrum   113

6   The governance quality conundrum   139

7   The contexts for transformation: practice architectures   161

8   The contexts for transformation through a spatial lens   183

9   Modelling ITE practice   201

Index   *213*

ACKNOWLEDGEMENTS

This research would not have been possible without the generosity and support of the many teacher educators who kindly agreed to take part and support me throughout. Particular thanks go to Fiona Ell, Simone White, Terry Bourke, Linda Eager, Maria Teresa Tatto, David Montemurro, Kathy Broad, Reuben Moore and colleagues at Teach First. A very special mention goes to my long-suffering colleagues at the UCL Institute of Education, particularly Piers Saunders and Carole Scott who endured my many questions and probing. I am also very grateful to all the teacher educators, partners and student teachers who agreed to talk to me during my visits and who were so generous with their time and honest in their opinions. I am also very grateful to those institutions for allowing me access to their teacher educators, their premises, students and partners, and their programmes. During the writing of this book, I also relied on the counsel and guidance of friends and colleagues: huge thanks to Jo McIntyre, Martin Mills, Trevor Mutton and Jane Perryman for their critique, feedback and support.

1

QUALITY CONUNDRUMS IN INITIAL TEACHER EDUCATION

During March 2020, after returning from a site visit to a university in Arizona to my London home, in the middle of the coronavirus pandemic, the country went into lockdown. Confined to my home, surrounded by swathes of data I had collected on my site visits, I reflected on the role of universities in teacher education before the pandemic struck and even more so after. In England, two-thirds through the academic year, student teachers were withdrawn from their placements. Teacher educators got together to consider what this meant for those student teachers, for their progress, qualification and future careers. How would this affect their studies, their learning and how could we support them and our partner schools? In times like this core values become important: what could we do that would be the best possible outcomes for all involved? Parts of the teacher education infrastructure, such as inspections and regulations around minimum periods of school experience, were rapidly disregarded. It felt, at the time, like universities with their specialist expertise were taking a lead. This was empowering, but it was also striking in how working in such an independent way felt unusual.

As a former Head of Initial Teacher Education (ITE), and having been involved in teacher education in a number of ways for 28 years, I have seen the recognition of the expertise of teacher educators change, particularly in the light of government policy changes, changes in schooling, and variations in how teachers are viewed and how their work is defined. In particular, the growing culture of compliance, accountability and governance has affected what teacher educators have been able to do. Commentators such as Connell (2009), Sachs (2015) and Mayer (2017) have criticised how accountability emphasises technical approaches to teaching. They advocate forms of professionalisation which elevate teachers beyond a narrow craft definition but as informed and autonomous professionals. Nevertheless, such accountability forces persist, and arguably it is becoming more and more difficult to counter, as many teacher educators take up the accountability mantra themselves: showing off their labels of achievement, adhering without question and adding additional internal checks to ensure compliance. Undergirding these trends are questions about quality: what does quality teacher education look like? How can it be achieved, monitored and recognised, and how can teacher educators be held accountable and to whom does their accountability lie? Who are the best teacher educators to make it happen?

The research, upon which this book is based, examined teacher education programmes in five different countries. Through exploring the university-based teacher education provision in each place, I have seen how the answers to these quality questions vary from place to place (as the chapters in this book will reveal). Common to all is a strong message that university involvement in ITE is crucial, but complex. It is particularly crucial when educational environments require teachers to do more than perform a set of routines or behaviours, but are looking for teachers who are able to act with integrity, autonomy and to make situational judgements; in these cases, teachers require preparation which is profoundly *educational*. This distinction elevates teacher education beyond the notion of teacher *training*, a term often used in the English policy context, and teacher *preparation*, a term common in the US. Both of these terms emphasise the technical and practical dimensions of teaching. Without doubt the development of practical skills is important for new teachers. However, training and preparation emphasise skill development at the exclusion of the understanding and judicious application of those skills. In that sense, they align with Biesta's critique of "learnification" (2010) – that it lacks a sense of the educational purpose. Teacher education that equips teachers with the range of knowledges they need to make good situational judgements is an educational and therefore moral enterprise.

This is not a new argument, and one that unsurprisingly is often made by teacher educators based in universities. It is not my intention to repeat that argument, but to augment it by demonstrating how the changing contexts of educating teachers today, internationally, makes this more and more important. The rise of accountability regimes in all aspects of the education sector, in the diversification of teacher education providers and the increase in education stakeholders (sometimes with commercial interests) means that it has never been more important for universities to take an *educational* stance in their engagement with teachers.

Undoubtedly, I have a self-interest in this view: I am a university-based teacher educator. The research upon which this book is based is exclusively focused on university-based teacher education. It may be the case that non-university-based teacher educators may be able to make similar claims, and I am certainly not seeking to downplay the crucial role that schools play in the education of teachers. The argument presented here is orientated specifically to what goes on in universities. Universities are special and unique places. Their specific status as a civic enterprise makes them a key site equipped to provide teacher *education*: an education which can stand up in the face of the challenges facing teaching today, particularly those that stem from neoliberal education policies around accountability, governance and performativity. This is not to say that universities are not without influence from neoliberal policies (indeed, this constitutes a theme throughout the book), but that other organisations without a commitment to academic freedom and civic responsibility are more susceptible to these forces. Universities have the capacity to provide a context for educational possibilities.

The professionalisation narrative

There has been a lot of interest recently in teacher education quality which originates from the argument that teachers are important because they are the single most influential variable in student's achievement. This point stems from the Organisation for Economic Co-operation and Development (OECD) pronouncement that "teachers matter" following their report on the determinants of student learning, which concluded that the largest variation in outcomes is attributable to social background and the students themselves, but the most important influence "potentially open to policy influence" is teaching, and especially "teacher quality" (OECD, 2005, p. 26). Connell (2009) highlights that it is significant that the OECD do not consider social factors to be within policy influence. But the idea that teachers are the most important factor has been widely taken up by commentators from across the political spectrum.

The focus on teacher education in this book deliberately does not adopt that argument. Teachers are undoubtedly important, because they make up a significant part of the educational infrastructure. But teachers are often not alone in deciding how they undertake their work. Teaching is subject to a range of influences and controls: inspection regimes, testing, reward structures and managerial interventions. Intentionally or not, these affect teachers' work. Saying that teachers are the most influential factor focuses the attention on discussions about improving education and educational disadvantage firmly onto teachers, making them the "subject of reform" (Ball, 2008). To focus the attention onto teachers ignores the role that the infrastructure, society and wider influences around teachers can play in creating the conditions in which they undertake their work.

The idea that quality teacher education will further professionalise teaching is related to a professionalisation narrative, which needs to be thoroughly questioned. Whitty (2008) highlights that to qualify as a profession, occupations usually require specialist theoretical knowledge, certification, a code of professional conduct orientated towards the "public good" and a powerful professional organisation. Whitty also notes that as teachers have never fully achieved this status, there are aspirations to professionalise teaching through what he calls the "professional project". However, occupational professionalisation does not occur just because of the introduction of professionalisation strategies: an emphasis on research, a focus on academic knowledge, contextualising practice within a theoretical frame or because qualification takes place in a university, overseen by a teacher educator who holds a doctorate. Professionalisation is part of a wider and dynamic set of influences and relationships: hence why, together with Wisby, Whitty refers to a fourfold typology of teacher professionalisms: tradition, managerialist, collaborative and democratic (2006). Where teacher professionalism falls within this typology is related to the context in which it occurs, the affordances and autonomy teachers are given, in the same way that teacher quality can also be enabled or constrained by the contexts in which it occurs.

The spatial importance of context

To understand how educational contexts vary, it is important to start by recognising the role that education plays in the production and reproduction of inequalities. Research in teacher education often refers to the importance of context, but rarely examines that context conceptually, often seeing context as an interactional or representational problem (Dourish, 2004). This is despite a growing body of work that recognises the importance of space and place in uneven development, and in particular in the production and reproduction of inequalities (Smith, 2010). Expressed simply, some places are more affluent than others, and so some places afford more opportunities than others. Geographers, such as David Harvey, have written extensively about the "geography of it all", showing how the flow of capital requires space, and how the arrangement of space is fundamental to flows of capital and by extension the equitable distribution of opportunity (2010). Education contributes to these flows through supporting access to social capital, cultural capital and intellectual capital.

But capital is not free-flowing: the movement of capital is controlled often by the elite in society who seek to affect how and where it flows in order to retain their advantage. The implication for education is that affluent populations have better schools, with better teachers and more funding, thereby students that go through this system (often the sons and daughters of the elite) are better prepared to take up roles as the elite and powerful when it is their turn. Less affluent populations have schools with less funding, teachers who are perceived as poorer quality and their students will end up being less prepared to take up similar powerful and influential roles. These patterns are borne out by empirical research: evidence from the US and the UK have highlighted how more disadvantaged communities tend to have less well-prepared teachers (Allen & Sims, 2018; Burgess, 2016; Hanushek & Rivkin, 2012), although the degree of preparation does not necessarily mean teachers are of a poorer quality.

It would seem logical then to conclude that the provision and availability of high-quality teachers are important in opening up educational opportunities. But teachers alone are unable to change the infrastructure which affects the flow of capital. Recognising the influence of such flows is central to understanding the accountability infrastructure around teaching and teacher education: in other words, the conditions that make up how teachers can do their "work". In order to understand teacher education, we need to understand the wider context within which teaching and teacher education operates.

Teachers are not solely responsible for "equalising" society or for counteracting the material, social and cultural deprivation experienced by some communities. The availability of high-quality teachers is just one factor in the production and reproduction of inequalities. However, recognising this broader context helps to highlight a range of factors that affect the availability of high-quality teacher education: these include locational factors (such as the local employment market) as well as policy changes which can influence the distribution of teacher education. For example, factors such as the inequitable (public) funding of teacher education in universities versus alternative programmes such as Teach First (part of the Teach for All movement) will affect the provision of teacher education in some places; accountability regimes can penalise large-scale providers with wide geographical reach (and universities tend to have a wider geographical reach than other providers), debates which privilege local or practical knowledge over that discussed on university programmes will all emphasise quality for some providers over others. These are more than contextual factors, but are spatially orientated factors, which can create a hostile climate for universities involved in teacher education, thereby disrupting their role in supporting a more equitable flow of capital.

Context is therefore incredibly important to understand teacher education. However, context should not just be seen as a container, within which teacher education sits, but as a series of significant and pervasive influences that can affect teacher education practice in a particular place. This is more than the accountability regimes alluded to above, but also includes other aspects of education more broadly: that which Kemmis and colleagues have called the Education Complex (2014). To fully understand teacher education, it is important to recognise the range of social, political, cultural and geographical factors which influence education, schools and all their interrelated components. In doing so, we need to ask what are our communities like? What needs do they have? What demands does this place on schooling? And what do teachers need in order to be effective in these contexts? In addition, there are questions specific to teacher education: what are the dominant ideas of being a good teacher? What debates are happening about education, qualifications and employability, and how do these influence what happens in our schools? And how are these influences affecting the experiences of individuals, the local community, regions, nations and global discourses? In other words, in order to understand teacher education, we also need to understand more than the context but the complex spatial factors occurring in the locations where it is taking place. It is this ambitious goal that this work seeks to undertake, to emphasise and highlight the spatially orientated factors which impede and support how teacher education is understood and how it is judged as being "high quality". Through examining the education and preparation of teachers within specific locations, it is possible to understand the barriers and constraints to providing high-quality teachers to all, and to highlight the spatially orientated factors that impede or encourage the flow of high-quality teachers.

Current trends affecting university-based initial teacher education

One could be forgiven for thinking that the odds are stacked against university-based teacher education, particularly in the light of its criticisms highlighted below from international commentators. These criticisms, particularly when made at a public and policy level, have an impact on funding and oversight arrangements, and skew merging "markets" of teacher education provision, privileging non-university-based providers.

The role of universities in ITE has never been uncontested. In most systems, ITE has been a fairly recent introduction to the university system, and as Labaree notes, it has never really sat comfortably within the academy (2006). Internationally, moving teacher education into universities from Teachers Colleges and Normal Schools was intended to professionalise teaching and raise its status. This promise was partly to do with aligning teacher education with educational research but has not yielded the promised results. This has been exacerbated in the US by critics who argue that university-based teacher education produces inadequate teachers; that it is disconnected from practice; and that it is overly theoretical (as outlined in the Holmes Group report, 1986). Whilst the debate cites evidence from newly qualified teachers who feel ill-prepared or concerns from parents and school principals, the criticism became public with the involvement of significant figures such as Arthur Levine (from Teachers College) and Arne Duncan (education advisor to President Obama). Their concerns, similar to those raised in the Holmes Group report which was critical of teacher education for the reasons cited above, have been staunchly defended by Zeichner (2017), and are widely regarded as politically motivated and subject to what he has described as the misquoting of evidence, echo chambers and knowledge ventriloquism. However, Zeichner acknowledges that there are wide variations in the quality of teacher education provision across universities, and Goldhaber (2018) acknowledges that there may be some empirical evidence to the criticisms raised. However, as Zeichner highlights, this is not an even playing field: non-university-based providers can gain access to private and public monies, such as those raised from venture philanthropy, which are not matched by public funding and which are not available to universities. Zeichner argues that the focus of the criticisms and the hostile funding environment privileges alternative providers across the US.

Although the situation is more advanced in the US, similar trends can be seen elsewhere. The 1998 Hillage Report noted similar concerns with university-based teacher education in England, which was also seen as being over-theorised, fragmented and unhelpful for teachers' professional practice. Traditionally, in England, the defence of university-based teacher education has been formulated around its proximity to research. However, the Carter Review in 2015 highlighted that even in research-intensive universities, researchers were not fully engaged in teacher education programmes. It is also true to note, as

Pring (2017) does, that the research that has had substantial impact on teaching (he uses the examples of the impact of social disadvantage, quantitative analysis and the uses of IQ tests) has often come from other faculties outside (teacher) education. In England, hostility towards university-based teacher education has taken a particular shape and form as the former Secretary of State for Education Michael Gove described such teacher educators as the Blob and the enemies of promise, contributing to what Furlong refers to (using a phrase from Ball, 1990) as the "discourse of derision" (Furlong, 2019). Successive education policies have deliberately sought to foreground school-led teacher education designed to destabilise and decentre universities from teacher education (Department for Education, 2010). However, again, internally there is a recognition that universities have been somewhat passive in their response, leaving some to call for a reinvigorated approach to teacher education (Ellis, Souto-Manning, & Turvey, 2018; Teacher Education Exchange, 2017). These concerns are echoed elsewhere. Sachs (2015), Ling (2017) and Connell (2009) have highlighted the same trends across Australia, and policy papers make reference to similar concerns in New Zealand.[1] Back in 2008, Grossman warned that if teacher educators failed to take these criticisms seriously, other organisations would seek to replace the universities' monopoly on the preparation of teachers. Such trends are symptomatic with marketisation and centralisation which Mayer has described as neoliberal education policies (2017). The language of neoliberalism ties up such approaches by using seemingly benign terms: marketisation, choice, deregulation and accountability. But these policies are not benign: they add to the hostile climate for universities who are often ill-prepared to respond.

The trends are international too, part of what Sahlberg referred to as the Global Education Reform Movement (GERM) (Sahlberg, 2010) and which results in a limited repertoire of policy interventions which have been widely adopted (Mayer, 2017). The policy interventions include the introduction and dominance of Teacher Standards, accreditation procedures for teacher education providers, and the provision of inspection regimes to monitor their compliance. These make up what Ball (2008) describes as technologies of performativity that lead to patterns of governance rather than government. For example, the deregulation of teacher education combined with a centralisation of accreditation opens up teacher education to new and alternative providers as long as the criteria for accreditation is met (as has been seen in several international contexts). Subsequently, globally there has been a growth of alternative providers such as those aligned with the Teach for All network and the new Graduate Schools Education (Cochran-Smith et al., 2020). These trends are in line with the "turn to practice" (Furlong, 2013) which has dramatically changed the landscape for teacher education. For example, despite the well-documented move to a school-led teacher education system in England (since the 2010 White Paper *The Importance of Teaching*), the government inspection agency Ofsted reports that four-fifths of "trainees" (the UK government's preferred term for new teachers) in 2018/2019 were trained through partnerships with a higher education institution (2018).

And yet, the power and influence of universities in driving teacher education has diminished substantially (McIntyre, Youens, & Stevenson, 2017). For example, some Russell Group universities have moved their teacher education provision away from the more research-intensive Faculty or Department of Education and changed the staffing structure to preclude academics in ITE from the responsibility to undertake research. Other university providers have teamed up with other local providers such as the Yorkshire First initiative led by Sheffield Hallam University: as a way of trying to even out regional pockets of over- and under-supply of teachers. Other providers have had to dramatically change or restructure their provision in the light of increased competition. The impact is that whilst universities are still involved in teacher education, the ways in which that involvement is situated have changed dramatically, and more importantly, the ability of universities to influence teacher education has reduced even more so.

At the same time, the influence and number of stakeholders who now have a vested interest in teacher education provision have increased, a situation that Ling, in relation to Australia, has described as one of supercomplexity (2017). Schools have been long-standing partners with universities in teacher education. Teacher education is now often overseen by various regulatory bodies, sometimes government departments for education at a state or national level. Teacher standards and accreditation processes may be "owned" by these bodies or certification councils, bodies or professional associations. These organisations have wide-ranging powers influencing the content, approach, assessment and formation of a teacher education programme. In addition, there is increasing complexity in accrediting who becomes a provider of teacher education, who condones and awards the qualification for individual teacher candidates, and who inspects and regulates the provision.

These complex webs of stakeholders make up policy technologies, to use Ball's term, which have made teacher education the "subject for reform", and so have destabilised the financial, intellectual and authoritative base of the university involved in teacher education. This is a particular issue for universities as they also have their own internal processes of programme validation, accreditation and governance. University-based providers have to ensure that their programmes meet the internal benchmarks of quality and quality assurance within the university governance structure, but also adhere to (often external) requirements. In Australia, there are national standards and state-based interpretations which operate alongside the university system of award assessment. In England, there is the Department for Education mandated content for teacher education (the Core Content Framework), statutory requirements around recruitment and programme parameters. The Teacher Standards, which have to be met in order for the award of Qualified Teacher Status, sit alongside a rigid and prescriptive inspection regime (through Ofsted). However, for university programmes, the award (such as the Post Graduate Certification of Education) belongs to the university. In practical terms, questions about who judges or assesses the teacher's progress in practical teaching can lead to questions of the ability of universities to control and oversee their academic awards as well as to take ownership of the consistency and rigour of assessment. This can put the university structures in tension with other accountability frameworks which, in the case of England, privilege partnership working and the shared ownership of judgements between schools and universities. As Moon comments, teacher education is unrivalled in political interference, arguing that "Ideas about academic freedom and university autonomy seem to stop at the door of the education faculty" (2016, p. 253).

All of these infrastructural and governance concerns are tied up with ideological and political pressures which promote particular views of teacher education and which permeate not just the public discourse about teacher education, but also the ways in which teacher education has been subjected to reform. Accountability regimes have now become a ubiquitous part of the teacher education landscape which underplay important values around democracy, equity and social justice, and focus on narrow outcome measures described as "attainment". In the light of these reforms, the role that universities play in teacher education is changing, and in order to understand teacher education, these influences, along with their resultant effects, need to be re-evaluated and reassessed. The focus of this book is this changing landscape, how it affects ITE, and how universities respond.

Different ways of understanding quality

With this increasingly hostile landscape in mind, asking the question of what high-quality teacher education looks like becomes critical, along with an examination of how that definition of high quality is changing. Unsurprisingly, this question has been asked and answered in a number of ways, by various groups, but with little consensus. This lack of consensus, I argue, is due to the different ways in which quality and its associated concepts of standards and quality assurance are understood by different stakeholders. This argument stems from Harvey's work (2007) in his exploration of quality within the higher education sector, where he distinguishes between quality, standards and quality assurance. Harvey argues that quality assurance mechanisms do not (in themselves) enhance the provision of education, but perform functions around accountability, control and compliance.

Quality assurance is a process of governance and compliance and so should not be confused with quality itself:

> It should be noted that the processes of quality assurance are quite separate from the concept of quality. Quality is to quality assurance what intelligence is to IQ tests. Quality, in higher education is, for example, about the nature of learning. Quality assurance is about convincing others about the adequacy of that processes of learning.
>
> *(Ibid., p. 5)*

This distinction is often absent in discussions about education and teacher education, where the focus on quality orientates around discussions of the most appropriate metrics and indicators used to judge quality rather than the learning itself (Bartell, Floden, & Richmond, 2018; Firestone & Donaldson, 2019; Gewirtz, Maguire, Neumann, & Towers, 2019; Skedsmo & Huber, 2019). In a similar vein, Harvey distinguishes between definitions of quality and that of standards (see Table 1.1). Standards (denoted forthwith as uncapitalised), as defined by Harvey, are distinct from the more specific Teacher Standards (capitalised) which are dominant in the field.

TABLE 1.1 Definitions of quality and standards

Quality	Definition
Exceptional	A traditional concept linked to the idea of "excellence", usually operationalised as exceptionally high standards of academic achievement. Quality is achieved if the standards are surpassed.
Perfection or consistency	Focuses on process and sets specifications that it aims to meet. Quality in this sense is summed up by the interrelated ideas of zero defects and getting things right first time.
Fitness for purpose	Judges quality in terms of the extent to which a product or service meets its stated purpose. The purpose may be customer-defined to meet requirements or (in education) institution-defined to reflect institutional mission (or course objectives). *NB: There are some who suggest that "fitness of purpose" is a definition of quality, but it is a specification of parameters of fitness and not itself a definition of the quality concept.*
Value for money	Assesses quality in terms of return on investment or expenditure. At the heart of the value-for-money approach in education is the notion of accountability. Public services, including education, are expected to be accountable to the funders. Increasingly, students are also considering their own investment in higher education in value-for-money terms.
Transformation	Sees quality as a process of change, which in higher education adds value to students through their learning experience. Education is not a service for a customer but an ongoing process of transformation of the participant. This leads to two notions of transformative quality in education: enhancing the consumer and empowering the consumer.
Standards	
Academic standards	The demonstrated ability to meet specified level of academic attainment. For pedagogy, the ability of students to be able to do those things designated as appropriate at a given level of education. Usually, the measured competence of an individual in attaining specified (or implied) course aims and objectives, operationalised via performance on assessed pieces of work. For research, the ability to undertake effective scholarship or produce new knowledge, which is assessed via peer recognition.

Standards of competence	Demonstration that a specified level of ability on a range of competencies has been achieved. Competencies may include general transferable skills required by employers; academic ("higher level") skills implicit or explicit in the attainment of degree status or in a post-graduation academic apprenticeship; particular abilities congruent with induction into a profession.
Service standards	Are measures devised to assess identified elements of the service provided against specified benchmarks? Elements assessed include activities of service providers and facilities within which the service takes place. Benchmarks specified in "contracts" such as student charters tend to be quantified and restricted to measurable items. *Post hoc* measurement of customer opinions (satisfaction) is used as indicators of service provision. Thus, service standards in higher education parallel consumer standards.
Organisational standards	Attainment of formal recognition of systems to ensure effective management of organisational processes and clear dissemination of organisational practices.

Source: Epistemology of Quality. Lee Harvey Paper presented at the Biennial Conference of the International Network of Quality Assurance Agencies in Higher Education, Toronto, April 2007. Subsequently published as Harvey (2007). Adapted from Harvey, 1995m © Lee Harvey, 2007.

With high levels of governance and oversight, teacher education is prone to certain definitions of quality which are easier to define in terms of quality assurance (or standards), as they lead to metrics, measures and indicators more readily. Other dimensions of quality, such as transformation, are more difficult to quantify as they are less observable, less immediate in terms of impact and more personal to the individual (Evans, 2011; Halász & Looney, 2019). Harvey argues that this difficulty in measurement should not mean that they get forgotten.

And yet, discussions about quality in ITE are not always clear on how quality is being defined. For example, the provision of Teacher Standards and student satisfaction surveys denote differing interpretations of what is valued rather than being based on empirical evidence that some Standards are inherently "better" than others. Notions of exceptional or excellence may refer to exclusivity and reputation (such as being associated with a prestigious institution) and may be more related to perceptions and access to social networks rather than the transformational nature of the learning experience.

So there is a need to explore the underpinning assumptions about why something is considered to be "quality", as that reveals assumptions about how it is defined. To suggest that quality can be determined by achieving a range of (professional) Standards suggests a cause and effect relationship: that those Standards are in themselves an authoritative account of better quality, which reveals:

> an explicit view that complying with requirements will result in competent graduates, a process that can be checked through measurable, observable variables.

(Harvey, 2007, p. 13)

This claim can of course be challenged. Sleeter (2019) notes how definitions of quality are likely to be defined by those that have power. Others have argued that teacher educators should "reclaim accountability" and foreground alternative values, such as democracy and social justice (Cochran-Smith et al., 2018), or to focus on the "core practices" that teachers need (Grossman, 2018; Grossman, Kavanagh, & Dean, 2018; Grossman & Pupik Dean, 2019). These arguments, whilst avoiding the limiting conception of standards, are still unable to fully describe the transformative element of teacher education.

Transformation: the key to teacher education

Transformation has often been used in relation to learning, particularly adult learning in higher education (see, for example, Meizrow's (2000) ideas of transformational learning and Netolicky's (2019) conception of transformational professional learning). A view of education as transformation requires an assessment and re-evaluation of currently held beliefs and actions, and through an educative process, those beliefs and actions undertake a change in form. It is this change in form that Harvey and Knight argue is distinctively *educational* (1996). The idea of transformation has been widely taken up in some part of the higher education community, and used in ITE as a way of supporting an activist orientation (as outlined by Kennedy (2018), drawing on Sachs' (2003) idea of the activist professional). Kennedy highlights that this approach enables new teachers to engage in a professionally authentic experience where they are supported in taking responsibility for their own learning, working as part of both university and school communities throughout the programme, enabling genuine integration of theory and practice. In this vein, transformation is about changing the form of someone who is not a teacher into that of being a teacher.

Such an approach to education is difficult to measure because, as Harvey argues, it is more aligned with a critical-dialectic epistemology:

> One aspect of quality assurance is improvement of the learning process. When this is informed by a transformation view of quality with radical views of learner-focused or autonomous learning, then the role and nature of the teacher and the privileged position of discipline knowledge starts to be deconstructed. This also moves to the hazy hinterland of quality assurance processes as none of the existing systems does more than nod in the direction of transformative learning. Not surprisingly, quality assurance processes are uncomfortable with this fundamentally critical-dialectical approach because there are no simple indicators, no self-evident or taken-for-granted and easily assimilated criteria for judging how students are empowered as critical reflective learners.
>
> *(Harvey, 2007, p. 10)*

A focus on quality as accountability leads to a compliance culture which detracts from processes of transformation: it is, in effect, anti-educational. However, in the same way that ice changes form into water or steam, education as transformation requires a qualitative change, which Harvey and Knight align with cognitive transcendence. This, they argue, requires enhancing and empowering the participant. The legislative and regulatory structure that surrounds ITE makes such an empowerment extremely challenging.

Seeing learning as transformation is not itself neutral, but influenced by visions of what the outcome of that transformation should look like. Moore (2004) recognises that discussions about the "good teacher" are underpinned by dominant discourses prevalent in popular media representations as well as policy texts. Although Moore's work is now over 20 years old, the discourses he identified (the Charismatic subject, Competent craftsperson and the Reflective practitioner) are still relevant in ITE. Connell (2009) has argued that auditability has become a dominant feature of being a teacher, whilst Cordingley (2008) has suggested a further discourse around collaborative practice and Sahlberg (2019) argues that the most recent phase of education is dominated by discourses of well-being and equity. The influence of these discourses is likely to relate to local concerns and priorities. For example, in New Zealand where there is a national concern about distribution of educational achievement after being described by the OECD as a "high-achievement, local equity" nation, there is a growing emphasis on teachers who can address issues of equity in the classroom (Cochran-Smith et al., 2016). In England, there is a dominant discourse of crisis particularly in teacher recruitment and retention, which is then reflected in policies that encourage diversification of routes into teaching, educational privatisation, allowing unqualified teachers to teach in state schools and an emphasis on teachers who are subject specialists over expert pedagogues, although the logic of this argument has been contested (Ellis, Mansell, & Steadman, 2020; Ellis & Spendlove, 2020). In other words, conceptions of quality, even around transformation, in ITE are highly contextual.

Quality, measures, standards and accountability

Even if, as I have suggested above, teacher educators see teacher education as being about transformation, this does not change the way that ITE is dominated by accountability regimes, indicators, metrics and measures of quality (Bartell et al., 2018; Sloat, Amrein-Beardsley, & Holloway, 2018; Watson, 2018). Cochran-Smith and colleagues (2018) highlight the rise in such metrics as part of the "era of accountability" which they attribute to five broad developments:

1 unprecedented global attention to teacher quality, tied to neoliberal economics;
2 a continuous public narrative asserting that "traditional" university-sponsored teacher education was failing to produce effective teachers who were prepared to respond to the demands of contemporary classrooms;

3   the conceptualization of teacher education as a public policy problem wherein it was assumed that getting the right policies in place would boost teacher quality and the national economy;
4   the teacher education establishment's turn toward accountability, which was consistent with a conception of teacher quality defined as effectiveness and linked to the human capital paradigm; and
5   the belief that the reform of public education, rather than other social policies, was the major tool for redressing inequality and eradicating poverty in the United States.

(Ibid., p. 17)

No doubt these accountability regimes have an enormous impact on the ability of teacher educators to effect transformation in their work; indeed, this makes up the production of spatial inequalities outlined above. It is key, however, to understand the discourses that underpin these indicators, so that their influence on teacher education can be understood.

Suzanne Wilson, in her lecture at the American Educational Research Association in 2018 seeking to make sense of the various accountability frameworks across the US, made a list of all the quality measures she had encountered in teacher education. These quality measures share similar features, and so have been categorised into the groups shown in Table 1.2.

The set of indicators around **Input measures** assumes that the quality of a teacher is related to the pre-programme experience and prior educational achievement of the candidates. These characteristics do not directly correlate to the categories of either quality or standards. The idea that these characteristics are an indication of quality is flawed but popular (see, for example, Francis et al. (2019) who use the metric of qualifications despite acknowledging its flaw as an indicator of teacher quality), as there is no direct correlation between prior attainment and quality of teaching (Day, 2019a; McNamara, Murray, & Phillips, 2017; Vagi, Pivovarova, & Barnard, 2019; Zhao, 2018; Zumwalt & Craig, 2005). The outlier in this group, Graduate diversity, points to a different conception of

TABLE 1.2 Categories of "quality" measures used in ITE

Input measures	*Process measures*	*Output measures*	*Perspectival measures*
Quality of entrants	Placements	Attainment against Standards (criteria)	School ratings of graduates
Degree class	Programme Cohesion	Employment rates	Graduates' self-report
Undergraduate institution		Measures of content knowledge	Graduates' evaluation
Graduate diversity		Graduates using "high leverage practices"	Student ratings
		Graduates' ethical behaviour	

teacher quality: one that suggests that representativeness of a diverse community is an important feature in the perceived quality of a teacher candidate. Whilst there is some research evidence that concurs that teacher diversity can have a positive influence on student outcomes (Sleeter, 2001), this variable suggests that quality is determined by the characteristics of teacher candidates (or applicants) rather than what happens during the process of ITE itself. This assumption downplays the educative or transformative potential of ITE.

The list of indicators under the heading of **Output measures** are similarly flawed, and are characterised by a range of cause and effect assumptions: for example, that (Teacher) Standards are adequate and accurate descriptions of teacher (or teaching) quality; that measures of content knowledge correlate to high-quality teaching; or that only the best teachers are recruited into employment. There is some research and anecdotal evidence for these indicators, but they are not conclusive (Day, 2019b; Ingvarson, 2019). Using employment rates as an indicator of quality is severely compromised in times of teacher shortage, when the demand for teachers outstrips the supply. Indeed, the English government's inspectorate Ofsted cites this as a reason for moving away from output indicators of quality in their revision of the ITE inspection framework (Ofsted, 2018). Even in times of a more selective employment market, it would not be accurate to assume that teachers are employed based on a rigorous analysis of the quality of their teaching. In addition, these metrics are short term: employment, or assessment against a set of Standards relate to a specific point in time. They do not record the impact on teachers in the long term.

A fairly recent addition in the Outputs category is the introduction of value-added metrics, where the quality of teacher education is directly linked with the attainment of their pupils. Despite the political attractiveness of this idea, it has been widely criticised for its lack of awareness of other factors to affect pupil attainment and simplistic linear logic, and validity (Noell, Burns, & Gansle, 2018; Sloat et al., 2018). The Output indicators are more convincing, however, than the input indicators as they do have a (cause and effect) logic to them, even though they are mainly focused on standards rather than quality.

In some systems, the awareness of the weaknesses of output data has led to supplementing them with what I have called **Perspectival data**: data drawn from the perspectives of student teachers themselves (evaluating their programme or their own efficacy and competence), or from employers, partners or pupils. There are questions about the reliability of this information: its accuracy and consistency (van der Lans, 2018). Gaertner and Brunner (2018) show that student perceptions of teaching quality are influenced by situational factors such as context and timing. Some school systems promote coherent identities (such as Multiple Academy Trusts in England or Charter School Chains in the US) which feature strong narratives about quality; as such judgements may be more driven by conformity and coherence to a prescribed set of values than a more rounded, holistic (and even critical) notion of a quality teacher or quality teaching. Rauschenberger, Adams and Kennedy's (2017) literature review on quality measurements in ITE notes that quality indicators are driven by values, which, in turn, drives practices: in other words, perspectival data reveals what responders think is important, and are not reliable indicators of either quality or standards.

The smallest list in the categorisations, that of programme features or **Processes**, is perhaps the least common and well developed, although becoming increasingly popular as policymakers seek to prescribe ITE curriculum content (see, for example, the new Core Content Framework in England and the inclusion of Key Tasks in the New Zealand teacher education accreditation requirements). Here the work of Darling-Hammond and colleagues (2006) on the characteristics of teacher education in well-regarded programmes has been influential, along with the further distillation into three points by Hammerness (2013):

1 Promotion of a clear vision of teachers and teaching;
2 Programme coherence, both conceptually and structurally, "reflecting a shared understanding of teaching and learning among faculty and students" (linked to formation of professional identity); and
3 A strong core curriculum that is closely linked to opportunities for learning that are grounded in teaching practice.

However, even these characteristics are vague (Rauschenberger, Adams, & Kennedy, 2017). Hammerness and Klette (2015) have produced indicators for each category, but highlight that their data does not reveal the quality of the opportunity afforded but the likelihood that it exists. In other words, they represent opportunities to learn, but not the transformative potential of the experience.

Drawing on Harvey's categorisation, ITE metrics, measures and indicators are predominantly quality assurance standards. They are proxies for quality rather than being representative of quality itself. Moreover, the focus on indicators detracts from an understanding that quality in a learning context is about transformation and as such is a descriptive, relative concept – not an absolute entity, and not one that can easily transfer to other contexts. However, such metrics are endemic and part of the limited range of policies around teacher education which seem to influence international and national debates (Mayer, 2017).

Transformation and pedagogy

For teacher education to be regarded as *educational*, it needs to be understood within how it seeks to change the form of someone who is yet to be a teacher to become one. This requires both an understanding of what is meant by being a teacher and also the processes of change required. In education, a change in form happens through pedagogy.

Loughran (2006) argues that whilst pedagogy is sometimes used as a synonym for teaching, it is much more than that as it requires a detailed understanding of the relationship between learning and teaching. Alexander differentiates between "...teaching is an *act* while pedagogy is both act and *discourse*" (2000):

> Pedagogy encompasses the performance of teaching together with the theories, beliefs, policies and controversies that inform and shape it.
>
> *(Ibid., p. 540)*

Alexander goes on to argue that pedagogy can be seen as an expression of the context in which teaching and learning takes place as well as the decisions that frame both. Linklater (2010, cited in Warwick, Warwick, Linklater, & Coltman, 2013) developed a spectrum of pedagogical thinking to reflect the complexity of this practice so it can be seen as a layered process, where individual acts of teaching and learning are contextualised within both philosophical and actual contexts.

Pedagogy on a programme of teacher education encourages a change in form through the movement of ideas. These ideas may stem from a variety of sources: they may come through the experience of practice, through knowledge shared by a teacher educator, through engagement in readings, research or discussion. For the change in form to occur, the movement of ideas needs to elicit a change in the person itself: so through their engagement in the pedagogical activities, they undergo some form of change, perhaps through adopting a different viewpoint, understanding or engaging in a practice differently.

This is not to suggest that pedagogy necessarily determines changes in identity. The movement of ideas which may change, say a classroom practice, may not result in a wholescale identity shift. For someone to become a teacher, however, they do need to make changes in how they undertake teaching as they move from a novice to becoming more accomplished. For those changes to occur, a shift must take place which is prompted through the movement of an idea. Pedagogy provides the context for that movement of ideas to take place.

This view of teacher education pedagogy is broad. The ideas which necessitate the changes to occur can come from a variety of sources, and as such this view of teacher education pedagogy includes learning which can stem from practice as well as from other sources. It is the pedagogical intervention which enables the idea to affect the would-be teacher. It is common for teacher educators to refer to this shift as occurring through reflection, but the reflection itself needs to be stimulated by the movement of an idea.

The movement of ideas then can be seen as a form of intellectual capital, which is mobilised through teacher education pedagogy. This movement can be enabled or constrained by the way that the teacher education is organised, described by Kemmis and colleagues (2014) as the practice architecture. The teacher education practice architecture comprises of the programme infrastructure as well as the political and discursive aspects and the accountability measures, referred to as the material-economic, cultural-discursive and social-political arrangements (ibid.). These arrangements can enable or constrain the practice of teacher education, or to use the language adopted here, the flow of ideas within a programme of teacher education.

Conceptualising teacher education pedagogy as a flow of ideas deliberately focuses attention onto the knowledge that teachers have as a form of intellectual capital. This framing is intended to recognise the specialist status of that knowledge, but also to recognise how important it is for teachers to have access to it. For example, in 2020, Ofsted introduced a new framework for the inspection of ITE. It was stated in this framework that new teachers should be taught the reading strategy of synthetic phonics at the exclusion of other strategies. When this was announced under consultation, there was a great deal of concern that this proscribed teacher educators from introducing new teachers to other, alternative forms of ways of learning to read. In other words, this framework was seeking to deny new teachers access to intellectual capital: knowledges of other ways of learning to read. This argument can be used for other important knowledges for teachers: theories of learning, findings from cognitive science or community knowledges. All of which are aspects of the intellectual capital that teachers might need.

An important consideration is how the flow of intellectual capital, the movement of knowledge and ideas, gets played out in space. In their articulation of their theory of practice and practice architecture, Kemmis and colleagues (ibid.) draw upon Schatzki's notion of "site-ontologies" to emphasise that education happens in particular locations. In the case of teacher education, those site ontologies are particularly important and complex, as teacher education tends to occur in both universities and schools, and in addition, those organisations are situated in specific places. These geographical contexts have unique features, such as access to certain groups, types of schools or arrangements of populations, which may enable or constrain the flow of knowledge. For example, the demand for teachers is not the same everywhere: in areas where teacher demand is high, the emphasis on practical skills and being classroom-ready is more prominent than in areas where there may be a surplus of teachers, and more emphasis is given to the knowledgeable and research-orientated teacher. As outlined above, to understand teacher education, understanding this broader context is vital.

I am suggesting then that there is a relationship between the factors which influence the movement of ideas and the space in which it occurs, and that these factors can influence teacher education pedagogy. This argument goes further than other teacher education research which seeks to tell a single story promoting a particular pedagogical approach, by suggesting that the types of pedagogical approaches that teacher educators use will be related to the myriad of contextual factors they need to take into account. This is one of the reasons why the indicators of quality outlined above cannot be applied to a wide variety of contexts and situations. It also goes some way to explaining why, even though the trends affecting teacher education may be international, the ways those trends are experienced and enacted locally can vary, and are often misunderstood. It is these misunderstandings around quality that I have called quality conundrums.

Quality conundrums

A quality conundrum is an idea that is intended to raise or enhance quality, but has the potential to do the opposite: to damage its transformative potential. In my exploration of teacher education provision, I found that there were a number of quality conundrums that worked across a range of universities; these were ideas with an inherent logic when simply expressed, but often, when incorporated into a narrative of quality, they get taken to an extreme and can damage teacher education. The damage occurs because when overemphasised, the quality conundrum limits the flow or movement of ideas. Chapters 2 to 6 explore some of these conundrums, in turn, through an example of how a university has sought to navigate the conundrum and situate its practice in relation to it. Each conundrum is different, but they share similar features:

- A quality conundrum is aligned to an idea, with an internal logic that seeks to make teacher education "better" in some way;
- As such, it is based on an assumption or presumption about a flaw in current provision;
- It is often aligned to a narrative about quality that stems from what Jones and Ellis (2019) have called a "simple" view of teacher development;
- And is given extra power and emphasis when it becomes part of the accountability and governance structure;
- However, when enacted, the quality conundrum can limit the flow of alternative forms of knowledge, ideas or intellectual capital, which a teacher may need.

These quality conundrums are part of the hostile environment for universities involved in teacher education as they create the dominant narratives about how practice should be. When combined with accountability structures, they affect the flow of capital. Universities have to navigate these structures in order to "do" teacher education – and this study set out to find out how.

Quality at scale in initial teacher education: the research project

In 2017, I took up the position of Head of Initial Teacher Education (ITE) at the UCL Institute of Education (IOE), an institution I had worked in (predominantly in teacher education roles) since 2001. At the time I was also Head of a large department, many of the faculty of which were involved, in some way in teacher education. My rationale was that as Head of ITE, I could be more effective as a Head of Department. The ITE provision, however, was at a breathtaking scale: working with around 2,000 new teachers every year, across a range of phases from Early Years to Post Compulsory. Immediately I became aware that as part of a research-intensive university, and an institution which had been ranked as Number 1 in the world for Education in the QS World Rankings consistently since 2014, and rated as Outstanding by Ofsted, the main issue was how to ensure that we were consistently providing high-quality teacher education at scale and across a range of programmes, whilst also contributing to the university's vision, mission and research expectations. Including schools in the Teach First partnership (at the time of the data collection the IOE was Teach First's largest partner, making up over a third of their overall provision), we were working with 700 schools across London. The variety of schools, the different priorities, identities and approaches to education embedded in these 700 schools, alongside the desire for a coherent vision of teacher education amongst our large and varied team of teacher educators, seemed overwhelming. As I started to understand more about our provision, I began to recognise that my team had developed a range of strategies, approaches and principles which made quality at scale possible that enabled them to work with and around different interpretations of quality from the field, the university and the ITE accountability infrastructure. This exploration became the first site for this research. After my three-year term as Head of ITE, my desire to understand quality at scale in ITE took me to explore the practices at a number of other large-scale but highly regarded institutions. In doing so, I began to draw upon my background, in geography education in particular, to view teacher education as a spatial practice. Adopting a spatial lens offered a unique perspective on how these universities were undertaking the practice of teacher education in the light of their spatial context.

The research focused on the question: *What are the features of high-quality, large-scale ITE?* Data were collected on the ITE practice of five universities (see Table 1.3). Each university was chosen as a (relatively) large ITE provider in their jurisdiction (in terms of teachers graduated and in comparison to other local providers) and as part of an institution renowned for its quality (according to local or international league tables). Inclusion was limited to predominantly English-speaking nations (Australia, England, Canada, New Zealand and the US), due to the advantages of exploring practices from a shared linguistic tradition. Many of the terms used in teacher education can be variously interpreted even within one linguistic environment and translation would add a further complication. However, this inclusion criteria skews the research to a relatively narrow, anglicised and postcolonial hub of countries. Whilst this dilutes the diversity of the contexts included, it does also illustrate the diversity inherent in teacher education in a group of countries with some shared cultural heritages.

The incidence of the global pandemic coronavirus in 2020 halted the data collection, so the data collection for the Ontario Institute for Studies in Education (OISE) of the University of Toronto, Canada, was conducted remotely, and plans to include two further universities, one in France and the other in China, had to be abandoned.

For the purposes of sampling, scale (high volume) was determined by the numbers of enrolled students relative to other providers in the region. For some areas, such as England and New Zealand, the region was identified as nationally. In the US, Canada and Australia, the region was defined as the States or Provinces to which governance of teacher education was devolved. Scale was determined by publicly available data. The measures of quality are outlined in Table 1.3.

TABLE 1.3 Universities and the teacher education programmes

University	Location	Type of Teacher Education	Ranking measure used	Teacher Standards	Accreditation authority
Queensland University of Technology	Australia	Post-graduate and undergraduate, Early Years, Primary and Secondary education	Australian Good Universities Guide	Australian Professional Standards for Teachers (APST) developed by the Australian Institute for Teaching and School Leadership (AITSL)	Queensland College of Teachers (QCT)
Ontario Institute for Studies of Education (OISE), University of Toronto	Canada	Masters of Teaching (post-graduate two-year programme)	Macleans and Times Higher Education ranking	Ontario College of Teachers	Ontario College of Teachers
University of Auckland	New Zealand	Graduate and under-graduate programmes in Early Childhood Education, Primary and Secondary education	QS World University Rankings	Standards and Code for the profession (Teaching Council)	Teaching Council of Aotearoa New Zealand (TCANZ)
UCL Institute of Education, University College London, London	UK	Post-graduate programme in EY, Primary, Secondary and Post-Compulsory education. Also partner with Teach First	QS World University Rankings	National Teacher Standards (defined by UK government Department for Education)	Department for Education regulations and designation of "providers"; Ofsted inspection
Mary Lou Fulton Teachers College, Arizona State University, Tempe Arizona	USA	Post-graduate and undergraduate, Early Years, Primary and Secondary education: but with an emphasis on the new undergraduate programme	US News rankings	Arizona State Standards	Arizona Department of Education. Schools are also accredited by the Council for the Accreditation of Educator Preparation (CAEP)

Different university ranking systems draw upon different criteria, and many of the ranking systems around university quality do not relate directly to the quality of the teaching or to teacher education. For example, the US News ranking methodology includes assessments from peers and educational professionals as well as the qualities of enrolled students, the faculty resources and the research activity. The QS World Rankings focus on both academic and employer reputation, numbers of international faculty and students as well as the faculty to student ratio and citations ration. In other words, there are no metrics directly related to the transformative effect of teaching. University ranking is therefore not taken as a proxy for quality in teacher education, but indicates universities that have a reputation for high quality generally. Such universities are likely to be concerned with maintaining status and ensuring their reputation for quality continues, which will influence how a university may value teacher education and the levels of trust and autonomy it affords to its teacher educators.

Data were collected through interviews with teacher educators, and where possible school partners and student teachers (or teacher candidates), around 50 in total. Where feasible, taught sessions were observed, and I participated in other related activities (such as meetings, seminars and related conferences). Relevant documentation was also included, such as programme handbooks, media announcements and review documents. Both the data collection and the analysis were checked and verified by a local representative acting as gatekeeper, who also supported access as necessary and acted as a critical friend to ensure my reading of the data was not influenced by my own ethnocentric gaze. Ethical approval was granted by my home institution, and where necessary local ethical approval was sought by the host institution.

The data were analysed to reveal the pertinent discourses around quality as well as the difference between "universal" understandings of quality in teacher education at scale and those which are localised. The research adopted a framework influenced by three conceptual approaches:

- A perspective on quality debates that views it as a way of knowing about practice and policy rather than as a discrete entity in and of itself (taken from Harvey, 2007), and explored earlier in this chapter;
- A theory of practice and practice architectures (taken from Kemmis et al., 2014) that enables the laying out of a practice and the influences which affect it (more on this in Chapter 7);
- Ideas about scale, space and the reproduction of space (taken from Lefebvre, 1991; Harvey, 2004), and outlined in detail in Chapter 8.

The data analysis focused on the different discourses around quality in each location, and looked specifically at how quality was being articulated and the relationship between quality and quality assurance from different influences on practice drawing on Harvey's categorisation.

In addition, the analysis involved a "laying out" of the practices of teacher education and how they have been shaped by the various practice arrangements and traditions, as outlined in the theory of practice and practice architectures by Kemmis et al. (2014) and discussed in more detail in Chapter 7. Kemmis and colleagues recognise that practices occur in particular sites which have their own traditions and practices, which, in turn, make up the arrangements of practice. Practices can be understood by exploring the cultural-discursive (the *sayings* of a practice), material-economic (the *doings*) and social-political arrangements (the *relatings*). Taken together, these arrangements reveal the practice architectures which can enable and constrain action and interaction. The theory of practice and practice architectures was used in the analysis as a way of laying out the practice in each site, and the approach provided a way of understanding the practice in each location, and how it was beholden to different factors (such as governance and accountability arrangements) as well as different partnerships and practice traditions. The findings of this laying out were then analysed further using the ideas of scale, relative space and representational space adopted from Lefebvre (1991) and Harvey (2004).

A spatial lens does more than just identify that location matters or that context plays a role in defining practices. Several disciplines have adopted a spatial turn in order to enrich their understanding of the different ways in which context and location can influence practice (Schatzki, Cetina, & Von Savigny, 2005). A spatial lens has been a key approach to reveal trends which contribute to uneven development (Smith, 2010). In education, it has been argued that schools in some of the poorest areas attract the lowest "quality" teachers (although the definition of quality in this context requires some careful handling). This is not due merely to location, but also due to the ways in some places are situated in relation to each other in both terms of significance as well as geographical location (known as relative space). For example, schools located in certain areas adjacent to other more attractive areas will find their comparative location as a disadvantage. Additionally, the representational space, how places (and in this case teaching) are represented has a spatial expression. Spatial theory, therefore, offers three rich conceptual lenses (location in space, relative space and representational space) that were used to interrogate the practice architectures in order to understand the particular influences on each practice (see Chapter 8). This becomes important when policymakers evoke ideas that become parts of the quality conundrum, as they assume that their policy will be enacted in a uniform way, and fail to recognise the distinct ways in which practices vary across space, and the complex array of reasons which can affect how those practices respond to trends and influences. In this sense, policy assumes conformity: that all schools need the same thing, in the same way, at the same time, which belies individual (and I would argue spatial) patterns and trends. The unique situation of each provider produces different challenges and problems, each of which has a spatial expression. Each provider is also beholden to a different infrastructure or architecture of quality measures, indicators and priorities, some of which may be sourced locally and others may come from regional, national and global debates. The working-through or practice of teacher education is contingent upon these factors, whilst also influenced by the location of the practice of learning to teach itself: the site of the university, school or other learning spaces. In each of the cases featured in this research, as the chapters will show, this triad of spatial practices come together to form the unique experience of learning to teach within these institutions.

The counterpoint of this argument is that we focus too much on the individual or local, and this is problematic too as it can hide important wider trends. I would argue that much current research in teacher education is guilty of this, adopting an overly individualised account can ignore some of the social, cultural, economic and political trends which affect education. The use of a spatial lens allows us to see the site of the individual situated within these wider scales.

Book outline

This chapter has outlined three of the key ideas that underpin this book: that quality in teacher education should be seen as a process of transformation rather than standards or indicators of quality assurance; that transformation occurs through the flow of ideas enacted through teacher education pedagogy; and that when ideas about quality get taken up, they can turn into quality conundrums which will affect practices. The next five chapters take each of these quality conundrums in turn, exploring how that conundrum gets manifest and how one of the universities studied works in and around that conundrum.

- Chapter 2 explores the practice quality conundrum through a comparison of the practices of a post-graduate teacher education programme and the Teach First employment-based programme both located at the UCL Institute of Education in London, UK;
- Chapter 3 looks at the research quality conundrum through the lens of the research-orientated programmes at Ontario Institute for Studies in Education (OISE), of the University of Toronto, Canada;
- Chapter 4 explores the knowledge quality conundrum, and in particular how it is addressed at Queensland University of Technology, Brisbane, Australia;
- Chapter 5 asks the question who are the best people to work with new teachers: the teacher educator quality conundrum, looking at Mary Lou Fulton Teachers College, Arizona State University, in the US;
- Chapter 6 looks at how to deal with the accountability quality conundrum, using the example of the University of Auckland, New Zealand.

The experiences across these five universities and across the five identified quality conundrums are then brought together in two further chapters. Chapter 7 explores the practice architectures and the practice arrangements pertinent to teacher education and how these arrangements enable and constrain university-based teacher educators' practices. In effect, these factors influence what practices are possible and which are not. Chapter 8 then uses the spatial lens to look at how the location, relative and representational nature of teacher education gets played out through these practices. Finally, these themes are drawn together in Chapter 9 which posits a model of ITE practice: a diagrammatic representation of how universities are able to "do" teacher education within the highly complex, stratified and challenging environments they find themselves in. The model is intended to illustrate the opportunities and responsibilities available to universities, to help them navigate the complex landscapes in which teacher education takes place. The model is also intended to be a useful way for universities to reconsider their role in teacher education: how they can leverage their influence, exercise their expertise and ensure that as new quality conundrums appear the transformational potential of teacher education is not lost.

A note on terminology

Terminology about ITE varies enormously around the globe, reflecting the different views on and status of teacher education provision. For this reason alone, adopting a unified terminology to describe stakeholders and programme structures can be challenging. The choice of terminology is political in itself.

In England, the term "initial teacher education" is the phrase preferred by university providers, in contrast to the narrower and more technical phrase of "initial teacher training" as preferred by the Department for Education. In the US, the phrase "teacher preparation" is more commonly used. As this research is set in universities, I have adopted the phrase initial teacher education, teacher education (or the abbreviation ITE) throughout to reflect the *educational* nature and the distinctive component that universities provide which goes beyond technical or skill-based training or generating classroom-ready teachers. Similarly, I will refer to "universities" instead of using the term "providers", unless making specific reference to alternative providers outside the university sector. On the whole, the use of "teacher educator" is reserved for those working in the university sector many of whom will have different designations such as lecturer, tutor, sessional tutor, academic and so forth. Where differentiation is needed between teacher educators, such as between tenure-track, adjunct or sessional, these will be clearly signposted. School-based colleagues involved in ITE will be referred to as "mentors" or the specific name given by their university (such as "lead teacher") where it denotes a different role or responsibility. I appreciate that many would argue that school-based mentors are also teacher educators; however, I agree with White (2018): that for this study, a distinctive term is needed to differentiate their work from those employed at a university with specific expertise, roles and responsibilities around teacher education. When necessary, reference will be made to university-based teacher educators or school-based teacher educators. The research predominantly deals with pre-service programmes, although Teach First is an in-service or employment-based route into teaching, hence participants on those programmes will be referred to as "student teachers"; this also denotes their enrolment on a university programme and differentiates them from both "students", qualified "teachers" and from pupils. Finally, universities use a variety of names for their teaching programmes and how they are differentiated; for ease of comparability, I will refer to "programmes" and "modules". Where local terminology varies (such as describing courses or units instead of modules), this will be made clear to enable understanding.

Note

1 https://teachingcouncil.nz/content/teacher-registration-and-certification-policy-review.

References

Alexander, R. J. (2000). *Culture and pedagogy: International comparisons in primary education.* Oxford: Blackwell.

Allen, R., & Sims, S. (2018). Do pupils from low-income families get low-quality teachers? Indirect evidence from English schools. *Oxford Review of Education*, 44(4), 441–458. doi:10.1080/03054985.2017.1421152

Ball, S. J. (1990). *Politics and policy making in education: Explorations in policy sociology.* London: Routledge.

Ball, S. J. (2008). Performativity, privatisation, professionals and the state. In B. Cunningham (Ed.), *Exploring professionalism* (pp. 50–72). London: Bedford Way Papers.

Bartell, T., Floden, R., & Richmond, G. (2018). What data and measures should inform teacher preparation? Reclaiming accountability. *Journal of Teacher Education*, 69(5), 426–428. doi:10.1177/0022487118797326

Biesta, G. (2010). *Good education in an age of measurement: Ethics, politics, democracy.* Boulder, CO: Paradigm.

Burgess, S. M. (2016). *Human capital and education: The state of the art in the economics of education.* Retrieved from Bonn, Germany: http://ftp.iza.org/dp9885.pdf

Carter, A. (2015). *Carter review of initial teacher training (ITT).* Retrieved from London. https://assets.publishing.service.gov.uk/government/uploads/system/uploads/attachment_data/file/399957/Carter_Review.pdf

Cochran-Smith, M., Carney, M. C., Keefe, E. S., Burton, S., Chang, W.-C., Fernández, M. B., ... Baker, M. (2018). *Reclaiming accountability in teacher education.* New York: Teachers College Press.

Cochran-Smith, M., Ell, F., Grudnoff, L., Haigh, M., Hill, M., & Ludlow, L. (2016). Initial teacher education: What does it take to put equity at the center? *Teaching and Teacher Education*, 57, 67–78. doi:10.1016/j.tate.2016.03.006

Cochran-Smith, M., Keefe, E. S., Carney, M. C., Sanchez, J. G., Olivo, M., & Smith, R. J. (2020). Teacher preparation at New Graduate Schools of Education; studying a controversial innovation. *Teacher Education Quarterly*, 47(2), 8–37.

Connell, R. (2009). Good teachers on dangerous ground: Towards a new view of teacher quality and professionalism. *Critical Studies in Education*, 50(3), 213–229. doi:10.1080/17508480902998421

Cordingley, P. (2008). Research and evidence-informed practice: Focusing on practice and practitioners. *Cambridge Journal of Education*, 38(1), 37–52. doi:10.1080/03057640801889964

Darling-Hammond, L. (2006). *Powerful teacher education: Lessons from exemplary programs.* San Francisco, CA: John Wiley & Sons.

Day, C. (2019a). Policy, teacher education and the quality of teachers and teaching. *Teachers and Teaching, 25*(5), 501–506. doi:10.1080/13540602.2019.1651100

Day, C. (2019b). What is teaching about? Professionalism and the limitations of standards and competences. *European Journal of Education, 54*(3), 315–318. doi:10.1111/ejed.12348

Department for Education. (2010). *The importance of teaching* (9780101798020). Retrieved from London. https://assets.publishing.service.gov.uk/government/uploads/system/uploads/attachment_data/file/175429/CM-7980.pdf

Dourish, P. (2004). What we talk about when we talk about context. *Personal and Ubiquitous Computing, 8*(1), 19–30. doi:10.1007/s00779-003-0253-8

Ellis, V., Mansell, W., & Steadman, S. (2020). A new political economy of teacher development: England's Teaching and Leadership Innovation Fund. *Journal of Education Policy*, 1–19. doi:10.1080/02680939.2020.1717001

Ellis, V., Souto-Manning, M., & Turvey, K. (2018). Innovation in teacher education: Towards a critical re-examination. *Journal of Education for Teaching, 45*(1), 2–14. doi:10.1080/02607476.2019.1550602

Ellis, V., & Spendlove, D. (2020). Mediating 'School Direct': The enactment of a reform policy by university-based teacher educators in England. *British Educational Research Journal.* doi:10.1002/berj.3607

Evans, L. (2011). The 'shape' of teacher professionalism in England: Professional standards, performance management, professional development and the changes proposed in the 2010 White Paper. *British Educational Research Journal, 37*(5), 851–870. doi:10.1080/01411926.2011.607231

Firestone, W. A., & Donaldson, M. L. (2019). Teacher evaluation as data use: What recent research suggests. *Educational Assessment, Evaluation and Accountability, 31*, 289–314. doi:10.1007/s11092-019-09300-z

Francis, B., Hodgen, J., Craig, N., Taylor, B., Archer, L., Mazenod, A., ... Connolly, P. (2019). Teacher 'quality' and attainment grouping: The role of within-school teacher deployment in social and educational inequality. *Teaching and Teacher Education, 77*, 183–192. doi:10.1016/j.tate.2018.10.001

Furlong, J. (2013). *Education – An anatomy of the discipline: Rescuing the university project.* Abingdon: Routledge.

Furlong, J. (2019). The Universities and initial teacher education; Challenging the discourse of derision. The case of Wales. *Teachers and Teaching, 25*(5), 574–588. doi:10.1080/13540602.2019.1652160

Gaertner, H., & Brunner, M. (2018). Once good teaching, always good teaching? The differential stability of student perceptions of teaching quality. *Educational Assessment, Evaluation and Accountability, 30*(2), 159–182. doi:10.1007/s11092-018-9277-5

Gewirtz, S., Maguire, M., Neumann, E., & Towers, E. (2019). What's wrong with 'deliverology'? Performance measurement, accountability and quality improvement in English secondary education. *Journal of Education Policy*, 1–26. doi:10.1080/02680939.2019.1706103

Goldhaber, D. (2018). Evidence-based teacher preparation: Policy context and what we know. *Journal of Teacher Education, 70*(2), 90–101. doi:10.1177/0022487118800712

Grossman, P. (2008). Responding to our critics: From crisis to opportunity in research on teacher education. *Journal of Teacher Education, 59*(1), 10–23. doi:10.1177/0022487107310748

Grossman, P. (2018). *Teaching core practices in teacher education.* Cambridge, MA: Harvard Education Publishing Group.

Grossman, P., Kavanagh, S., & Dean, C. (2018). The turn to practice in teacher education. In P. Grossman (Ed.), *Teaching core practices in teacher education* (pp. 1–13). Cambridge, MA: Harvard Education Press.

Grossman, P., & Pupik Dean, C. G. (2019). Negotiating a common language and shared understanding about core practices: The case of discussion. *Teaching and Teacher Education, 80*, 157–166. doi:10.1016/j.tate.2019.01.009

Halász, G., & Looney, J. (2019). Teacher professional competences and standards. Concepts and implementation. *European Journal of Education, 54*, 311–314. doi:10.1111/ejed.12351

Hammerness, K. (2013). Examining features of teacher education in Norway. *Scandinavian Journal of Educational Research, 57*(4), 400–419. doi:10.1080/00313831.2012.656285

Hammerness, K., & Klette, K. (2015). Indicators of quality in teacher education: Looking at features of teacher education from an international perspective. In G. K. LeTendre & A. W. Wiseman (Eds.), *Promoting and sustaining a quality teacher workforce* (pp. 239–277). Bingley: Emerald Publishing.

Hanushek, E. A., & Rivkin, S. G. (2012). The distribution of teacher quality and implications for policy. *Annual Review of Economics, 4*(1), 131–157.

Harvey, D. (2004). *Space as a key word*. Paper presented at the Marx and Philosophy Conference, Institute of Education, London. http://frontdeskapparatus.com/files/harvey2004.pdf

Harvey, D. (2010). *The Enigma of capital and the crises of capitalism*. Oxford: Oxford University Press.

Harvey, L. (2007). The epistemology of quality. *Perspectives in Education, 25*(3), 1–13.

Harvey, L., & Knight, P. T. (1996). *Transforming higher education*. Bristol: Open University Press.

Hillage, J., Pearson, R., Anderson, A., & Tamkin, P. (1998). *Excellence in research on schools*. Sudbury: Department for Education and Employment.

Holmes Group. (1986). *'Tomorrow's teachers: A report of the Holmes Group*. East Lansing, MI: Holmes Group.

Ingvarson, L. (2019). Teaching standards and the promotion of quality teaching. *European Journal of Education, 54*(3), 337–355. doi:10.1111/ejed.12353

Jones, J., & Ellis, V. (2019). Simple and complex views of teacher development. In *Oxford Education Research Encyclopedia*. Oxford: Oxford University Press. https://doi.org/10.1093/acrefore/9780190264093.013.418

Kemmis, S., Wilkinson, J., Edwards-Groves, C., Hardy, I., Grootenboer, P., & Bristol, L. (2014). *Changing practices, changing education*. Springer Science & Business Media.

Kennedy, A. (2018). Developing a new ITE programme: A story of compliant and disruptive narratives across different cultural spaces. *European Journal of Teacher Education, 41*(5), 638–653. doi:10.1080/02619768.2018.1529753

Labaree, D. F. (2006). *The trouble with ed schools*. New Haven, CT: Yale University Press.

Lefebvre, H. (1991). *The production of space* (D. Nicholson-Smith, Trans. Vol. 142). Malden, MA: Oxford Blackwell.

Ling, L. M. (2017). Australian teacher education: Inside-out, outside-in, backwards and forwards? *European Journal of Teacher Education, 40*(5), 561–571. doi:10.1080/02619768.2017.1385599

Linklater, H. (2010). *Making children count? An autoethnographc exploration of pedagogy*. PhD, University of Aberdeen, Unpublished.

Loughran, J. (2006). *Developing a pedagogy of teacher education: Understanding teaching & learning about teaching*. Abingdon: Routledge.

Mayer, D. (2017). Professionalizing teacher education. In *Oxford research Encyclopedia of education* (Vol. 1). Oxford: Oxford University Press. https://doi.org/10.1093/acrefore/9780190264093.013.96

McIntyre, J., Youens, B., & Stevenson, H. (2017). Silenced voices: The disappearance of the university and the student teacher in teacher education policy discourse in England. *Research Papers in Education, 34*(2), 153–168. doi:10.1080/02671522.2017.1402084

McNamara, O., Murray, J., & Phillips, R. (2017). *Policy and research evidence in the "reform" of primary initial teacher education in England.* Cambridge: Cambridge Primary Review Trust.

Meizrow, J. (2000). *Learning as transformation: Critical perspectives on a theory in progress.* San Francisco, CA: Jossey-Bass a Wiley Company.

Moon, B. (2016). Building and agenda for reform of teacher education and training within the University. In B. Moon (Ed.), *Do Universities have a role in the education and training teachers? An international analysis of policy and practice* (pp. 251–262). Cambridge: Cambridge University Press.

Moore, A. (2004). *The good teacher: Dominant discourses in teaching and teacher education.* London: RoutledgeFalmer.

Netolicky, D. M. (2019). *Transformational professional learning: Making a difference in schools.* Abingdon: Routledge.

Noell, G. H., Burns, J. M., & Gansle, K. A. (2018). Linking student achievement to teacher preparation: Emergent challenges in implementing value added assessment. *Journal of Teacher Education, 70*(2), 128–138. doi:10.1177/0022487118800708

OECD. (2005). *Teachers matter: Attracting, developing and retaining effective teachers.* Paris: Organisation for Economic Co-operation and Development (OECD) Publishing.

Ofsted. (2018). Building great teachers? Initial teacher education curriculum research: Phase 2. Retrieved from https://www.gov.uk/government/publications/initial-teacher-education-curriculum-research/building-great-teachers

Pring, R. (2017). Research and the undermining of teacher education. In Peters, M.A (Ed.) *A companion to research in teacher education* (pp. 609–620). Dordrecht: Springer.

Rauschenberger, E., Adams, P., & Kennedy, A. (2017). *Measuring quality in initial teacher education: A literature review for Scotland's MQuITE study* (S. C. o. D. o. E. (scde.ac.uk) Ed.). Edinburgh: Scottish Council of Deans of Education (scde.ac.uk).

Sachs, J. (2003). *The activist teaching profession.* Maidenhead: Open University Press.

Sachs, J. (2015). Teacher professionalism: Why are we still talking about it? *Teachers and Teaching, 22*(4), 413–425. doi:10.1080/13540602.2015.1082732

Sahlberg, P. (2010). Educational change in Finland. In *Second international handbook of educational change* (pp. 323–348). Dordrecht: Springer.

Sahlberg, P. (2019). *Leading together; how teacher leadership can be enhanced and supported.* Paper presented at the Sammon om Ledelse, Undervisningssektoren, Christianborg.

Schatzki, T. R., Cetina, K. K., & Von Savigny, E. (2005). *The practice turn in contemporary theory.* Abingdon: Routledge.

Skedsmo, G., & Huber, S. G. (2019). Measuring teaching quality: Some key issues. *Educational Assessment, Evaluation and Accountability, 31*(2), 151–153. doi:10.1007/s11092-019-09299-3

Sleeter, C. (2001). Preparing teachers for culturally diverse schools: Research and the overwhelming presence of whiteness. *Journal of Teacher Education, 52*(2), 94–106. doi:10.1177/0022487101052002002

Sleeter, C. (2019). Considering core assumptions about what it means to teach. *Teachers College Record, 121,* 1–4.

Sloat, E., Amrein-Beardsley, A., & Holloway, J. (2018). Different teacher-level effectiveness estimates, different results: Inter-model concordance across six generalized value-added models (VAMs). *Educational Assessment, Evaluation and Accountability*, *30*(4), 367–397. doi:10.1007/s11092-018-9283-7

Smith, N. (2010). *Uneven development: Nature, capital, and the production of space*. Athens: University of Georgia Press.

Teacher Education Exchange. (2017). *Teacher development 3.0; How we can transform the professional education of teachers*. London: Teacher Education Exchange.

Vagi, R., Pivovarova, M., & Barnard, W. (2019). Dynamics of preservice teacher quality. *Teaching and Teacher Education*, *85*, 13–23. doi:10.1016/j.tate.2019.06.005

van der Lans, R. M. (2018). On the "association between two things": The case of student surveys and classroom observations of teaching quality. *Educational Assessment, Evaluation and Accountability*, *30*(4), 347–366. doi:10.1007/s11092-018-9285-5

Warwick, J., Warwick, P., Linklater, H., & Coltman, P. (2013). Developing primary trainee teachers' professional identity on an initial teacher education course: Linking course structure, professional relationships and pedagogic understanding. In M. Evans (Ed.), *Teacher education and pedagogy: Theory, policy and practice* (pp. 60–79). Cambridge: Cambridge University Press.

Watson, C. (2018). From accountability to digital data: The rise and rise of educational governance. *Review of Education*, *7*(2), 390–427. doi:10.1002/rev3.3125

White, S. (2018). Teacher educators for new times? Redefining an important occupational group. *Journal of Education for Teaching*, *45*(2), 200–213. doi:10.1080/02607476.2018.1548174

Whitty, G. (2008). Changing modes of teacher professionalism. In B. Cunningham (Ed.), *Exploring professionalism* (pp. 28–49). London: Bedford Way Papers.

Whitty, G., & Wisby, E. (2006). Moving beyond recent education reform – And towards a democratic professionalism. *Hitotsubashi Journal of Social Studies*, *38*(1), 43–61.

Zeichner, K. M. (2017). *The struggle for the soul of teacher education*. Abingdon: Routledge.

Zhao, Y. (2018). The changing context of teaching and implications for teacher education. *Peabody Journal of Education*, *93*(3), 295–308. doi:10.1080/0161956x.2018.1449896

Zumwalt, K., & Craig, E. (2005). Teachers' characteristics: Research on the indicators of quality. In Cochran-Smith, M. and Zeichner, K. (Eds.) *Studying teacher education: The report of the AERA Panel on Research and Teacher Education* (pp. 157–260). Washington, DC: American Educational Research Association.

2
THE PRACTICE QUALITY CONUNDRUM

Teachers need to be effective practitioners. However, exactly how much practice new teachers need, of what type and the role this plays in teacher education pedagogy is still an area of debate. In this chapter, I argue that the debates around practice make up a practice quality conundrum, which is both political and pedagogical in nature.

In Chapter 1, I argued that high-quality teacher education requires transformation, and that the conditions for transformation are enabled through teacher education pedagogy. Reviews of the characteristics of well-regarded teacher education programmes note that it is not just the provision of practical experiences which is important but how those experiences are "carefully chosen to support the ideas and practices presented in simultaneously, closely interwoven coursework" (Darling-Hammond, 2006). Whilst this statement highlights the importance of practical experiences, it says less about the nature of those experiences, and it is in this lack of clarity that we find the practice quality conundrum.

The turn to practice

At the heart of the practice quality conundrum lies what has been called the "practice turn" in teacher education. A focus on practice theory, sometimes referred to as the practice turn, can be found in a large number of disciplines including philosophy, sociology, science, cultural theory and anthropology (Hui, Schatzki, & Shove, 2016; Nicolini, 2012; Schatzki, Cetina, & Von Savigny, 2005). However, in teacher education, the practice turn has taken on two specific meanings. One, which is prevalent in England, indicates a shift that began in the 1990s when government policy stipulated how much practical experience was required on a teacher education programme, the start of what then later became a privileging of school experience and oversight over other aspects of teacher education

(Ellis & Spendlove, 2020; Furlong, 2013; Heilbronn & Yandell, 2010; Jackson & Burch, 2018; Parker, 2015). The second is a movement which emerged in the US and is orientated around core practices and the science of learning, described by Jones and Ellis (2019) as a "simple" view of developing the practice of teaching. Core practices are discussed in more detail in Chapter 4.

Jones and Ellis (2019) highlight that some approaches which make up a simple view of teaching have a poor research base. For example, the "teacher moves" developed by Lemov (2010) are based on his experience and observations of "effective" teacher behaviours. New teachers often ask for more practical tips about teaching and books such as Lemov's *Teach like a Champion* which focus exclusively on teachers' behaviour are incredibly popular. However, the thinking, understanding, concepts and ideas that underpin these behaviours are largely invisible, as they focus explicitly on the visible part of teaching: what teachers do in the classroom – techniques, routines and behaviours. Developing a set of techniques and routines is important for any teacher; but an exclusive focus on them erroneously suggests that teaching is predominantly a set of skills, and that teacher education should focus on the rehearsal and adoption of these skills.

The idea that teacher development should be based on this "simple" view is symptomatic of the problems, which Labaree summed up as "teaching is a complex job that looks deceptively simple" (2006). Most of us have gone through some form of formal education and have an image of what teaching looks like, enshrined in images and metaphors from our own "apprenticeship of observation" (Lortie, 1975) as a pupil. These images are reinforced through media representations of teaching, which new teachers may seek to replicate through "cinematic pedagogies" (Henry, 2020). It is straightforward then to assume that all teaching requires is the development of these familiar behaviours by someone with adequate (subject) knowledge. This is a view of teaching often defined as a "craft" conception.

This limited or simple view of teaching as a craft has been encapsulated in England by the former Secretary of State Michael Gove (see Furlong, 2013). It represents a narrow and technical view of teaching, focusing on behaviours which has been widely criticised (Childs, 2013; Czerniawski et al., 2018; Edmond & Hayler, 2013; Ellis, Steadman, & Trippestad, 2018; George & Maguire, 2018; Knight, 2012; McIntyre, Youens, & Stevenson, 2017; McNamara, Murray, & Phillips, 2017; Mutton, Burn, & Menter, 2016). This is not to suggest that teaching skills are not important. Indeed, the majority of teacher education programmes emphasise the importance of practical experience, and to some extent all are a form of professional training (Furlong, 2013) or apprenticeship (Dunn, Hattie, & Bowles, 2018).

But the consequence of an overly simplistic view of practice is that it underplays the importance of teachers' knowledge and understanding, and can lead to a narrow conception of teaching. In that sense, it can limit the flow of ideas available to the new teacher, focusing on those ideas that relate to behaviours. For example, Tatto, Richmond and Carter Andrews (2016) suggest that this discourse around minimalist teacher education influenced by the practice turn is based on the idea that as long as teachers are prepared in their subjects, learning to teach only requires a short period of induction. This idea is pervasive even though, as they highlight, it runs counter to the research evidence. In addition, there is a concern that an overemphasis on technical practice is reductionist and does not prepare teachers well to practice the moral-ethical judgements and creative problem solving they need. An over-reliance on prescribed procedures and rule following can lead to inappropriate action or teaching that is performative and managerialist (Edwards-Groves & Grootenboer, 2015).

This view of teaching has a direct impact on the pedagogy of teacher education. Jones and Ellis (2019) connect the emphasis on teacher behaviours with the idea of deliberate practice, which they relate to Popkewitz's (1985) idea of industrial task analysis, which emphasises "what works" and oversimplifies it. Deliberate practice has been extremely influential in some forms of teacher education and features centrally in the Teach First's Leadership Development Programme principles (outlined below). Widely used in many spheres, deliberate practice was originally proposed by Ericsson, Krampe and Tesch-Römer in 1993 as a way of developing expert performance, and has been made popular through texts such as Gladwell's 2008 *Outliers* and Syed's 2010 *Bounce*, which both posits deliberate practice as a way of enhancing performance through focusing, with expert tuition, on specific areas of practice that need to be developed. Deliberate practice has become a popular way of viewing enhancing performance in many fields, including teaching. However, it is assumed that because it has been shown to be effective in music and sport that it has wide applicability in a variety of settings. Empirical studies have showed that its effectiveness in explaining variation in expert performance differs between fields, and fails to take into account other significant social and cultural factors (Hambrick et al., 2014). Its value for teacher education has yet to be substantiated; however, it grows in popularity.

Philip and colleagues (2018) outline that approaches like deliberate practice place an emphasis on what they call "prescriptive practices", a narrow range of pedagogies for teacher education. They quote Lemov, who has claimed that "everyone, and especially educators, can improve their performance through relentless and deliberate practice", and align this with Ball and Forzani's (2009) calls for "deliberate and unabashed prescriptiveness" in teacher training (p. 506). Philip and colleagues question the empirical base of approaches that promote deliberate practice, in particular the Deans for Impact (2016) publication *Practice with Purpose: The Emerging Science of Expertise*, noting that it mostly self-cites or draws on the work of members of the Core Practice Consortium (discussed in more detail in Chapter 4). Philip et al.'s critique is that this approach:

> de-emphasize teacher education's role in developing "the broad professional vision (deep knowledge of their students and of the cultural contexts in which their work is situated), and the relational skills they need to be successful in the complex institutional settings in which they will work"

(Zeichner, 2012, p. 379). Their technique-focused and reductive readiness approaches hold special appeal for charter schools that rely on short-term teaching and high turnover (Stuit & Smith, 2012; Toma & Zimmer, 2012)—another manifestation of the "new economy" that demands that education "constantly and consistently retrains … workers, quickly and at little to no expense for the employer" (Cottom, 2017, p. 12).

(Ibid., p. 5)

Jones and Ellis (2019) also highlight how pedagogies such as deliberate practice fail to ask questions about who practices work for and the underlying syntactic structure of teacher knowledge. It could be argued then that such a pedagogical approach is too narrow in the range of ideas that it emphasises and, by focusing on it too much, will diminish the range of other ideas that student teachers have access to. In this sense, it can limit the opportunity for transformation to occur, and can channel the transformation potential to a narrow range of behaviours and practices.

Reflective practice

A more expansive view of teacher education pedagogy is that of reflective practice. Traditionally, university-based teacher education programmes have focused on Schön's idea of the reflective practitioner as a key pedagogical approach (Furlong, 2013; Menter et al., 2010; Moore, 2004), sometimes supplemented by the idea of the inquiring teacher or inquiry as stance (Cochran-Smith & Lytle, 1993, 1999a, 1999b) as a pedagogical approach which promotes such reflection. Schön's conception of the reflective practitioner works across practical and academic settings, as it promotes reflection both in and of action, thereby taking place in the "white heat" of action as well as through carefully curated pedagogical interventions. Reflective practice, however, has been critiqued for being too introspective, and to be effective requires critical engagement (Eraut, 1994, 1995), and more recently for becoming a part of governance and oversight structures leading to performativity akin to the confessional (Fejes, 2011).

Pedagogies which feature reflective practice have to rely on two key factors. The learner is ably supported through extended forms of mentoring (which may include aspects of feedback similar to deliberate practice), and they are able to build on a specialist knowledge base. Both of these elements are key to elevate reflective practice beyond introspection, and for it to transform the knowledge, beliefs or actions of the student teacher. Without something to challenge existing beliefs, new teachers may be unaware of what is informing the judgements they make. In addition, such interventions can support them to develop expertise that goes beyond what can be gained through classroom experience alone. There is an evidence base – mostly qualitative in nature – that teacher education which seeks to do this has a lasting impact and value for teachers (see O'Kelly, 2019). However, it is notoriously difficult to "prove" one set of educational theories or approaches in teacher education against another (Mayer et al., 2015).

Pedagogical binaries and politics

So far I have drawn a fairly stark distinction between pedagogies which focus on behaviours and those which focus on reflection. As with all binaries, such a distinction is potentially dangerous and disingenuous. There is little empirical research that can inform teacher educators as to the best ways to bring these knowledges together for new teachers. Darling-Hammond and colleagues have led the field in seeking to define the characteristics of effective teachers alongside effective teacher education (Darling-Hammond, 2006, 2017; Darling-Hammond & Lieberman, 2013; Darling-Hammond et al., 2000; Darling-Hammond & Oakes, 2019). However, as discussed in Chapter 1, their categories are somewhat open to interpretation, and there is no consensus from the research about the best forms of teacher education (Kirby, McCombs, Barney, & Naftel, 2006; Mayer et al., 2015; Menter et al., 2010). The adoption of one approach over another is often aligned to the values system and situation of the teacher educators. For example, university-based programmes, with an emphasis on knowledge gained alongside practice, have adopted approaches aligned with reflective practice that seek to bring the two together (Moore, 2004). Similarly, universities with a research focus can emphasise clinical approaches to teaching (Menter, 2017). However, teacher education programmes, such as Teach First and Teach For America (TFA), or similar early entry or employment-based programmes are looking for pedagogical approaches which emphasise being classroom-ready in a shorter period of time (Jones & Ellis, 2019) and are more likely to advocate deliberate practice. For teacher educators, who are committed to professional learning rooted in reflection, reflexivity and professional practice, a deliberate practice approach can feel superficial. However, for teachers with a limited repertoire of approaches, deliberate practice on a few behaviours can feel useful and can encourage teachers to feel they are "classroom-ready". There is a danger to this binary conception, particularly when these pedagogical approaches are aligned with politics.

Ideas that emphasise the behaviour of teachers has also been encouraged through a focus on the "science of learning", of which deliberate practice often features, as illustrated in the US through the Deans for Impact in its report *Practice with Purpose: The Emerging Science of Expertise*. The Deans for Impact have been described by Cochran-Smith, Stringer Keefe and Carney (2018) as a group of managerial reformers, with connections to other neoliberal trends such as charter schools and the effectiveness agenda. The Deans for Impact have published widely on the Science of Learning and promote strategies, such as deliberate practice, to form part of the teacher education programmes. Studies of programmes which have adopted these approaches are highly critical, arguing that they represent an impoverished view of learning theories, and encourage the recruitment of poorly trained teachers in the areas of most need (Zeichner, 2016). The organisations which run such programmes are seen as politically motivated and well connected. This is also the case in England, where the science of learning movement is evident in a number of publications orientated around cognitive psychology, particularly promoted by the UK Minister for School Nick Gibb and from authors such as Willingham, Didau and Kirschner, who have made terms like dual-coding, interleaving and direct instruction popular, alongside promoting a knowledge-rich curriculum. These approaches are described as "scientifically proven" whilst being practical and useful for teachers.

This debate is highly politicised, particularly in England. The emphasis, characterised by the "simple" view of teacher education, focuses on "what works" and teacher behaviours. This is reflected in a number of policy outputs such as the Early Career Framework and the Initial Teacher Training (ITT) Core Content Framework, which claims to emphasis research-based approaches, but draw upon a narrow definition of "acceptable" research (mostly from the Education Endowment Foundation which fund evaluative, randomised controlled trials). This aligns with the scepticism of the Minister for Schools Nick Gibb, with what he has described as an overly ideological preference for theories in initial teacher education (ITE) promoted particularly from university-based teacher educators.

However, some of these approaches have certainly enriched teacher education programmes. Indeed, Darling-Hammond and colleagues have summarised the implications from this body of work for school and classroom practices (Darling-Hammond, Flook, Cook-Harvey, Barron, & Osher, 2019). There is a danger then that the strategies of teacher education such as deliberate practice, which may indeed have value for new teachers, get rejected because of their alignment with political and ideological movements, or alternatively that they get overemphasised through policy and political discourses, squeezing out the flow of other important knowledges and ideas.

The value of practice as part of learning to teach is widely recognised. The controversy comes in how that practice becomes part of the learning experience. There is a danger that the practice turn can place too much emphasis on the behavioural (what teachers do) rather than the attitudinal (their "service" orientation) and the intellectual (what teachers think) (Pachler, 2013). Winch has argued (2017) that conceptual understanding is crucial for the transfer to professional practice, and that consequently practice itself is only a successful strategy depending on what is being practiced or the content and application of the practice rather than the skill itself (McKenney & Schunn, 2018). Therefore, adopting deliberate practice, whilst it has the backing of some research, does not fully address the question of the best way to educate teachers. It is not the practice itself that is key, but what is being practiced, the quality of that experience and how that contributes to learning to be a teacher.

The quality conundrum then is whether an emphasis on practice, with the intention of improving the preparation of teachers, can actually limit their repertoire and understanding through restricting their access to a range of knowledges and ideas. In answering such a question, we need to consider what kinds of experiences new teachers need in order to be able to teach well and to be "adaptive" to new or novel situations. Advocates of approaches such as deliberate practice consider that it will enhance and improve teacher education by helping teachers to develop practical skills. The danger is that if such an approach is too narrow, it will, in the long term, de-professionalise teaching, as teachers will have only a limited knowledge base upon which to draw.

This debate is particularly rife in England, and in the rest of this chapter, I will explore how this conundrum is manifest at one university (UCL Institute of Education [IOE]) which works with a traditional clinical practice model of teacher education, the PostGraduate Certificate of Education (PGCE), but who also work in partnership with Teach First on their Leadership Development programme that is influenced by deliberate practice. Both programmes seek to develop high-quality teachers, but adopt very different pedagogies: one through a process of gradual immersion through appropriately paced school placements, and the other as an employment-based route with a pre-service intensive five-week programme seeking to ensure classroom-readiness. The juxtaposition of these two programmes is intended to debate this quality conundrum, how it is manifest and the purposes it serves, and is not to determine the veracity of the claims of either.

A note on insider research

The study of the teacher education provision at UCL Institute of Education (IOE) was the first one I conducted, largely because it was my own institution and the one I had greatest access to. At the time of the data collection, I was the Head of Initial Teacher Education at the IOE, with oversight of all the ITE programmes. I was in the last year of a three-year term-of-office, but I also have a long history of association with IOE's teacher education provision. I was a student teacher at the IOE and have subsequently undertaken roles as a school-based mentor, subject tutor and leader, and eventually taking on overall ITE leadership. My account therefore needs to be viewed through this lens: I am committed to ITE and to the institution, but have been an insider for 28 years, and so have seen the provision from a variety of angles. I was conscious in my data collection that it was very difficult for me to set aside this wealth of insider knowledge (Perryman, 2011). In some cases, my background with the programme was longer and more detailed than those I interviewed. Also when talking to colleagues from Teach First, I was conscious of listening to their accounts whilst comparing them to my experience of working with the programme from inside the IOE. There is no doubt that my experience influences my reading and the analysis of the data, despite my attempts to rely on the data and to ensure that all accounts were verified, and so the following needs to be read in that light: I am aware it could be seen both as a partial insider analysis or as an authoritative insider account. In my attempts to be the latter, I have ensured that the contents below have mostly come from sources in the public domain (such as programme handbooks and publications) and have been corroborated by at least two of the interviewees, and drafts of this chapter were shared with colleagues both inside and outside the IOE to check for veracity and that the analysis rings true to them.

The English context

The English teacher education system can be characterised by high levels of centralised oversight and control. The UK Government's Department for Education (DfE) allocates all providers in England with a target number of places for teacher "training" (the DfE's preferred term for teacher education). The DfE also writes and publishes the Teacher Standards through which a new teacher can gain Qualified Teacher Status. Guidance and regulations on teacher training provision are circulated by the DfE, and each provider is part of an inspection cycle, from the government's inspection agency Ofsted (Office for Standards in Education, Children's Services and Skills). There have been moves to standardise and control teacher education provision through the Carter Review (for a critical account, see Mutton et al., 2016), which outlined the content of teacher education and a set of standards for mentors, and more recently (and published after the data for this study was collected), the ITT Core Content Framework (and corresponding changes to the Ofsted framework for inspection of ITE). The English teacher education system has been described as a highly regulated environment despite a rhetoric of deregulation (Mutton et al., 2016). These accountability regimes and policy technologies apply to all providers, including the Teach First provision.

Despite this rigid accountability regime, England has a tradition of teacher education as professional formation, and one where professional autonomy has been widely prized (Heilbronn & Yandell, 2010). Commentators suggest that this may no longer be the case in some institutions (Furlong, 2013), but it has always been a tradition at the UCL Institute of Education.

UCL Institute of Education

The IOE is the largest teacher education provider in England, and one of the oldest. Established in October 1902 as the London Day Training College, teacher education (and training) has been a constant at the IOE. In December 2014, the IOE merged with University College London (UCL) and became a single Faculty School, with the new name of UCL Institute of Education. As a result of merger, UCL became the biggest higher education institution in London and the largest postgraduate institution in the UK.[1]

The IOE is widely regarded in the area of education: it has been ranked as the World's number one for education worldwide from 2014 to 2020 inclusively in the QS World University Rankings and awarded the 2015 Queen's Anniversary Prize. In the most recent Research Excellence Framework assessment of university research, the IOE was top for "research power" (quality of outputs multiplied by the size of the entry) in education.

With regards to teacher education, in 2014, the IOE secured "outstanding" grades from Ofsted on every criterion for its initial teacher training, across primary, secondary and further education programmes. However, the IOE has also been singled out for criticism by the Minister for Schools Nick Gibb for being particularly ideological in its approach. For the year this research was conducted (2019), the IOE was England's largest teacher education provider, with 1,430 students enrolled on university-led (785), School Direct fee-funded (90) and School Direct Salaried (130) and Teach First (420) programmes.[2] Including the number of second-year Teach First students (it is a two-year programme), the IOE works with around 2,000 new teachers each year and employs around 350 teacher educators.

The partnership between Teach First and UCL Institute of Education needs to be understood in the light of ITE policy shifts in England. As Rauschenberger (2016) notes, the IOE was instrumental in the development and conceptualisation of Teach First, although they were not selected to be partners during the first Teach First London cohort. The decision by IOE to seek to become key partners for the London region was partly influenced by the changing landscape of teacher education in England and the shift away from university-led provision, as outlined in the White Paper *The Importance of Teaching* (2010). Such a move can be seen as part of the impact of the changing English teacher education system at the time, and particularly the impact of the policy shift towards school-based teacher education (Brown, 2017; Parker, 2015), and the increased diversity and complexity of the teacher education landscape (Whiting et al., 2018). The influence of organisations such as Teach First in policy networks and third-sector organisations has been strong on the English system (Ball & Exley, 2010; Olmedo, Bailey, & Ball, 2013). However, the shift to a school-led system has not fully taken hold, and the challenges facing teacher recruitment have meant that university-based providers are still an important part of the teacher supply model because of their capacity to train large numbers of student teachers (Ofsted notes that four-fifths of new teachers have been involved with a higher education institution (2018)).

Teach First

At the time of study, the IOE was Teach First's largest partner, making up over a third of its national provision. Teach First is a charity organisation aligned with the global Teach For All movement. Teach First is often described as having been modelled on Teach For America (TFA), although Rauschenberger's analysis of the origins of Teach First (2017) shows some distinct differences between them, not least the influence of the McKinsey and Company corporate strategies around identifying and nurturing leadership potential, the focus on developing a corporate infrastructure and the influence of Mike Totterdell and Geoff Whitty (both of the IOE at the time) in helping the Teach First innovators develop the teacher education vision and navigate the policy landscape. Brett Wigdortz, the founder of Teach First, co-founded Teach For All with the founder of TFA, Wendy Kopp. Teach For All is now a global movement with 52 independent partner organisations (https://teachforall.org/).

The distinctive features of Teach First, replicated in the Teach For All movement, is a focus on attracting high-quality graduates into teaching, and encouraging them to work in schools in "challenging circumstances" for a short period (two years), and then to become ambassadors for education in their subsequent careers. Teach First was the first so-called adaptation of TFA, appearing in England in 2002, and supported by London's business community as a way to address underachievement in disadvantaged London schools (ibid.). The idea spread beyond London and, at the time of the data collection, is a national programme working with eight universities across England (and one in Wales) and with a target recruit figure of 1,750 participants (or student teachers).

Both Teach First and TFA have received intense criticism. In the US, TFA received a scathing assessment by Darling-Hammond (1994) who accused TFA of harming minority students and attempting to de-professionalise teaching. Other critiques of the international movement have paid particular attention to the rhetoric that underpins the programme that includes a saviour discourse which ignores social and economic reasons for underachievement (Ellis et al., 2015). Rhetorical analysis of this discourse reveals the messages that these programmes are focused on "othering" disadvantaged students and encouraging participants in this scheme to "teach other people's children, elsewhere, for a while" (Ellis et al., 2015).

Much of the criticisms around Teach First are based on the rhetoric of the programme, the way it conceptualises challenging schools and disadvantaged students and its disruptive influence on the teacher education landscape. However, there have been more positive reviews of Teach First as both a leadership development programme (Blandford, 2014) and as a form of alternative certification (Muijs, Chapman, & Armstrong, 2012, 2013). The Teach First programme for the London region was also rated as Outstanding in its most recent Ofsted inspection; however, this inspection and the reviews of the programme were related to a former iteration of the programme to the one featured in this research. The current version outlined here has yet to be inspected by Ofsted.

Demand for teachers in London

Neither Teach First's London provision nor the IOE's scale and diversity can be fully understood without a sense of the teacher recruitment and retention situation in London. The joint report by the National Foundation for Educational Research (NFER) and Nuffield Foundation (Worth, De Lazzari, & Hillary, 2017) on teacher Workforce Dynamics in England, emphasised that the "teacher supply challenge in London is particularly acute when compared to other geographic areas". These findings are supported by Sibieta (August 2018),[3] whose analysis of the trends shows that the supply of teachers with certain subject specialisms is exacerbated by location.

However, the education landscape does look somewhat different to other parts of the country. The NFER and Nuffield Foundation report found that London's teacher labour market faces a particularly acute challenge over the coming decade and that this challenge is specific to London rather than a general pattern across other large English cities. This is due to a forecast growth in pupil numbers and the demographics of London teachers: London has more new entrants to its teacher workforce each year, but these are not enough to replace the many teachers who leave teaching in London, particularly as London has a higher rate of young teachers leaving the profession and a steady outflow of teachers in their 30s and 40s to teach elsewhere. Higher proportions of schools with vacancies and of unqualified teachers employed in London, compared to other areas, suggest that the labour market is already experiencing significant shortages in many areas.

While the vibrancy of London and the pace of change in its education system seem to initially attract younger teachers, there are factors that discourage teachers from remaining in London in their 30s and beyond. The most important factor driving low teacher retention in London is higher housing costs. In addition, early career teachers are accelerated into middle leadership positions more quickly in London than they are in other areas, which is perhaps due to a lack of more experienced teachers to fill these roles. While these opportunities for quick progression can initially attract teachers to London, it may leave teachers feeling underqualified and therefore overwhelmed by their extra responsibilities. Middle leaders are more likely to leave the profession in London than in other areas, and more move out of London to teach elsewhere than move into the capital.

Additionally, schools in London have consistently outperformed and added greater value than other schools across England (although the gap appears to be closing). The reason for this "London factor" is not entirely clear (Baars et al., 2014) and has been attributed to various factors, including the London Challenge initiative which partnered high-performing schools with those in need. The high performance of London schools does mean that expectations of teachers in London, both from parents, communities and school leaders, are high. These factors have a significant impact on the preparation of new teachers, and are reflected in the diversity and academic rigour of the teacher education programmes at the IOE.

Diverging approaches to teacher education

One of the most distinctive differences between the IOE and Teach First as teacher education providers is their diverging approaches to teacher education. Whilst others have noted that the Teach For All movement, despite a rhetoric of doing things differently, has borrowed heavily in both pedagogy and content from traditional teacher education programmes (Schneider, 2013); the IOE's flagship PGCE programme is very different in style and approach to the Teach First Leadership Development Programme.

Following the policy shift towards school-led teacher education, the IOE diversified its portfolio of ITE programmes. Traditionally, the core of the teacher education provision has been the Primary and Secondary PGCE, a ten-month post-graduate programme which results in Qualified Teacher Status and 60 Masters credits (a third of a Masters degree). These programmes remain the largest teacher education programmes within the IOE with approximately 240 students on the Primary programme and 700 students on the Secondary programme spread across 18 different subject specialisms. In addition, the IOE runs PGCE programmes for early years (called EYITT: Early Years Initial Teacher Training), and for the Post Compulsory sector (focusing mainly on education for those over the age of 16). At the time of data collection, the IOE had a large School Direct Salaried programme, which is an employment-based programme which awards Qualified Teacher Status only (although a PGCE top-up programme is available), and worked in partnership with a number of School Centred Initial Teacher Training providers – six at the time of the data collection. Within the internal structure of the IOE, teacher education spans four academic departments. The range of programmes can also mean that the IOE may work with school partners with new teachers on a variety of programmes. Including the schools partnered with the London Region of Teach First, the IOE works with over 700 schools across London.

One of the key challenges within this diverse landscape is to have a unified vision for ITE that speaks to the values and mission of the IOE, whilst also recognising the different needs and requirements of teachers on different programmes. The following extract from the IOE's Strategy for ITE articulates how this is conceived:

> ITE provision at the IOE encompasses five programmes across age ranges from Early Years to Post-Compulsory phases. All programmes are underpinned by the vision of an "IOE teacher" as someone who is prepared to achieve excellence in all aspects of their future career in education. As such, all programmes go beyond the development of technical teaching competence, requiring all students to apply the broader theoretical background to learning and teaching and to engage in scholarly reflection on policy and practice. Whilst sharing common goals, programmes are structured and sequenced to achieve this in different ways, reflecting the particular emphasis and needs of each programme. Each programme type is designed to provide different opportunities for learning in a structure and composition and which may appeal to different teacher candidates.
> *(IOE's ITE Strategy, 2019)*

A key dimension to the IOE's distinctive approach is its emphasis on specialisation: a feature made possible by its large scale and diversity. This is indicative of a characteristic of the IOE's recruitment strategy for teacher educators which emphasises specialisation and encourages teacher educators to work across and between programmes. Teacher educators, particularly who work on the secondary provision, might also find themselves working on other post-graduate programmes (such as subject specialist Masters in Education) and/or research projects.

The variety and complexity of the IOE's provision makes it hard to reflect the distinctive characteristics of each programme. The longest running flagship programmes of the Primary and Secondary PGCEs are the two largest programmes. Both these programmes were developed in the late 1990s, and were amended in the mid-2000s in response to the Bologna Agreement and changes needed to make the PGCE a Masters-level programme (Heilbronn & Yandell, 2010). Whilst there are similarities between the two programmes, they are differently structured but share a core philosophy around teacher education pedagogy based on the idea of developing practice through specialist knowledge and critical reflection. What follows below is a brief pen portrait of these two programmes and how they aim to develop specialist knowledge in their student teachers.

Primary PGCE

The Primary PGCE is a large programme of 240 student teachers (in 2019) who work with over 40 tutors (teacher educators), many of whom have been recruited because of a specific area of interest or specialism. The programme curriculum is divided into two modules: Teaching and Learning and Professional Studies. Within Teaching and Learning, student teachers are able to gain experience of a range of specialist subject areas, and are encouraged to choose one in which to specialise. Every student is a member of a tutor group, supported by a Supervising Tutor who take on a personal tutoring role and have responsibility for school-based visits and observations. Some supervising tutors also teach on particular modules to the whole cohort (although this is organised on a carousel basis and so teaching sessions are still in small groups). One of the guiding principles of the programme is that the experience for the students should be high quality, and so great store is placed on recruiting high-quality tutors.

The programme has a singular identity: the assessment and expectations are the same regardless if you choose to specialise in geography or music. The core values of the programme are focused on unifying ideas and principles: that of the spiral curriculum underpinned by a Reflective, Teaching and Learning cycle that allows the student teachers to deepen their understanding as they gain experience. The programme also places an emphasis on criticality: encouraging the student teachers to think critically about the practice they experience in schools through the challenges they are exposed to by the specialist IOE input. This emphasis is borne from the key ideas that underpin the programme – a commitment to preparing teachers who can "practice" but are not restricted to the contexts they have experienced, but have developed a deep and critical understanding of teaching that will enable them to practice and work in a variety of contexts.

> In the learning and teaching module, students are constantly encouraged to think very critically ... I think it would be very dangerous for new teachers to go into primary schools in the current climate and not have a good level of criticality. From what we see from them from the beginning

of the year to the end, their ideas about what good practice is changes quite dramatically, particularly as they start to see beyond what teachers do in the classroom.

(IOE Interview, 2019)

This is how the programme sees the relationship between theory and practice – experience is gained through practice, and the programme content is designed to enhance and develop the understanding of that practice. In addition, students are encouraged to experience a range of contexts, including some primary institutions overseas, and to use the programme content in their critical reflection on these experiences. The structure of supervising tutors and tutor groups enables the programme to feel intimate, as a programme member reflected:

there's actually no difference between 30 students and 240 in that regard. Absolutely none.

(IOE Interview, 2019)

The scale of the programme does mean, however, that there is a separation between theory and practice (as the tutor who undertakes the school visit and observation may not be teaching a large part of the programme) and maintaining partnerships with schools is challenging. Primary schools in England tend to be small, and often only have the capacity to support one or two student teachers. The programme therefore works with a wide range of primary schools across London, some of which vary in their experience and expertise in teacher education. Maintaining coherence across this broad partnership is a challenge, particularly as school budgets have tightened, schools are less likely to release mentors for ITE training. The programme team have responded by taking ownership of the professional studies element of the programme in-house to ensure quality and consistency and are developing a new strategy of working with hubs of school to improve partnership involvement.

The Secondary PGCE

The Secondary PGCE programme is organised in a hierarchical structure, with high levels of responsibility devolved to subject teams. Some aspects of the course are common to all subjects and make up the backbone of the programme. This would include the

- Timetable structure;
- Partnership agreements;
- Assessment and Modular structure;
- Assessment Record File, Trackers, Lesson observation sheets; and
- Gradual immersion approach to teacher education.

Other aspects are individual to particular subjects, such as:

- How the timetable is organised and structured;
- Layout of the teaching days;
- Interpretation of the assessment elements;
- Module assignments; and
- Integration of subject content knowledge, subject-specific pedagogy and teacher education pedagogy.

The structure and design of what is devolved to subject teams reflect the focus on subject-specific understanding which underpins the Secondary programme. The programme philosophy is that a good quality teacher of a secondary subject needs a detailed knowledge of their subject, specialist subject pedagogy and conceptions of progression and understanding as understood by that subject. This focus on subject specialism also affects the range of experiences that are offered on the programme which seek to connect the student teachers with the wider subject community. This might consist of fieldtrips, guest speakers from subject associations and other specialist connections, which are described as enrichment experiences that delve into what it means to be a subject specialist beyond the teaching and assessment of that subject. The aim here is to develop a subject teacher identity beyond a narrow definition of classroom practice.

The Secondary PGCE programme is rooted in an approach originally outlined by Totterdell and Lambert (1998) as the "reflective professional" who is able to think strategically and in an informed way, with the support and challenge offered by theories, research as well as through experienced colleagues. The learning stems from engagement with subject specific concepts and practical experience, developed through metacognition aligned to professional formation, so that the student teachers can think about teaching "as well as, but distinct from, thinking about tomorrow's lesson" (ibid., p. 359). The course structure developed by Totterdell and Lambert has been adapted substantially, but the pedagogical approach can still be seen in the programme today through a range of profile tasks regarding developing teacher identity, structured curriculum planning-implementation-evaluation tasks and the provision of "thinking frameworks" such as the "challenging review" of lesson observations. The emphasis on subject specialism is also supported by a range of reviews of teacher education which advocate that strong specialist knowledge is an important dimension of teacher education (Darling-Hammond, 2006; Darling-Hammond et al., 2000; Korthagen, Loughran, & Russell, 2006; Schleicher, 2012). The focus of the programme is to use a range of ideas generated from experience, theory and collaboration to enable student teachers to question their understanding of teaching. In the Secondary programme, this is emphasised through the lens of the subject specialism.

Each of the 18 subject specialisms is led by a team of subject specialists with varying subject-specific pedagogy expertise and classroom experience. The curriculum and pedagogy are adjusted according to those subject specialisms. For example, the Music PGCE might look quite different from the Science PGCE, even though they follow the same format of a gradual immersion approach to learning to teach. The assumption is that through the expertise of the subject team and the targeted input on particular aspects of subject pedagogy, the student teachers, already graduates and subject specialists, will be able to develop a high degree of understanding about how to teach their subject and what learning and progression looks like within it. This approach is similar to Shulman's concept of pedagogical content knowledge (1986), but differs in that it does not see teacher education as the transformation of content knowledge into pedagogical forms. Instead, this approach places specialist knowledge as the centre of the teacher education experience, viewing the subject as a disciplinary lens through which educational experiences are built.

Both the Primary and the Secondary PGCE have been developed with phase- and subject-specific approaches to teacher education in mind. On the Secondary PGCE, there is a great deal of flexibility for the subject specialist teams in design of content and pedagogy. On the Primary PGCE, there is a focus on sharing expertise alongside personalised support. On both programmes, subject and phase experts also act as personal tutors, and conduct school visits, observations and progress reviews for each of their tutees.

For the Primary PGCE, additions to the tutor team is seen as an opportunity to recruit tutors with particular expertise in areas such as phonics, PE or cognitive psychology that have become statutory contents for the teacher education curriculum. The Primary team is also able to have a range of subject experts who specialise in subject areas within the primary curriculum; this is unusual across England, as such subject expertise is often not possible with smaller programmes (see Catling (2017), for example, from geography education). The same is true to a greater extent for the Secondary PGCE. A member of the programme team explains:

> It [specialisation] brings multiple perspectives. It brings a richness to the course ... I think for many subjects it also brings different perspectives through tutors with different takes, different expertise ... There's a lot of expertise that comes from individual research interests and I think having a large course also balances and diffuses the risk of having one person with a focus just on a particular thing ... There's a benefit too with the students working in large cohorts of peer groups where they can share ideas and they've got a lot of different backgrounds and experiences to draw on.
>
> *(IOE Interview, 2019)*

Subject specialisation is a particular dimension of the IOE's approach, affecting how the Secondary PGCE programme is structured, how staff are recruited and deployed and the emphasis placed on what knowledges are valued. The subject specialist perspective is privileged over that of generic issues or concerns, which can mean that large subjects with more specialist teacher educators dominate the institutional discourse. Some smaller subjects can feel isolated and less connected.

This is also key in identity formation, as new teachers are socialised into subject communities and networks and taught to teach through the lens of their subject. Across the partnership, the closest arrangements are between school subject departments and the subject specialists at the IOE. The number of different schools across London adds to the diversity of this experience through a subject lens that the student body can draw upon and use to expand their understanding.

The pedagogical approach, then, around the development of specialisation can be seen not just in the programme curriculum, but also in the range of practice arrangements that constitute the programme: recruitment of new teacher educators, programme structure and quality assurance mechanisms. The approach can be challenging in relation to authentic partnership working. A small proportion of partnership schools will be involved in partnership boards (at a subject, phase or institutional level), but as the entire provision reaches across 700 schools with around a 30% turnover each year, this is challenging to sustain. It is also difficult to establish institutional-level partnerships at this scale, and so much partnership working is undertaken at an individual level, with teacher educators forming long-term and strong relationships with mentors in partner schools, enabled by the principle that all teacher educators at the IOE undertake extensive school visits with all partner schools.

However, all of these elements are orientated around the idea of building a professional base for the new teachers: connections with their subject community, a specialist body of expertise and a critical perspective on research, practice and educational issues. These pedagogic elements are aimed at professional formation (Heilbronn & Yandell, 2010).

Such an approach is significant for the context of London. Whilst the macro trends of London were outlined above, there is a wide range of variation across London: schools in affluent communities will look incredibly different from schools in more disadvantaged communities. The changing demographic of London also means these characteristics can shift quickly, as gentrification and a buoyant housing market can result in rapid changes in the character of an area and the catchment of a local school. The growing significance of Multiple Academy Trusts can also influence these relationships, as schools become part of Academy chains and adopt their educational emphases, so the relationship between those schools and the IOE has to develop and change. The IOE has developed an internal infrastructure of Partnership Co-ordinators and Institute Partnership Managers to ensure clear communication between subject teams and school organisations, and that the programme continues to adapt and provide the support needed to become a professional teacher in London.

Such an approach places a high level of trust and autonomy in individual teacher educators and is reliant on their individual expertise. Whilst there are quality assurance processes and procedures in place (aligned with the highly regulative inspection system by Ofsted), these are retrospective and so the institution has to trust in the expertise of its teacher educators to adapt as issues arise during a programme.

The Teach First leadership development programme

One of the challenges in reviewing the quality of the Teach First programme is that the programme itself has changed substantially over time. The programme stems from a contract which Teach First is awarded directly from the Department of Education and therefore is regularly up for retendering and renewal. The initial programme, supported by Canterbury Christ Church University, was limited to a small number of teachers in the London region. Each retendering offers an opportunity to restructure the programme, review its financial arrangements and its subcontracted relationship with partners. In the first iteration of the programme, Teach First took on the role of a recruiting organisation and the teacher education was provided largely by their university partner, Canterbury Christ Church University; over time, and with various contract iterations, Teach First has reduced the input and involvement of university-based specialist teacher educators and increased their role and input to the programme. It is therefore important to be specific about which version of the programme is being discussed.

The data for this research was collected in 2019; this was the second year of a new contract and new version of the Leadership Development Programme, which had just been validated as a PGDip (Post Graduate Diploma – worth 120 Masters credits or two-thirds of a Masters degree), a two-year employment-based route into teaching. The new programme was a significant departure from the previous iteration: some teacher educator roles (previously known as Professional Tutors and based in the university partner organisations) were removed and substituted by Participant Development Leads (PDLs) directly employed by Teach First, with a broader remit which included teaching on the programme as well as undertaking school visits. The increase in the role Teach First played in the teaching of the programme varied between half and two-thirds on the accredited elements. Therefore, the role and function of the university partner within the Teach First infrastructure had changed significantly.

Teach First is a national provider of teacher education, operating with eight university partners in England and one in Wales (at the time of data collection). The organisation and structure of the Teach First programme is therefore situated around a number of centralised elements. For example, student teachers, or participants as they were called, are recruited through a central Recruitment Centre(s) (renamed to Development Centre) and allocated to various regions. The programme is designed centrally by a national team but executed locally by Teach First staff (PDLs), who are organised regionally and contribute to the programme alongside school- and university-based colleagues. There is some regional variation, particularly in the university dimension of the course, but the programme is organised around central processes, systems and curriculum with an emphasis on consistency.

This is evident in the eight programme principles developed by Teach First and circulated to partners. The preamble to the Principles states:

> Teach First's Programme Principles set out 8 principles that we think will enable participants to make the most progress, the most quickly on the

Leadership Development Programme. They are based on a significant research base, and are updated annually in line with evidence from the sector, feedback from individuals using them and evaluation data about their impact.

(Teach First Programme Principles, 2019)

The eight principles are listed as:

- Alignment, consistence [sic] and simplicity;
- We are explicit about what we do and why;
- We include exposure to a wide range of debates in the system ensuring each is rooted in the most robust evidence around what constitutes effective practice;
- We ensure the curriculum meets the needs of the particular audience it is intended for;
- All curricula are appropriately sequenced;
- Deliberate practice is an explicit component of our programmes;
- Our programme is rooted in the most robust evidence around how pupils, and especially pupils from disadvantaged backgrounds, learn best; and
- A broad and balanced curriculum and the importance of knowledge and skills.

Teach First refers to research as a means for understanding the best way to both teach and learn to teach. The focus on deliberate practice is a key example of this not only as a principle in its own right, but with respect to how it is elaborated:

- Deliberate practice (in various forms) sits at the heart of development – a large body of research tells us why this type of practice is effective in supporting skill development.
- We believe that deliberate practice (and associated feedback from experts) towards carefully crafted targets, and supported by access to a range of outstanding practice, helps participants build clarity in confidence in all areas of their work.
- When combined with carefully structured reflection, deliberate practice is a powerful drive of development.

There is an explicit goal of "effectiveness" both in teaching and in teacher education, and with an emphasis on speed – although the parameters of this effectiveness remain undefined. The call to research (in this document un-referenced) sits alongside polemic affirmations ("we believe").

The leadership dimension of the Teach First programme has also been a unique and controversial aspect of the programme. Whilst there are some who have argued for the importance of seeing teachers as leaders (Blandford, 2014), the focus of leadership for the Teach First programme relates to the two-year commitment to teaching, and what graduates of the programme will have gained personally through their involvement and that will be of subsequent benefit to them when they leave the programme. The conflation of the ideas of leadership and training are problematic with an employment-based programme with relatively little taught content. This has been highlighted as a concern for their sister organisation TFA:

> Still, TFA can only do a fraction of what traditional teacher education programs do, given their brief five week window. The brevity of their training is the product of necessity, brought about by the fact that TFA corps members commit to teach for only two years. But it was once also a product of philosophy – a manifestation of the belief that bright and energetic novices could be quickly prepared for classroom success. That, however, no longer appears to be the case, and TFA employees refer internally to the 'dirty little secret' that great teachers cannot be produced in such a short period (Lewis 2008). Limits on TFA's growth, then, may send a powerful message about how long it takes to prepare a teacher to enter a classroom ready for work.
>
> *(Schneider, 2013)*

The Teach First programme is different to that of TFA, and in the iteration of the Teach First programme at the time of the data collection, the taught component of the programme was taught in part by both Teach First staff and UCL teacher educators. A member of the IOE team noted that this was a distinctive feature of the programme in relation to its academic content:

> So I think the quality of the Teach First program relies heavily on the quality input from the university. I think it's always been the case.
>
> *(IOE Interview, 2019)*

The Teach First Leadership Development Programme is an employment-based route, so the majority of the programme, outside of the initial five-week Summer Institute, is focused on schools where participants are employees and spend the majority of their time, and there is limited input to the programme that is not aligned with the Masters level parts of the programme. The structural arrangements of the programme therefore mean that for the majority of their time on the programme, student teachers (or participants) are engaged in employment as teachers and are undertaking classroom practice. This is addressed in the structure of the programme: where participants are introduced to some key teaching skills during the Summer Institute, and these are reinforced through a pedagogy of deliberate practice, facilitated through the mentoring particularly of PDLs and school-based colleagues to support these new teachers to develop a repertoire of functional skills.

Does the difference in approach matter?

As the programme outlines above demonstrate, the IOE's PGCE programmes and the Teach First Leadership Development Programme both adopt very different approaches to programme design, based on a different emphasis, and understanding of professional learning, and the different needs of their students. This is not uncommon, as Rauschenberger, Adams and Kennedy (2017) note that programmes are often orientated around contextual needs and what is valued. The early entry nature of the Teach First programme requires that teachers are able to start teaching at the start of the academic year, necessarily equipped with a limited range of strategies and approaches. The emphasis on deliberate practice, whilst shown to have minimal impact on professional fields outside of sport and music, could be seen to be appropriate for a conception of teaching as a skill or craft executed for a limited period of time. The IOE's focus on developing specialist expertise, at either a phase or subject level, is orientated to a different perception of need and conception of teacher education for a career-long profession.

There is much value in the "horses for courses" argument: recognising that different programmes have identified contrasting needs, different audiences and purposes, and so the pedagogy they have chosen reflects that. However this argument underplays the significance of ideology in the formation of the problems and the solutions that the programmes are addressing. For example, the Teach First programme is overt about the "problem" it seeks to address: educational disadvantage. The programme targets schools in challenging circumstances and participants who share their vision. The formation of the problem: that high-performing graduates can make a substantial difference even with minimum training, feeds into the education discourse of the current and recent governments, who are suspicious of university departments of education (Gibb, 2016)[4] and have expressed concern at the calibre of graduates who go into teaching (Department for Education, 2010). The adoption of a pedagogical strategy such as deliberate practice can be seen as a solution which aligns with this ideological position.

The position of the IOE is also political. As part of a research-intensive university, with a formidable reputation and with over 100 years' experience of preparing teachers for London, the IOE reflects a traditional view of teacher education that privileges research. The "problem" of teacher education for the IOE is also about quality and preparing teachers for London schools (which are high performing but also diverse and dynamic), but the emphasis at the IOE is about supporting local communities to address those challenges through a long-term career-orientated approach: offering research and critical perspectives that enable the teacher to adopt a stance in relation to their professional practice that will be generative throughout a teacher's career.

In this sense, they address the practice conundrum in different ways: for the IOE, practice is seen as a part of the transformational experience of learning to teach – a source of ideas that can challenge preconceptions; for Teach First, the emphasis is on being ready to practice – adapting behaviours to those that are considered most effective. These contrasting responses are rooted in their relationship to the areas they serve. The IOE has a long tradition as a London provider, preferring former London teachers as teacher educators, and generating the curriculum around the experience of teaching in London schools. This approach explicitly celebrates the diversity of both those schools and the pupils who attend them and views that diversity as a valuable source of knowledge that can positively influence teaching. Teach First is a national programme, and whilst has remained rooted in London since its inception, its focus is more on schools in challenging circumstances (although that criteria has been relaxed when they have had difficulty finding school placements). Schools are the practice site for the new teachers alongside having a responsibility to them as their employers.

In terms of the relative space, it is significant that both organisations are the largest two providers of teacher education nationally (at the time of the data collection). Teach First is part of a significant policy network (Olmedo et al., 2013) and an international Teach For All network. Teach First is often represented on DfE Working groups and other influential policymaking opportunities and are widely connected with Multiple Academy Trusts and educational social enterprises (particularly as they many include Teach First Ambassadors). The IOE is also influential but in a different sphere: with wide connections nationally and internationally as part of the Russell Group of universities, research networks and regular attendance at many international conferences and events. Former IOE Directors have also been present in policymaking circles. Across London, the IOE works with around 700 schools, and with teacher educators undertaking all site visits, the IOE sustains significant knowledge on what happens in those schools. Teach First works with a range of schools nationally that meet their criteria. This status and hierarchy gives both organisations considerable influence and prestige. Both are important in supporting the supply of teachers for London and have wide networks, which they tend to exploit in different ways.

Nationally, Teach First places significantly more emphasis and financial resources into marketing (than the IOE), and have a wider and more effective presence in the public consciousness. Teach First are able to exert more soft power, both in relation to the public awareness and in policy circles. The IOE's influence is more in the research sphere. In this sense, the IOE contributes differently to the representational space of teacher education, and in particular in how teachers are viewed. In a city like London, arguably there is space for both, and taken together they could be seen as balance: the dynamic and enthusiastic sitting well alongside the considered and thoughtful. However, this only works if they are indeed in balance. And recent developments would suggest that this balance is shifting.

Teach First have diversified their policy on recruitment. Originally, Teach First sought to recruit "participants" who might not have previously considered teaching an option. The veracity of this claim has been questioned (see Rauschenberger, 2016). Nevertheless, Teach First originally sought to recruit participants achieving good degrees (a 2:1 or above) from prestigious universities such as those from the Russell Group. As the target numbers for Teach First increased, so they had to move away from what the leadership referred to as "Tier One" towards "Regional" universities. This was attributed to the growth of the programme to cover all areas of England and the desire for some graduates to remain in the area where they studied. The IOE Programme team noted that increasingly they were seeing participants with lower A'level (the public examination required for university entrance) grades, and that participants were finding the course more demanding and experiencing more mental health issues, and ultimately achieving lower results (than in previous years and also in relation to other student teachers on commensurate IOE teacher education programmes). The changing nature of the Teach First participants raises questions as to whether the programme remains a short-term experience programme for high-performing graduates that emphasises a practice-based orientation. If participants are likely to view Teach First as an alternative route to a teaching career and less as a steppingstone to a career elsewhere, then questions do need to be raised as to whether this would require a rethinking of their pedagogical strategy.

Practice is political

The IOE and the Teach First have responded differently to the practice quality conundrum. The IOE's focus is to equip teachers with the intellectual and specialist resources they need in order to be able to reflect on practice in a critical and informed way throughout their career. This is based on an assumption that the nature of practice will change, and so teachers will need resources to adapt to those changes. In that sense, the programme seeks to balance an emphasis on practice by focusing on what is needed for career-long development, and to introduce student teachers to a range of knowledges and ideas that will challenge and potentially transform them. This leads to a challenging and demanding programme. The Teach First approach is to focus on teaching as leadership and on being classroom-ready for the duration of their commitment to schools. Their response to the practice quality conundrum is to focus on quality in the short term: to be classroom-ready. The use of deliberate practice focuses the scope of transformation to classroom practice. Should teachers continue after their two years, Teach First offers other leadership programmes for development. There is an orientation to practice here which is not just pragmatic, but also, I would argue, political.

As outlined above, Teach First is an influential organisation within the English education policymaking (see Olmedo et al., 2013) and has direct influence with the government. Papers from influential think tanks such as the Education Policy Institute hail the Teach First approach as the way forward to address the "problems" of the supply of quality teachers in England (Freedman, Lipson, & Hargreaves, 2008). Teach First, as part of the Teach For All movement, is often seen as the answer to many policy-related problems around teacher education – university-based teacher education as the cause.

In contrast, the IOE has a different reputation, and has been considered part of the Blob, an unflattering term used by Conservative politicians and their supporters to describe the education establishment (McIntyre et al., 2017; Menter,

2017; Whiting et al., 2018). Ball and Exley (2010) note the "clear ambivalence towards academia" (p. 153) expressed in government and think tank literature. The IOE is part of a research-intensive university, with a formidable reputation for education, therefore could be guilty of the criticism of similar organisations:

> There is a sense that academics remain unhelpfully out of touch with real and practical policy problems; that they are detached, cynical and more concerned with peer review, the Research Assessment Exercise and spending time thinking than with getting on and doing.
>
> *(Ibid., p. 153)*

Within this context, adopting deliberate practice as a dominant pedagogical approach acts as a signifier to a particular type of education ideology dominant in the English education system. The polarisation of educational approaches characterises progressive, child-centred education and discovery or enquiry learning on one side, and knowledge-rich curriculum, direct instruction and a focus on deliberate practice on the other. By signalling their support for direct instruction, knowledge-rich curriculum and using the pedagogy of deliberate practice, Teach First is also sending a clear signal that it is different from other teacher education providers. This pedagogical statement aligns it to other disruptors in the field of teacher education, along the lines of the Deans for Impact in the US. In this sense, the pedagogical approach is not just about the best way to learn to teach or for developing a pedagogy for transformation, but is also a political message.

However, is this the best way to support the transformation of new teachers? Teach First's emphasis on deliberate practice and being classroom-ready aligns with their formation as an early entry programme, an employment-based route. The pedagogical approach focuses on classroom behaviours. This is appropriate for the needs of their participants at that particular time. The PGCE at the IOE is a programme of gradual immersion into teaching. The year-long programme is designed to expose new teachers to a range of ideas, theories and experiences that will challenge them with a view to affecting transformation for the long term. Whilst both programmes have adopted a pedagogical strategy suitable for the needs of their students, the question remains as to whether they are commensurate professional preparation for a career in teaching.

Notes

1 https://www.ucl.ac.uk/ioe/about-ioe/history-ioe.
2 Provider tables: ITT trainee number census 2018–2019.https://www.gov.uk/government/statistics/initial-teacher-training-trainee-number-census-2018-to-2019.
3 https://epi.org.uk/publications-and-research/the-teacher-labour-market-in-england/.
4 https://researched.org.uk/tom-bennett-speaks-to-nick-gibb/.

References

Baars, S., Bernardes, E., Elwick, A., Malortie, A., McAleavy, T., McInerney, L., ... Riggall, A. (2014). *Lessons from London schools: Investigating the success*. Reading: CfBT Education Trust.

Ball, S. J., & Exley, S. (2010). Making policy with 'good ideas': Policy networks and the 'intellectuals' of New Labour. *Journal of Education Policy, 25*(2), 151–169. doi:10.1080/02680930903486125

Blandford, S. (2014). Leading through partnership: Enhancing the teach first leadership programme. *Teacher Development, 18*(1), 1–14. doi:10.1080/13664530.2013.863801

Brown, T. (2017). *Teacher education in England: A critical interrogation of school-led training*. London: Routledge.

Catling, S. (2017). Not nearly enough geography! University provision for England's pre-service primary teachers. *Journal of Geography in Higher Education, 41*(3), 434–458. doi:10.1080/03098265.2017.1331422

Childs, A. (2013). The work of teacher educators: An English policy perspective. *Journal of Education for Teaching, 39*(3), 314–328. doi:10.1080/02607476.2013.799848

Cochran-Smith, M., & Lytle, S. L. (1993). *Inside/outside: Teacher research and knowledge*. New York: Teachers College Press.

Cochran-Smith, M., & Lytle, S. L. (1999a). Chapter 8: Relationships of knowledge and practice: Teacher learning in communities. *Review of Research in Education, 24*(1), 249–305. doi:10.3102/0091732X024001249

Cochran-Smith, M., & Lytle, S. L. (1999b). The teacher research movement: A decade later. *Educational Researcher, 28*(7), 15–25.

Cochran-Smith, M., Stringer Keefe, E., & Carney, M. C. (2018). Teacher educators as reformers: Competing agendas. *European Journal of Teacher Education, 41*(5), 572–590. doi:10.1080/02619768.2018.1523391

Cottom, T. M. (2017). *Lower ed: The troubling rise of for-profit colleges in the new economy*. New York: The New Press.

Czerniawski, G., Gray, D., MacPhail, A., Bain, Y., Conway, P., & Guberman, A. (2018). The professional learning needs and priorities of higher-education-based teacher educators in England, Ireland and Scotland. *Journal of Education for Teaching, 44*(2), 133–148. doi:10.1080/02607476.2017.1422590

Darling-Hammond, L. (1994). Who will speak for the children? *Phi Delta Kappan, 76*(1), 41–54.

Darling-Hammond, L. (2006). *Powerful teacher education: Lessons from exemplary programs*. San Francisco, CA: John Wiley & Sons.

Darling-Hammond, L. (2017). Teacher education around the world: What can we learn from international practice? *European Journal of Teacher Education, 40*(3), 291–309. doi:10.1080/02619768.2017.1315399

Darling-Hammond, L., Flook, L., Cook-Harvey, C., Barron, B., & Osher, D. (2019). Implications for educational practice of the science of learning and development. *Applied Developmental Science, 24*(2), 97–140. doi:10.1080/10888691.2018.1537791

Darling-Hammond, L., & Lieberman, A. (2013). *Teacher education around the world: Changing policies and practices*. Abingdon: Routledge.

Darling-Hammond, L., Macdonald, M. B., Snyder, J., Whitford, B. L., Ruscoe, G., & Fickel, L. (2000). *Studies of excellence in teacher education: Preparation at the graduate level*. Washington, DC: ATCEE.

Darling-Hammond, L., & Oakes, J. (2019). *Preparing teachers for deeper learning*. Cambridge, MA: Harvard Education Press.

Deans for Impact. (2016). *Practice with purpose: The emerging science of teacher expertise*. Austin, TX: Deans for Impact.

Department for Education. (2010). *The importance of teaching* (9780101798020). Retrieved from London. https://assets.publishing.service.gov.uk/government/uploads/system/uploads/attachment_data/file/175429/CM-7980.pdf

Dunn, R., Hattie, J., & Bowles, T. (2018). Exploring the experiences of teachers undertaking Educational Design Research (EDR) as a form of teacher professional learning. *Professional Development in Education, 45*(1), 151–167. doi:10.1080/19415257.2018.1500389

Edmond, N., & Hayler, M. (2013). On either side of the teacher: Perspectives on professionalism in education. *Journal of Education for Teaching, 39*(2), 209–221. doi:10.1080/02607476.2013.765193

Edwards-Groves, C., & Grootenboer, P. (2015). Praxis and the theory of practice architectures: Resources for re-envisioning English education. *Australian Journal of Language and Literacy, 38*(3), 150–161.

Ellis, V., Maguire, M., Trippestad, T. A., Liu, Y., Yang, X., & Zeichner, K. (2015). Teaching other people's children, elsewhere, for a while: The rhetoric of a travelling educational reform. *Journal of Education Policy, 31*(1), 60–80. doi:10.1080/02680939.2015.1066871

Ellis, V., & Spendlove, D. (2020). Mediating 'School Direct': The enactment of a reform policy by university-based teacher educators in England. *British Educational Research Journal*. doi:10.1002/berj.3607

Ellis, V., Steadman, S., & Trippestad, T. A. (2018). Teacher education and the GERM: Policy entrepreneurship, disruptive innovation and the rhetorics of reform. *Educational Review, 71*(1), 101–121. doi:10.1080/00131911.2019.1522040

Eraut, M. (1994). *Developing professional knowledge and competence*. London: Falmer Press.

Eraut, M. (1995). Schön Shock: A case for reframing reflection-in-action? *Teachers and Teaching: Theory and Practice, 1*(1), 9–22.

Ericsson, K. A., Krampe, R. T., & Tesch-Römer, C. (1993). The role of deliberate practice in the acquisition of expert performance. *Psychological Review, 100*(3), 363–406.

Fejes, A. (2011). Confession, in-service training and reflective practices. *British Educational Research Journal, 37*(5), 797–812. doi:10.1080/01411926.2010.500371

Freedman, S., Lipson, B., & Hargreaves, D. (2008). *More good teachers* (9781906097301). Retrieved from London. https://policyexchange.org.uk/wp-content/uploads/2016/09/more-good-teachers-apr-08.pdf

Furlong, J. (2013). *Education – An anatomy of the discipline: Rescuing the university project*. Abingdon: Routledge.

George, R., & Maguire, M. (2018). Choice and diversity in English initial teacher education (ITE): Trainees' perspectives. *European Journal of Teacher Education, 42*(1), 19–35. doi:10.1080/02619768.2018.1544613

Gladwell, M. (2008). *Outliers: The story of success*. London: Penguin.

Hambrick, D. Z., Oswald, F. L., Altmann, E. M., Meinz, E. J., Gobet, F., & Campitelli, G. (2014). Deliberate practice: Is that all it takes to become an expert? *Intelligence, 45*, 34–45. doi:10.1016/j.intell.2013.04.001

Heilbronn, R., & Yandell, J. (2010). *Critical practice in teacher education: A study of professional learning*. London: Institute of Education, University of London.

Henry, J. (2020). The cinematic pedagogies of underprepared teachers. *Teaching and Teacher Education, 89*, 102990. doi:10.1016/j.tate.2019.102990

Hui, A., Schatzki, T., & Shove, E. (2016). *The nexus of practices: Connections, constellations, practitioners*. Abingdon: Taylor & Francis.

Jackson, A., & Burch, J. (2018). New directions for teacher education: Investigating school/university partnership in an increasingly school-based context. *Professional Development in Education, 45*(1), 138–150. doi:10.1080/19415257.2018.1449002

Jones, J., & Ellis, V. (2019). Simple and complex views of teacher development. In *Oxford research Encyclopedia, education*. Oxford: Oxford University Press. https://doi.org/10.1093/acrefore/9780190264093.013.418

Kirby, S. N., McCombs, J. S., Barney, H., & Naftel, S. (2006). *Reforming teacher education; something old, something new*. Retrieved from Santa Monica: https://www.rand.org/content/dam/rand/pubs/monographs/2006/RAND_MG506.pdf

Knight, R. (2012). The emerging professional: An investigation into teacher education students' developing conceptions of the relationship between theory and classroom practice before, during and after a postgraduate teaching programme. *Journal of Education for Teaching, 38*(2), 209–210. doi:10.1080/02607476.2012.656446

Korthagen, F., Loughran, J., & Russell, T. (2006). Developing fundamental principles for teacher education programs and practices. *Teaching and Teacher Education, 22*(8), 1020–1041. doi:10.1016/j.tate.2006.04.022

Labaree, D. F. (2006). *The trouble with ed schools*. New Haven, CT: Yale University Press.

Lemov, D. (2010). *Teach like a champion: 49 techniques that put students on the path to college*. San Francisco, CA: Jossey-Bass.

Lewis, A. 2008. "Personal Recollection." Unpublished Electronic Document. Teach For America, New York. Cited in Schneider, J. (2013). Rhetoric and practice in pre-service teacher education: The case of Teach For America. *Journal of Education Policy, 29*(4), 425–442. doi:10.1080/02680939.2013.825329

Loewenberg Ball, D., & Forzani, F. M. (2009). The work of teaching and the challenge for teacher education. *Journal of Teacher Education, 60*(5), 497–511. doi:10.1177/0022487109348479

Lortie, D. C. (1975). *Schoolteacher*. Chicago, IL: University of Chicago Press.

Mayer, D., Allard, A., Bates, R., Dixon, M., Doecke, B., Kline, J., ... White, S. (2015). *Studying the effectiveness of teacher education*. Dordrecht: Springer.

McIntyre, J., Youens, B., & Stevenson, H. (2017). Silenced voices: The disappearance of the university and the student teacher in teacher education policy discourse in England. *Research Papers in Education, 34*(2), 153–168. doi:10.1080/02671522.2017.1402084

McKenney, S., & Schunn, C. D. (2018). How can educational research support practice at scale? Attending to educational designer needs. *British Educational Research Journal, 44*(6), 1084–1100. doi:10.1002/berj.3480

McNamara, O., Murray, J., & Phillips, R. (2017). *Policy and research evidence in the 'reform' of primary initial teacher education in England*. Cambridge: Primary Review Trust Cambridge.

Menter, I. (2017). *The role and contribution of higher education in contemporary teacher education*. Retrieved from http://www.scde.ac.uk/wp-content/uploads/2017/05/Report-Ian-Menter-2017-05-25.pdf

Menter, I., Hulme, M., Elliot, D., Lewin, J., Baumfield, V., Britton, A., ... McQueen, I. (2010). *Literature review on teacher education in the 21st century* (S. G. S. Reserach Ed.). Glasgow: University of Glasgow.

Moore, A. (2004). *The good teacher: Dominant discourses in teaching and teacher education*. London: RoutledgeFalmer.

Muijs, D., Chapman, C., & Armstrong, P. (2012). Teach first: Pedagogy and outcomes. The impact of an alternative certification programme. *Journal for Educational Research Online, 4*(2), 29–64.

Muijs, D., Chapman, C., & Armstrong, P. (2013). Can early careers teachers be teacher leaders? A study of second-year trainees in the teach first alternative certification programme. *Educational Management Administration & Leadership, 41*(6), 767–781. doi:10.1177/1741143213494188

Mutton, T., Burn, K., & Menter, I. (2016). Deconstructing the Carter review: Competing conceptions of quality in England's 'school-led' system of initial teacher education. *Journal of Education Policy, 32*(1), 14–33. doi:10.1080/02680939.2016.1214751

Nicolini, D. (2012). *Practice theory, work, and organization: An introduction.* Oxford: Oxford University Press.

O'Kelly, J. (2019). *The value of initial teacher training: Generating controlled or activist professionalism?* UCL Institute of Education, Unpublished EdD thesis.

Ofsted. (2018). Building great teachers? Initial teacher education curriculum research: Phase 2. Retrieved from https://www.gov.uk/government/publications/initial-teacher-education-curriculum-research/building-great-teachers

Olmedo, A., Bailey, P. L. J., & Ball, S. J. (2013). To infinity and beyond …: Heterarchical governance, the Teach For All network in Europe and the making of profits and minds. *European Educational Research Journal, 12*(4), 492–512. doi:10.2304/eerj.2013.12.4.492

Pachler, N. (2013). 'Interesting times' or teacher education and professionalism in a 'brave new world'. In M. Evans (Ed.), *Teacher education and pedagogy: Theory, policy and practice* (pp. 23–40). Cambridge: Cambridge University Press.

Parker, G. (2015). School direct: A critique. *Power and Education, 7*(1), 106–112. doi:10.1177/1757743814567390

Perryman, J. (2011). The return of the native: The blurred boundaries of insider/outsider research in an English secondary school. *International Journal of Qualitative Studies in Education, 24*(7), 857–874. doi:10.1080/09518398.2010.529842

Philip, T. M., Souto-Manning, M., Anderson, L., Horn, I., J. Carter Andrews, D., Stillman, J., & Varghese, M. (2018). Making justice peripheral by constructing practice as "core": How the increasing prominence of core practices challenges teacher education. *Journal of Teacher Education, 70*(3), 251–264. doi:10.1177/0022487118798324

Popkewitz, T. S. (1985). Ideology and social formation in teacher education. *Teaching and Teacher Education, 1*(2), 91–107.

Rauschenberger, E. (2016). *Reconstructing the emergence of teach first: Examining the role of policy entrepreneurs and networks in the process of policy transfer.* Doctor of Philosophy, The University of Edinburgh, Edinburgh.

Rauschenberger, E., Adams, P., & Kennedy, A. (2017). *Measuring quality in initial teacher education: A literature review for Scotland's MQuITE study* (S. C. o. D. o. E. (scde.ac.uk) Ed.). Edinburgh: Scottish Council of Deans of Education (scde.ac.uk).

Schatzki, T. R., Cetina, K. K., & Von Savigny, E. (2005). *The practice turn in contemporary theory.* Abingdon: Routledge.

Schleicher, A. (2012). *Preparing teachers and developing school leaders for the 21st century: Lessons from around the world.* Paris: OECD Publishing.

Schneider, J. (2013). Rhetoric and practice in pre-service teacher education: The case of Teach For America. *Journal of Education Policy, 29*(4), 425–442. doi:10.1080/02680939.2013.825329

Shulman, L. (1986). Those who understand: Knowledge growth in teaching. *Educational Researcher, 15*(2), 4–14.

Stuit, D., & Smith, T. (2012). Explaining the gap in charter and traditional public school teacher turnover rates. *Economics of Education Review, 31*(2), 268–279.

Syed, M. (2010). *Bounce.* London: Collins.

Tatto, M. T., Richmond, G., & Carter Andrews, D. J. (2016). The research we need in teacher education. *Journal of Teacher Education, 67*(4), 247–250. doi:10.1177/0022487116663694

Toma, E., & Zimmer, R. (2012). Two decades of charter schools: Expectations, reality, and the future. *Economics of Education Review, 31*(2), 209–212.

Totterdell, M., & Lambert, D. (1998). The professional formation of teachers: A case study in reconceptualising initial teacher education through an evolving model of partnership in training and learning. *Teacher Development, 2*(3), 351–371. doi:10.1080/13664539800200066

Whiting, C., Whitty, G., Menter, I., Black, P., Hordern, J., Parfitt, A., ... Sorensen, N. (2018). Diversity and complexity: Becoming a teacher in England in 2015–2016. *Review of Education, 6*(1), 69–96. doi:10.1002/rev3.3108

Winch, C. (2017). *Teachers' know-how: A philosophical investigation*. Chichester: John Wiley & Sons.

Worth, J., De Lazzari, G., & Hillary, J. (2017). *Teacher retention and turnover research: Interim report*. Slough: NFER.

Zeichner, K. (2012). The turn once again toward practice-based teacher education. *Journal of Teacher Education, 63*(5), 376–382.

Zeichner, K. (2016). *Independent teacher education programs: Apocryphal claims, illusory evidence*. Boulder, CO: National Education Policy Center.

3
THE RESEARCH QUALITY CONUNDRUM

The previous chapter questioned the role of practice in teacher education. In a similar vein, questions can be asked about the role of research and the extent to which it enhances initial teacher education (ITE), or if an overemphasis on research detracts from practice knowledge and experience. As Bullough Jr. has argued, the term research, and that of researcher, is an honorific, embodied with status and authority (2014). Research is often placed in opposition to practice: as an intellectual activity that can "get in the way" of teachers focusing on their practical skills, and so as an unnecessary distraction to ITE. This binary thinking is largely due to a lack of clarity in how research (in its various forms) can contribute to teacher education. The quality conundrum in this chapter is whether research enhances teacher education or that too much emphasis on research can actually distract new teachers focusing on developing their classroom practice.

Research in teacher education can take many forms (Menter, 2017), not all of which are directly related to the teacher education pedagogy. In the previous chapter, I highlighted the turn towards practice, which by implication indicates a turn away from something, potentially research. However, before exploring the contribution that research can make to ITE specifically, it is important to consider the link between research and universities. Research is an activity undertaken by universities but is also a signifier of power and status: the contribution of research to teacher education has implications for the role that universities can play within teacher education.

Universities and teacher education

In some places, universities have been somewhat side-lined from the debates around ITE, sometimes ignoring the key role they play in the provision for new teachers (Ellis, Steadman, & Trippestad, 2018; Zeichner, 2017). For example, despite the well-documented move to a school-led teacher education system in England (since the 2010 White Paper *The Importance of Teaching*), Ofsted report that four-fifths of "trainees" in 2018/2019 were trained through partnerships with a higher education institution (Ofsted, 2018). Even in highly diversified systems, the supply of new teachers often relies on the participation of universities in teacher education.

Universities have not always been central in teacher education. The history of ITE in different international contexts notes that the move from Teachers Colleges and Normal Schools into universities is a fairly recent occurrence (Furlong & Whitty, 2017; Labaree, 2008; Pring, 2017). Shifting teacher education into universities can be seen as a way of raising the status of teachers and to enhance their perceived professionalism. Making universities central to teacher education places greater emphasis on the development and sharing of a specialist, expert and often research-based body of knowledge. Initially, this stemmed from the so-called foundational disciplines of philosophy, psychology, history and sociology, but has since diversified into academic, practical and integrated knowledge traditions (Furlong & Whitty, 2017).

However, as Labaree (2008) notes, moving ITE into universities has not always been a satisfactory arrangement. From the viewpoint of universities, teacher education is considered a weak discipline with a poor track record of research. From the perspectives of teacher educators, who come from a different career trajectory to most academics (see Chapter 5), there are challenges in meeting the criteria for a successful career in academia. Labaree's pessimistic account quotes Theodore Sizer and Arthur Powell (writing as the dean and associate dean of the Harvard Graduate School of Education) who describe the professor of education as "pathetic ... gentle, unintellectual, saccharine, and well-meaning, the bumbling doctors of undiagnosable ills, harmless if morosely defensive" (Labaree, 2006, quoted on page 111). The discipline of education suffers from a lack of status in the academy.

A specialist body of knowledge is reliant upon knowledge generation either through theory-building or empirical research. Universities provide the context for the development of such research. Although not always part of universities' remit (Collini, 2012; Connell, 2019; Watson, Hollister, Stroud, & Babcock, 2011), the capacity to undertake and verify research sets universities apart from other organisations. Even today, when multiple organisations, including schools, engage in research, universities offer a special role and function as the home of disciplinary communities and a key authority in the ethical oversight, validation and verification of knowledge (Furlong & Whitty, 2017). Young and Muller (2014) have argued that such a perspective is necessary to counter the anti-intellectualism of professional development (often found in fields which emphasise expertise over knowledge).

However, the relationship between universities and education research is not set in stone or universal. In England particularly, schools and third-sector organisations are becoming increasingly prominent in educational research.

This has been exacerbated by the approach of the English government's main education research funding body, the Education Endowment Foundation (EEF), which funds a narrow range of research and through a narrow range of research methodologies (Randomised Control Trials), described as overly instrumentalised (Ellis et al., 2018; Godfrey, 2017; Hulme, Wood, & Shi, 2020; Turvey, 2018; Turvey & Pachler, 2020). The types of research funded and produced by the EEF has been described by Turvey (2018) as dehumanising because of its overemphasis on data and lack of recognition of the human dimension of education. There is also a strong trend towards schools increasing their engagement with research, both through ensuring aspects of their work are research-informed but also that they become research-engaged, and drive their own research agendas (Godfrey, 2017; Greany & Brown, 2015; Greany et al., 2014; McAleavy, 2016; Wisby & Whitty, 2019).

At the same time the sorts of research that are often referred to in teacher education and to education more broadly are rarely attributed to university departments of teacher education. Pring (2017) notes how the most significant theories affecting education are more likely to come from faculties outside teacher education such as from sociology or psychology. Indeed, research stemming from educational faculties has been widely criticised and education academics as being uninterested in the concerns of policymakers (Ball & Exley, 2010). Whilst education's performance in university-based research-assessment exercises have been defended (Furlong, 2013), these trends are exacerbated by the perception of teacher education research as being of low quality and lacking in robust theory or reliant on weak methodologies.

However, research orientation is not the only reason for situating ITE within universities. As Freidson (2001) has argued, universities also play a key role as gatekeepers for entry to a profession (thus maintaining its exclusionary status) and offer a context for professional socialisation, through induction into the professional culture, or accepted ways of behaving ethically within the profession. These features, Friedson argues, are key in distinguishing professions from other occupations and are central to why university-based education is a prerequisite to professional status. However, these features of socialisation and gatekeeping are more often associated with the more traditional professions (such as law and medicine) which have more distinctive specialist bodies of knowledge and where the profession itself has more autonomy about setting entry requirements and professional codes of conduct. University-based socialisation and gatekeeping is not necessary with an occupation more commonly aligned with professional training than education, and where governments and external (to the profession) regulatory bodies determine who can join the profession and how they should behave.

The practice turn (outlined in Chapter 2) in education has changed the relationships between universities and schools. Universities are not as influential in ITE as they once were, particularly in England after the move to a school-led education system (see Brown, 2017). The relationship between universities and schools is also becoming increasingly fragmented, as federations of schools such as

Multiple Academy Trusts, Charter Chains and other third-sector and commercial organisations become more prominent in education. For example, analysis of networks of social enterprises (Ball, 2012), and in particular around the Teach for All/Teach First network, shows a range of connections and relationships between third-sector organisations which Olmedo, Bailey and Ball (2013) argue shows a shift in the governance of teacher education across Europe. In other words, these new networks are related nationally and internationally and differ to the traditional local affiliations between universities with a local network of partnership schools or with international disciplinary communities. In addition, schools are increasingly turning to third-sector organisations like ResearchED[1] to support research-based professional development and research updates.

The role of universities therefore is changing, and previously held assumptions about the importance of research, universities and prestige in relation to teacher education need to be considered in the light of this changing dynamic. With reference to teacher education, however, if the flow of ideas is central to the pedagogical approach that will bring about transformation, then the question comes as to where those ideas are generated. Universities, with the responsibilities towards professionalisation outlined above, reflect a view of knowledge that can be viewed as hierarchical. Knowledge generated by schools, either through research or experience, is often considered of lower status and may be less likely to gain wide recognition.

Research in teacher education

The role of research in ITE is widely defended. Darling-Hammond and colleagues have argued that a research orientation appears to be a strong feature of teacher education in so-called high performing systems (Darling-Hammond, 2006; Darling-Hammond & Lieberman, 2013; Darling-Hammond et al., 2000), and that it is increasingly important as teaching becomes more complex.

There are three common ways in which research can feature within ITE programmes:

- **Research as a form of academic engagement**: Reflecting a career continuum that sees engagement in academic research as progression route for teachers into teacher education or education research;
- **Research as content**: Making up the knowledge base for teacher education through research-informed or evidence-based findings about ways to teach; and
- **Research as pedagogy**: Using research as a way of learning about teaching both in the initial stages but providing a pedagogy of professional development and improvement throughout a teacher's career.

Perhaps the least common in this trilogy is the idea of research as a form of academic engagement, particularly for ITE. Whilst pursuing an academic career directly from graduation from ITE programmes is uncommon, it is not unusual to find some Masters programmes in education suggesting that doctoral studies or research trajectories are viable post-qualification options. It is also true that many teacher educators have engaged with research at a Doctoral or Masters' level and that many educational researchers have had some experience in the classroom. However, it is unusual to present a research career as a goal of *initial* teacher education.

It has become increasingly commonplace to suggest that teachers should be research-informed and that this should start with their initial induction to the profession. For example, the Carter Review of initial teacher training in England argued that there are limitations on trainees' abilities to engage fully in research, and positions them as "intelligent consumers of research who take an evidence-based approach to their own practice" (Carter, 2015, p. 21). The review recommends the creation of "synthesised executive summaries providing practical advice on research findings about effective teaching in different subjects and phases" (p. 8). The combination of both assertions places the teacher as a passive consumer of research who is also unable to make selections about the sorts of research they wish to engage with as this has been curated by the authors of these executive summaries. This argument is supported by both the short nature of ITE programmes (less than ten months duration in England) and the complex understanding of research and its associated methodologies needed in order to make informed judgements about the validity of research findings.

However, this does raise the question as to whether such curation is beneficial for new teachers. On the one hand, the curation of research can target and select the most appropriate research for teachers and present the findings and ideas therein in "digestible" form, allowing teachers to focus on how to use that research in their practice. On the other hand, such a selection will necessarily have omissions, limiting the range of ideas available to new teachers, and the opportunity to fully understand the parameters and limitations of the research, potentially limiting the opportunities for transformation. Some of this selection already takes place; the Carter Review noted that within research-intensive institutions, it is often the case that active researchers are not fully engaged in teacher education programmes. In other words, whilst those who did the research may do "guest lectures", the majority of teacher education was undertaken by staff who were not research active or actively engaged in research projects; research was more of content on those programmes than immersion as part of an active research community.

This position taps into a long-held concern about undertaking a programme of professional education in a research-orientated setting (such as a university) which may not devote sufficient time or attention to the training necessary to develop practical experience and teaching expertise. Even in universities, Furlong (2013) argues that all teacher education includes some form of training. The Carter Review positions the university or school providing teacher education as a curator of knowledge: selecting, synthesising and presenting research findings into consumable portions for novice teachers. This argument is replicated in the public discourse, and can be found on much of the social media criticisms of teacher education and in the titles of publications such as Sarah Mullin's book *What they didn't teach me on my PGCE* (2019).

However, this approach, with an on over-emphasis on practice, replicates a technical perception of teaching that underplays its complexity and situated nature. The idea of research as pedagogy places research somewhat differently within ITE as a form of learning. Within this category, there is not widespread agreement as to what research as pedagogy looks like. For example, Menter and colleagues' (2010) categorisation of different forms of teacher professionalism shows how different forms of ITE position research differently (and cumulatively). For example:

- The effective teacher: with an emphasis on meeting standards and competences, positions research as content to be digested and understood;
- The reflective teacher: with an emphasis on individual professional development achieved through practice, positions research as being a tool with which to challenge assumptions based on experience;
- The enquiring teacher: adopts an enquiry approach, which in some cases has veered towards a research orientation; and
- The transformative teacher: adopts an activist stance in relation to enquiries in order to contribute to social change and sees research as emancipatory.

Research can therefore be seen as a way of challenging assumptions about teaching, as a way of investigating and inquiring into practice, but also as a way of challenging issues of equity, and justice that exist within education and providing a range of ideas possible for transformation. This can be undertaken in a variety of ways. Toom et al. (2019) argue that focusing on incidences can help to trigger teacher development from research, whilst Farley-Ripple, May, Karpyn, Tilley and McDonough (2018) offer a conceptualising of the relationship between teacher development and research. So whilst research is viewed positively for ITE by many teacher educators (Afdal & Spernes, 2018), due attention needs to be paid to how it is used. For example, there are variations in how candidates respond to research-based ITE (Puustinen, Säntti, Koski, & Tammi, 2018), and the kinds of evidence which can affect teachers practice (Nutley, Walter, & Davies, 2003) and how practitioners situate themselves in relation to research findings (Biesta, 2007).

Clinical practice

One of the most popular ways of integrating research into practice is through the adoption of clinical practice. A landmark document in this debate is the BERA/RSA report (Burn & Mutton, 2013) which outlines the importance of research in teacher education, highlighting the distinction between teachers as producers and consumers of research and the implications this has for ITE. Whilst generated specifically within the UK, the report has had resonance internationally (White, Down, Mills, Shore, & Woods, 2020), as it outlines with examples that clinical practice, and in particular research-informed clinical practice, can have wide applicability in a range of contexts.

The clinical practice model has become a defining feature of many teacher education programmes (ATCEE, 2010; Burn & Mutton, 2015; Dunn, Hattie, & Bowles, 2018; Heilbronn & Yandell, 2010). It is often seen as a way of counteracting an apprenticeship model of teacher education (Dunn et al., 2018) and supporting teacher development that is more holistic and long lasting. Early iterations saw clinical practice as a way of elevating reflection-in-action into a more rigorous tool to support teachers to make decisions about practice (Lambert & Totterdell, 1996) and to appreciate the importance of context (Totterdell & Lambert, 1998). In other words, clinical practice was seen as a way of broadening the range of ideas that new teachers were exposed to, thereby linking theory and practice (Flores, 2018), bridging practices (Loewenberg Ball, 2000), elevating experiences from practice into meaningful learning about teaching (Cramp & Khan, 2018; Kostiainen et al., 2018) and enabling new teachers to gain a deeper understanding of their context (Alvunger & Wahlström, 2017).

However, there are some substantial differences in how clinical practice looks in practice. One of the most well-known theorisations of clinical practice is that of practical theorising as developed by Hagger and McIntyre on the Oxford Internship Scheme (OIS) (Hagger & McIntyre, 2006; McIntyre, 1990, 1995). The OIS particularly emphasises the partnership model recognising the distinctive (and equally valuable) knowledge and expertise held within schools. School partners therefore share responsibility for the support of the "interns" and share responsibility for the curriculum. The conception of practical theorising addresses problems with reflective practice as the main pedagogical strategy for teacher education, by recognising that practicum experiences are often not enough for genuine reflective practice. Through practical theorising, beginning teachers can learn from other people's ideas, both experienced practitioners and that of education scholars, and then submit them to critical examination (Hagger & McIntyre, 2006).

However, there have been criticisms of this approach to learning to teach and how it was developed (Ellis & Childs, 2019). The OIS has been characterised specifically by Ellis (2010) as the impoverishing of experience, and he questions whether close alignment enables both university teacher educators and student teachers (or interns) to critique school practice (Ellis, 2010). In other contexts, Tatto and Hordern (2017) note that different contexts place various emphasis on practice or disciplinary knowledge which can marginalise the focus on technical competence. Wieser (2018) has also questioned the research that teacher actually use in practice, whilst Puustinen et al. (2018) have argued that the connection between research and practice is not always clear. There are various ways of conceptualising research then in relation to practice and as part of a pedagogy for teacher education, and this is at the heart of the research quality conundrum: how and in what ways engaging with research can support or hinder the development of new teachers.

Research as pedagogy for professionals

The idea that research forms a part of the pedagogy for the formation of professionals is linked to the specialist status of professionals as stemming from their specialist body of knowledge. Within Winch, Oancea and Orchard's (2015) definition of a professional teacher, research is particularly important as it enables new teachers to develop situational judgement. Grace (2017) argues that exploring social, moral and ethical issues (at an initial stage of development) are key to avoid reducing teaching to a technical practice. Both these points are underpinned by a view of teachers as professionals who require adaptive expertise which is best gained through an engagement with research (Earl & Timperley, 2008; Hammerness & Klette, 2015). In this sense, research is seen as enabling teachers to connect theory and practice, to form meaningful generalisations and a deeper understanding of aspects of reality (Eisner, 1979). But that also requires a two-way dialogue between research and practice (Flynn, 2018).

Such a relationship between research and practice is contingent on the way they are situated within teacher education pedagogy and the way that research is perceived. Sachs (2003) makes the important distinction between the research conducted by practitioners and that conducted by academics. She notes that they ask different questions, use different methodologies and seek to undertake research for different purposes, as practitioners focus on practical problems and questions rather than contributing to the field. For new teachers on ITE programmes, conducting research is also tied up with certification and accreditation requirements: conducted through obligation perhaps rather than genuine curiosity. In relation to practitioner research, Furlong, Salisbury and Coombs (2003) have suggested that this affects the nature of the questions they ask as well as the resultant research they conduct. It has therefore been questioned as to whether this can then, indeed, be considered research at all, and so it is important to clarify in what ways that research can contribute to the transformation required within ITE.

Research conducted by new teachers is of a different type to that undertaken by researchers. It addresses questions of interest to the individual rather than of interest to the field; it often is less concerned with issues of validity and reliability and can be overly reliant on qualitative data methods. Consequently, it rarely yields robust insights into the phenomena under study. This does not mean however that it isn't personally transformative for the individuals that undertake it (Furlong et al., 2003). Undertaking research also encourages new teachers to ask critical questions, perhaps about the status quo, but this could be seen as a distraction from developing highly skilled practice. Research that asks questions about phenomena itself rather than about how to teach in a particular way is, as

Menter and colleagues argued, emancipatory and distinctively different to the research conducted as part of the "what works" agenda for research, which situates research as answering problems without recognising the situational judgement necessary for practice (Biesta, 2007).

The research quality conundrum therefore needs to be addressed in programme design: where the role of research in teacher education as a form of pedagogy or as a form of content can be integrated into the development of the student teachers, and how it contributes to the flow of ideas. The remainder of this chapter explores the teacher education provision at OISE at the University of Toronto, Canada, which foregrounds research as a key feature of their ITE provision, and how they have sought to address this quality conundrum to situate research as a valuable pedagogical tool.

OISE

OISE, an institution recognised for its innovative research into education, formally merged with the University of Toronto in 1996. Following changes in the teacher education provision in the Province in 2014, OISE repositioned itself as a graduate faculty of education, reflecting the priorities of the broader research-intensive university. This was in response to three external factors: the Government's decision to substantially reduce the enrolment of students in teacher education programs, to decrease the funding for each student and the shift towards a new four-term degree framework.[2] McDougall and colleagues (2017) have argued that the shift reflects the University of Toronto's "differentiated" role as Ontario's leading research-intensive university. As it stands, OISE is the only graduate-level entry teacher education programme in Ontario, and along with McGill University in Quebec, one of two across Canada (Baxan & Broad, 2017). This context gives OISE a rather special status and unique role in the teacher education landscape of the province.

OISE is a large-scale provider of teacher education: the Masters of Teaching (MT) programme has over 800 students and the MA in Child Study (also a pre-service teacher education programme) has around 200 students. OISE is the largest teacher education provider in Ontario, and only University of British Columbia is larger is Canada (with circa 1,300 students in 2017). OISE is part of the University of Toronto, the highest ranked university in Canada[3] and according to the Times Higher Education ranking.[4] This emphasis on both large scale and high quality should be seen within the broader context of education in Ontario, where the demand for teachers enables a strong orientation to research.

Context of teacher education in Ontario

In contrast to the other universities featured in this study, OISE is operating in a very different teacher supply context. Ontario has not experienced a teacher supply shortage to the same extent as many other places for some time. MacDonald outlined in a newspaper report in 2019 that in 2013, there was a first-year teacher unemployment rate of 38%. This rate has dropped substantially to 14% in 2017, and is considered to be in single figures now due to the changes in teacher education provision brought in by the Province. In 2015, the province of Ontario extended the period of teacher education, causing an immediate shortfall in the provision of new teachers, and in 2015 cut enrolment in Teachers Colleges by half, reducing the number of graduates in Ontario from 12,399 in 2015 to 5,480 in 2018 (Pfeffer, 2018). However, these high-level figures mask some underlying trends. A rise in the number of teacher retirements, increasing school enrolments and a "patchy applicant interest after years of hearing there were no jobs and region specific circumstances" (MacDonald, 2019) have all affected the trends around teacher supply and demand. However, it can still take a newly qualified teacher between five and seven years before finding a permanent teaching position. There is increasing demand for teachers of French, mathematics and science.

In Ontario, teaching is a highly respected and high-status profession, and in terms of salary fares comparatively well with others. The profession is supported by strong teacher unions, who have recently experienced success in well-publicised workforce disputes and local disagreements. Ontario is also well known for its success in the OECD's PISA tests scoring in the top ten ranked countries in all areas. The system is well known for its local (i.e., Provincial) accountability structure situated within a cultural context that values teachers highly, focuses on literacy and promotes equity and unity, and results in high academic performance of migrant children. This reflects the population profile of the area: Ontario is the largest province in Canada, with an area of around 400,000 square miles and a population of approximately 13 million or 40% of all Canadians. It is a highly urbanised province, with 80% of students located in metropolitan areas. In terms of diversity, 27% of Ontario students were born outside Canada and 20% are minorities. Toronto, the main city in Ontario, is one of the most diverse cities in the world (OECD, 2010). This diversity is reflected in the education system in Ontario which prioritises public support of minority languages and religious minorities, as echoed in the number of school boards for the publicly funded Catholic education and French-language schooling. However, Ontario still experiences structural inequities particularly affecting Black and Indigenous students.

Within this context, there is less of an emphasis on the supply of teachers and more about the importance of maintaining high standards and supporting the diversity of Ontario's population. These priorities are reflected in the approach to teacher education found on the OISE Masters of Teaching (MT) programme.

The MT programme

Research is an important theme in the MT programme, reflected in both the website and programme handbook. For example, on the website[5] Graduate Research is given equal emphasis with the other two aspects of the programme: Academic

Program and Practice Teaching. Research, and particularly scholarly research, also features heavily in the programme's vision:

> Teaching excellence and scholarly research are the mutually reinforcing pillars of the Master of Teaching program. The program prepares candidates to become outstanding teachers and leaders who consult, critique, create and mobilize educational research. As a community, our faculty, students and graduates share a deep commitment to all learners and the building of a more just, equitable and sustainable world.
> (MT Programme Handbook, 2020)

Research is also emphasised as being at the "core" of the programme:

> Research is at the core of the Master of Teaching degree program. A unique aspect of your experience as an MT student is that you have course-based opportunities to learn about educational research methodologies, to conduct research in an area of specialization that interests you, and to produce graduate level scholarship.
> (Ibid.)

This is manifest in two academic courses on Educational Research, one taken in each year of the programme and culminating in an original research paper. The evolution of this aspect of the programme shows the changing role of research across the teacher education provision. In the older version of the programme, the two research courses combined in something that "looked like" and was often described by students as a "thesis" in five chapters written across the two years. Such an approach reflects the need for the programme to "make ourselves distinctive, and demonstrate why we are different" (OISE, Interview, 2020) in the light of some controversy over the unique Masters-level designation afforded to the programme. This structure has now been adapted into Year 1 course on Research Literacy, where students learn how to access, critically evaluate and synthesise education research. This is achieved through engaging with a range of methods and methodologies, debates about knowledge production and dissemination practices and exploring the relationship between research and harm (including issues around resisting and refusing research, research and legacies of colonialism, research as mechanism for reproduction of structural and systemic inequities). The course also pays attention to reflexivity and research (emphasising the importance of positioning self in relation to beliefs about knowledge, and the research topic and participants). During this course, students choose a topic area to investigate and are supported in producing a literature review which results in a research paper and a Three Minute Research presentation. This Year 1 research work is intended to establish the foundation for the study they will design and conduct in the second year.

In Year 2, the Research Course is devoted entirely to supporting the individual research studies, and requires the student teachers (or teacher candidates) to start with a research informed problem statement (drawing on the foundation work they did in Year 1) and draft research questions. They design either an interview-based study or document analysis study and carry it out in full (including data collection and analysis). For this course, they write a research paper and present the findings at the annual conference.

The description of the research endeavours highlights the type of research focus on the programme:

> Findings from your research will inform your own teaching practice and professional identity as teacher-researchers. You will also be encouraged and supported to share your findings with the education community through avenues for publication and participation in educational research conferences.
>
> *(MT Programme Handbook)*

Within this statement, the programme documentation speaks to several of the concerns about research in teacher education: situating research as a way of both informing and developing practice, but also recognising its situation within the field. One teacher educator discussed how the student teachers (or teacher candidates as they are known), prioritise the research aspects of their programme:

> They literally have to prioritise research, of course, because they feel like that is one of the reasons they come to the program. It's a graduate programme and they are conscious of that, so they tend to prioritise research.
>
> *(OISE, Interview, 2020)*

However, this is not to denigrate the practical learning they achieve, as this teacher educator went on to say:

> And the practicum, of course, because that is where you must put so much of your energy as you're learning so much in those moments.
>
> *(OISE, Interview, 2020)*

Research within the programme does not just feature within those specific courses and assessment papers, but is also a feature of the taught component of the programme in a variety of ways:

> I think it is fair to say that there is a good degree [of research content]. There was a good degree of drawing on professional literature and research literature as in every course. There's varying degrees to which an instructor may intentionally make a course assignment more of a research driven process, as an inquiry project or an investigative project. But I think a lot of the faculty draw upon literature, and have students read the literature: there's a lot of reading, critical analysis, discussion of literature. There's less,

but still present, inquiry driven work where people are asked to draw upon the literature to explore their reflection on their own teaching practice. And then there's the stand-alone research courses.

(OISE, Interview, 2020)

The capacity to support the level of research expected in the programme needed to be adapted as the programme grew in size. Following the Province-wide changes to ITE, the decision was taken to close two large undergraduate teacher education programmes and to increase the size of the Masters programme. The MT programme then grew quickly from around 150 students to the current level of 840 (within four to five years). Such rapid growth inevitably required changes to the staffing of the programme, and to various practices embedded within it. As one of the programme team acknowledged, the increase in students and subsequent increase in staffing involves "a lot of humans and a lot of beliefs and values and biases and research orientations". In the older version of the programme, students were required to complete a research project/dissertation, which they were guided through under the supervision of a member of faculty with some expertise in this area (where this was possible). However, as the programme grew, there was no longer the capacity to offer this personalised supervision and research training for all students. Therefore the research courses were introduced to centralise the research training to cohorts rather than individuals and to free up opportunities for individual targeted supervision.

Another aspect of the programme development has been the staffing on the programme. OISE employs a small number of research faculty and faculty known as "teaching stream". The remainder of the staffing is made up of "sessional" staff, part-time lecturers who teach and supervise on the programme and some of whom may hold similar positions elsewhere. A recent external review estimated the number of sessional staff was over 80%, but teacher educators estimated the figure to be higher, as OISE faculty were often relieved of teaching courses for leadership roles, and sessional staff used to replace them. The external report emphasises the considerable work that has been achieved in integrating sessional staff more fully into the academic culture of the department. In my interviews, teacher educators emphasised the high quality of the sessional staff: they often hold doctorates in relevant fields and have extensive school experience. Some of the sessional staff have also been a key part of the OISE MT team for some years, having taught on some courses for 11 years or more. Indeed, the University of Toronto has introduced a ranking process to ensure that longer-serving sessional staff are guaranteed a certain number of courses to ensure consistency and to reward loyalty.

However, the process of being a sessional instructor is recognised as being challenging, with different levels of job protection and instability. In order to generate sufficient income, sessional staff have to teach more courses and so have high teaching loads. They are often asked to teach the research modules which are also considered to be highly labour intensive because of the personalised nature of the feedback required. The external review tentatively raised the question as to the impact of such changes on the research vision of the department:

> To date, in order to manage the immediate integration of the significantly expanded MT program, the department's organizational changes seem to have been driven largely by structural needs rather than research or scholarly visions of the department. Faculty remain strongly committed to the Department and its current leadership team and appear to be invested in continuing their conversations and planning to establish a unified front in their programmatic identities and vision.
>
> *(External Review)*

From my data, it was clear that the programme leadership took the research emphasis very seriously from the viewpoint of staff engagement as well as programme development. Research had been the focus of a recent professional development opportunity, where all staff were encouraged to discuss research in the programme:

> We talked more about research in the program and how do you take it up in your course and we looked at these expectations around scholarship, the expectations around professional knowledge and asked ourselves "how do those things fit together?". We thought about what are you doing with research and what are your colleagues doing? … It was really fascinating because there was about 60 people I think, in three groups, and the things that surfaced in every group were so similar: they all talked about wanting to have a deeper connection to the students' research and what they're developing.
>
> *(OISE, Interview, 2020)*

Across the faculty, including the sessional staff, there appears to be strong coherence about the role and value of research as part of the professional learning experience. However, even in the light of this coherence and agreement, the programme leadership continues to question and review the role of research on the programme:

> It's one of the key questions, I think. So, what does a research informed teacher education program or research at graduate level teaching program look like? How has the emphasis shifted? I think of how we assess students, and that most of them would see the research as isolated. So, it's a research intensive program, but the big question we were moving to is what does it mean to be masterly? What makes this program at a master's level?
>
> *(OISE, Interview, 2020)*

Such questions raise further issues about the degree to which the research courses on the MT programme are aimed at developing a deeper understanding of research methodology, or as a practical support for developing their own Masters-level research projects.

The programme team have been reflecting on the role of research in the programme leading to changes in the programme. There is a recognition that the old style of research output as a "thesis" over two years was not necessarily reflecting the perspective of "research as stance" (after Cochran-Smith & Lytle, 1999) or of seeing research as a form of scholarship for teachers preferred by the programme team. The team are now under a process of reviewing how research is being taught, through a programme-wide curriculum-mapping exercise, and by foregrounding other forms of research such as practitioner research. One of the team explains:

> I've always been trying to attend to 'research as stance' and practitioner research, trying to create opportunities where we can for students to enact it, even though there's so many barriers that get in the way of that ... We could do more around at least having the candidates understand what would research mean to you as a teacher, on an everyday level, not just when somebody comes in and says, I've got a project for you ... but what would it mean on an everyday level in terms of enquiry and asking questions and collecting evidence in an everyday classroom, teaching practice and assessment evaluation practices ... it's uncomfortable because we're contradicting ourselves in a lot of ways: like we're emphasising one and then we're asking them to do the other.
>
> (OISE, Interview, 2020)

As part of this development, the team are considering how to bring practicum and the research pieces together more closely, and building partnership with the school boards to enable research to be more central to the work they do with the student teachers. This is based on a view of research in teacher education as being more than curating research knowledge or developing research literacy. As one teacher educator commentated, it is:

> a commitment to the integrity of developing teachers as intellectuals ... I think that's got to be a defining feature of teacher education. It's got to be something about the professional status of teacher educators, whether they actually see that that's important, and regardless of what the market is doing.
>
> (OISE, Interview, 2020)

This is a view that seems to permeate with the teacher educators I spoke to. One teacher educator reflected on the research that was undertaken by students on the previous version of the programme (before the expansion):

> They did some wonderful, like, amazing projects. But I think there was necessarily a sense that everybody was going to take this project and they

might use it. It might well inform their teaching, and they might certainly share it with colleagues. And it would certainly make them such a valuable member of the team at a school. But, you know, I think even when research was more about becoming a researcher, it was still not entirely a comfortable fit. And it was, it certainly meant most for those who took it further.

(OISE, Interview, 2020)

There is a reference here to the idea of research within the programme as preparation for a career in research or academia, a path which very few pursue (it was estimated that only a few students who enjoy the research on the MT programme do seek to move straight to doctoral studies). Research, whether to enhance practice or as a form of apprenticeship, is an honorific, implying status and hierarchy. But there is a more fundamental question here about how research relates to the flow of ideas on teacher education programmes: whether research conducted by student teachers contributes to the canon of ideas in the field or if it acts as a pedagogy, offering opportunities for student teachers to see how different ideas can change perceptions of practice.

Whilst some of the student teachers were undoubtedly attracted to the MT programme because of the research emphasis and the reputation of OISE, the programme team also reflected that this did not necessarily mean that they fully embraced the idea of undertaking research from the outset. For example, one teacher educator recounted to me that she observed a pattern in her student teachers: for the majority of her students, it was in the presentations at the research conference towards the end of the programme, where they realised what they had achieved through undertaking the research and the transformative power of having gone through the research process.

During the time of my data collection, the programme team were considering how the role of research in their programme might look into the future, and there are suggestions for different types of education research courses which might focus on, for instance, practitioner research or research with a particular emphasis in themes such as sustainability or identity. The teacher educators I spoke to were passionate about such potential so that student teachers could:

Sink their teeth into something a little deeper than what we could do in a one-size-fits-all education research course.

(OISE, Interview, 2020)

However, they also saw that research in ITE was orientated as a pedagogy for learning and for professional development that could benefit teachers beyond their early career:

So I want my candidates to walk away with an inquiry mindset. And why do I call it inquiry, rather the research? Because I do want them to think of themselves as teacher researchers for sure. We do a lot of work and talk about action research. And I model that for them ... What I'm hoping is they walk away with an inquiry mindset that they know they have the skills to find answers to questions if they need it. But they can also lead their own students in that inquiry process and become co-inquirers together.

(OISE, Interview, 2020)

However, it was widely recognised that getting the balance right between how much and what type of research student teachers should conduct was a challenge. One teacher educator placed a great deal of emphasis on the politics of knowledge production and how central this was to the vision of the MT programme at OISE:

the politics of knowledge production of who is included, whose knowledge is considered common sense and whose knowledge is excluded; decolonising knowledge production in research, and all the implications of all of that, are really important for teachers' identities as knowledge workers. ... We have such an opportunity there for students to learn how to be reflexive about their own beliefs about knowledge, and the implications of that for equity are huge or indeed subtle and insidious.

(OISE, Interview, 2020)

Therefore, rather than seeing research as a pedagogy for teaching, it is also seen as important in the construction of teacher identity. In other words, as one teacher educator remarked, rather than seeing the research and practice as two elements to be kept in balance, there was need to view them as integrated. "Excellent practice is driven by intentional commitment to practice, and research without embrace of considerations of practice is limited." Another teacher educator commented:

I know that we do push the notion that we're a research program pretty heavily. But it's about the balance between theory and practice and helping our students understand that they're fully integrated. That's the kicker. I think a key part of that is the messaging around a research informed program, because we want our students to get that idea even when they're looking at the application criteria, right from the get-go. So when they come in, we don't get things like: "we can learn everything we need to know in the classroom." Well, you can learn part of that, and you can probably be an OK teacher. But if you want to be a really high-quality teacher, then what you really need to be teacher researcher. That's what's going to get you to be a really amazing teacher. So we hope that that consistent messaging gets out to them.

(OISE, Interview, 2020)

Such an approach necessitates that the faculty teaching on the programme are also active researchers. This was acknowledged by the teacher educators I spoke to, who talked about their own research interests but also in the funding made available to the sessional staff, without which they had little funding or opportunity to continue their own research interests.

Research and the field

The three perspectives on research outlined at the start of this chapter were echoed in my discussions with the programme leadership at OISE. There was a recognition that when the MT programme was smaller, the previous programme leadership had an approach to research that had "a certain narrowness" to how research was conceived, and the current team were now revising the ways in which research is featured, more along the lines of "inquiry as stance" (Cochran-Smith & Lytle, 1998, 1999), focusing on ways in which research in teacher education is aligned to research as pedagogy and that is more sustaining through a teacher's career. The team is strongly committed to celebrating students' research and making it accessible to the wider educational community, and it is here that the changes they are proposing to make to their journal reflects their shift:

> We launched a journal for the program a couple of years ago. And last year we looked through the articles and we realised the limitations of what we were doing ... So that was a good thing, I guess, because it made us question: what are we expecting when we say knowledge mobilization here? What kind of knowledge are they mobilizing? What spheres are we really thinking about this as being part of a scholarly community in that regard? Are we thinking of it as being more of scholarship that informs practitioner communities?
>
> *(OISE, Interview, 2020)*

Part of this reconsideration was also about what the programme team wanted the student teachers to gain from their engagement with research: either an inquiry stance, a practitioner focus or as consumers of research. In addition, the concern was about how this research emphasis was supporting their development to become good teachers. "we can't be focussed so much on a particular kind of outcome that we're missing the learning that they might need to do." This change was reflected in the editorial of the OISE journal designed for the MT students to publish their work:

> In looking back over the past two years since launching the MTRJ, we cannot help but reflect on the bigger picture and how we as a program help to cultivate the convening spaces where the dialogical work of educational knowledge production can happen. Publishing, as one instantiation of that dialogical work, is the result of an, often lengthy, journey to bring an article forward from submission to final print. Perhaps even more complex are the precipitating efforts to actualize an early idea into formal study, as the

novice investigator develops into an increasingly seasoned researcher and writer. While all of our teacher candidates undergo the leg of the research journey from idea to formal study, most of them do not end up engaging in the knowledge mobilization and dissemination beyond presenting their papers in the annual MT Research Conference. Yet, we would suggest that this could be considered a critical element of their professional apprenticeship as knowledge builders.

(MacKinnon, 2019, p. 2)

Reflecting on the role and contribution of research has led to a change in the journal's focus towards shorter articles, which foreground a key aspect of the research, but also that is written in a more accessible journalistic style. The hope is that this approach will enable a focus on the scholarly contribution of the research work that the student teachers undertake and will build on the scholarly dialogue encouraged on the OISE MT programme:

we're all kind of recognising that it's important to celebrate our research. It's important how the candidates engage in research. But we want to think about what, to what end, and what's this going to look like for them, not just for those who go into doctoral stream.

(OISE, Interview, 2020)

So OISE can be seen as an institution that is actively considering ways in which they can address the research quality conundrum, actively and productively focusing on the issues and seeking to find a way to integrate and enhance the learning experience with and through research. There are some contextual elements to the OISE programme which are important in how they are achieving this. The emphasis on research is based in their historical context as a research-based institution, their merger with a research-intensive university and their position as the only graduate teacher education programme in Ontario (and only one of two in Canada). In this context, the focus on research gives the MT programme a sense of status and prestige that is essential in a teacher market with low levels of demand; as one teacher educator described to me, prospective teachers considered that having a graduate-level qualification (presumably from a prestigious institution) might make them more attractive to school boards looking for new employees.

Resolving the research quality conundrum

However, the research focus at OISE is not just about competition for employment (a factor that some teacher educators at OISE were sceptical of anyway), but is also based on a value position about the importance of research for teacher professionalism. The programme team has a clear position in relation to the research quality conundrum: that research is an important part of becoming a better teacher as a knowledge worker who understands the politics of knowledge production. They acknowledge that not all their students embrace this notion throughout the programme (but that the research conference is a key opportunity where they see the value of this approach). The ongoing discussions are orientated about how research is supportive of that goal, particularly as the programme shifts and adapts to changing circumstances; so the team continues to consider how the fit of research within ITE needs deliberate and conscious consideration.

The role of research within teacher education is dominated with different positions around the relevance of research to teaching, and in particular whether teachers need to be able to evaluate complex research methodologies in order to be able to judge the validity of research outputs (or indeed have the time to do that), or whether teachers should be producers or consumers of research. There is a recognition that research is an important tool to help teachers gain a deeper understanding of their practice that may yield positive improvements for their pupils. But there is also a recognition that this kind of research is somewhat different to the work undertaken by academic researchers who seek to contribute knowledge back to the field.

So when an ITE programme puts forward research as a key part of their programme, there are questions as to the extent to which it penetrates the entire programme or is considered an additional component to meet the requirement for the programme to be at Masters level. The response at OISE demonstrates an approach where research is seen as integral to the teacher education programme as part of the rich flow of ideas that can support transformation, but also fundamental to teacher professionalism. The departmental focus on research reaches out to all teaching staff (including sessional staff), who all take responsibility for how they fulfil the programme expectations in relation to research, and how research features in their courses and their pedagogical practices.

It could be argued that OISE's position in relation to research is enabled by the teacher supply situation in Ontario. Other programmes, such as the Masters programme at the University of Melbourne, have found that some approaches to teacher education have been challenging financially. When there is a large demand for people to become teachers but a fairly limited employment opportunity, there is an advantage for programmes that seek to offer an enriched experience. As an anecdotal example, whilst in Arizona discussing the range of educational programmes available to potential teachers, a long-serving teacher commented to me that it didn't matter what programme you selected, as demand for teachers was so great that anyone was guaranteed a job regardless of the preparation they have received. In such a scenario, the benefits of undertaking a longer, more challenging and complex, research-orientated approach needs to be made clear to the prospective teacher.

However, it could also be the case that a focus on research is also seen as an institutional strategy to ensure that teacher education contributes to the research mission of the institute and university. Initial teacher education is sometimes considered a practice field, where scholarly inquiry can be inspired or rooted in practice and can yield insights which inform and deepen our understanding of that practice. Within such a scenario, there would appear to be an opportunity for practitioner research to make a contribution to the wider field. However, it is rarely able to make this contribution, and when practice-orientated fields lack prestige through their claim to philosophical and/or theoretical knowledge, so practitioner research is likely to be even less regarded. Within this context there is a question about the contribution that student teacher research makes, and to what extent research by teachers with little experience will be able to contribute understandings to the accumulated wisdom of the field. If research is understood as pedagogy, then engaging with research is situated within the field rather than actively contributing to it.

Within the representational space, however, focusing a programme on research makes a strong statement. Research is an honorific, speaking to a hinterland of assumptions about specialist knowledge, disciplinary engagement and intellectual endeavours. Aligning new teachers with a form of teacher preparation orientated around research enhances the professionalism of the individuals as well as to the profession as a whole. It elevates teaching from a solely action-based activity to an intellectual one.

Therefore, resolving the research conundrum by emphasising the value of research in teacher education, both as a form of pedagogy, the source of knowledge and content and as a career-enhancing form of professional development, as OISE has done, speaks to a commitment to teaching as a profession across time and space. Assuming, of course, the local market appreciates this added value.

Notes

1 In June 2020, a petition was launched in protest regarding the alliance between ResearchEd Canada and OSSTF/FEESO (two educational organisations in Canada).
2 https://www.oise.utoronto.ca/oise/About_OISE/History_Facts.html
3 https://www.macleans.ca/education/best-education-universities-in-canada-2018-ranking/.
4 https://www.timeshighereducation.com/student/best-universities/best-universities-canada#survey-answer.
5 https://www.oise.utoronto.ca/mt/Home.html.

References

Afdal, H. W., & Spernes, K. (2018). Designing and redesigning research-based teacher education. *Teaching and Teacher Education, 74*, 215–228. doi:10.1016/j.tate.2018.05.011

Alvunger, D., & Wahlström, N. (2017). Research-based teacher education? Exploring the meaning potentials of Swedish teacher education. *Teachers and Teaching, 24*(4), 332–349. doi:10.1080/13540602.2017.1403315

ATCEE. (2010). *The clinical preparation of teachers: A policy brief.* Retrieved from Washington, DC: American Association of Colleges for Teacher Education.

Ball, S. J. (2012). *Global Education Inc.: New policy networks and the neo-liberal imaginary.* London: Routledge.

Ball, S. J., & Exley, S. (2010). Making policy with 'good ideas': Policy networks and the 'intellectuals' of new labour. *Journal of Education Policy, 25*(2), 151–169. doi:10.1080/02680930903486125

Baxan, V., & Broad, K. (2017). *Graduate Initial Teacher Education – A Literature Review.* Retrieved from Toronto: https://www.oise.utoronto.ca/mtvisioning/UserFiles/File/Literature_Review_Chapter_1_Final.pdf

Biesta, G. (2007). Why "what works" won't work: Evidence-based practice and the democratic deficit in educational research. *Educational Theory, 57*(1), 1–22. doi:10.1111/j.1741-5446.2006.00241.x

Brown, T. (2017). *Teacher education in England: A critical interrogation of school-led training.* London: Routledge.

Bullough Jr., R. V. (2014). Toward reconstructing the narrative of teacher education. *Journal of Teacher Education, 65*(3), 185–194. doi:10.1177/0022487113519131

Burn, K., & Mutton, T. (2013). *Review of research-informed clinical practice in teacher education.* Paper submitted to the BERA-RSA Inquiry. London: BERA/RSA.

Burn, K., & Mutton, T. (2015). A review of 'research-informed clinical practice' in Initial Teacher Education. *Oxford Review of Education, 41*(2), 217–233. doi:10.1080/03054985.2015.1020104

Carter, A. (2015). *Carter review of Initial Teacher Training (ITT).* Retrieved from London. https://assets.publishing.service.gov.uk/government/uploads/system/uploads/attachment_data/file/399957/Carter_Review.pdf

Cochran-Smith, M., & Lytle, S. L. (1998). Teacher research: The question that persists. *International Journal of Leadership in Education, 1*(1), 19–36. doi:10.1080/1360312980010103

Cochran-Smith, M., & Lytle, S. L. (1999). The teacher research movement: A decade later. *Educational Researcher, 28*(7), 15–25.

Collini, S. (2012). *What are universities for?* London: Penguin UK.

Connell, R. (2019). *The good university: What universities actually do and why its time for radical change.* London: Zed Books Ltd.

Cramp, A., & Khan, S. (2018). The convivial space – Exploring teacher learning through practitioner research. *Professional Development in Education, 45*(3), 344–355. doi:10.1080/19415257.2018.1431957

Darling-Hammond, L. (2006). *Powerful teacher education: Lessons from exemplary programs.* San Francisco, CA: John Wiley & Sons.

Darling-Hammond, L., & Lieberman, A. (2013). *Teacher education around the world: Changing policies and practices.* Abingdon: Routledge.

Darling-Hammond, L., Macdonald, M. B., Snyder, J., Whitford, B. L., Ruscoe, G., & Fickel, L. (2000). *Studies of excellence in teacher education: Preparation at the graduate level.* Washington, DC: ATCEE.

Dunn, R., Hattie, J., & Bowles, T. (2018). Exploring the experiences of teachers undertaking Educational Design Research (EDR) as a form of teacher professional learning. *Professional Development in Education, 45*(1), 151–167. doi:10.1080/19415257.2018.1500389

Earl, L. M., & Timperley, H. (2008). *Professional learning conversations: Challenges in using evidence for improvement* (Vol. 1). London: Springer.

Eisner, E. W. (1979). *The educational imagination: On the design and evaluation of school programs.* New York: Macmillan.

Ellis, V. (2010). Impoverishing experience: The problem of teacher education in England. *Journal of Education for Teaching, 36*(1), 105–120. doi:10.1080/02607470903462230

Ellis, V., & Childs, A. (2019). Innovation in teacher education: Collective creativity in the development of a teacher education internship. *Teaching and Teacher Education, 77,* 277–286. doi:10.1016/j.tate.2018.10.020

Ellis, V., Steadman, S., & Trippestad, T. A. (2018). Teacher education and the GERM: Policy entrepreneurship, disruptive innovation and the rhetorics of reform. *Educational Review, 71*(1), 101–121. doi:10.1080/00131911.2019.1522040

Farley-Ripple, E., May, H., Karpyn, A., Tilley, K., & McDonough, K. (2018). Rethinking connections between research and practice in education: A conceptual framework. *Educational Researcher, 47*(4), 235–245. doi:10.3102/0013189x18761042

Flores, M. A. (2018). Linking teaching and research in initial teacher education: Knowledge mobilisation and research-informed practice. *Journal of Education for Teaching, 44*(5), 621–636. doi:10.1080/02607476.2018.1516351

Flynn, N. (2018). Facilitating evidence-informed practice. *Teacher Development, 23*(1), 64–82. doi:10.1080/13664530.2018.1505649

Freidson, E. (2001). *Professionalism, the third logic: On the practice of knowledge.* Chicago, IL: University of Chicago press.

Furlong, J. (2013). *Education – An anatomy of the discipline: Rescuing the university project.* Abingdon: Routledge.

Furlong, J., Salisbury, J., & Coombs, L. (2003). *The best practice research scholarship scheme: An evaluation. Final report to the DfES.* (C. U. S. o. S. Sciences Ed.). Cardiff: Cardiff University School of Social Sciences.

Furlong, J., & Whitty, G. (2017). Knowledge traditions in the study of education. In G. Whitty & J. Furlong (Eds.), *Knowledge and the study of education: An international exploration* (pp. 13–57). Oxford: Symposium.

Godfrey, D. (2017). What is the proposed role of research evidence in England's 'self-improving' school system? *Oxford Review of Education, 43*(4), 433–446. doi:10.1080/03054985.2017.1329718

Grace, G. (2017). Professions, sacred and profane: Reflections upon the changing nature of professionalism. In M. Young & J. Muller (Eds.), *Knowledge, expertise and the professions* (pp. 18–30). Abingdon: Routledge.

Greany, T., & Brown, C. (2015). *Partnerships between teaching schools and universities: Research report* (U. I. o. Education Ed.). London: UCL Institute of Education.

Greany, T., Gu, Q., Handscomb, G., Varley, M., Manners, P., & Duncan, S. (2014). *School-university partnerships: Fulfilling the potential. Summary Report.* Bristol: National Co-ordinating Centre for Public Engagement.

Hagger, H., & McIntyre, D. (2006). *Learning teaching from teachers: Realising the potential of school-based teacher education.* Maidenhead: McGraw-Hill Education (UK).

Hammerness, K., & Klette, K. (2015). Indicators of quality in teacher education: Looking at features of teacher education from an international perspective. In G. K. LeTendre & A. W. Wiseman (Eds.), *Promoting and sustaining a quality teacher workforce* (pp. 239–277). Bingley: Emerald Publishing.

Heilbronn, R., & Yandell, J. (2010). *Critical practice in teacher education: A study of professional learning.* London: Institute of Education, University of London.

Hulme, M., Wood, J., & Shi, X. (2020). Measuring up? Metrics and research assessment in UK teacher education. *Journal of Education for Teaching, 46*(2), 220–239. doi:10.1080/02607476.2020.1724658

Kostiainen, E., Ukskoski, T., Ruohotie-Lyhty, M., Kauppinen, M., Kainulainen, J., & Mäkinen, T. (2018). Meaningful learning in teacher education. *Teaching and Teacher Education, 71*, 66–77. doi:10.1016/j.tate.2017.12.009

Labaree, D. F. (2006). *The trouble with ed schools.* New Haven, CT: Yale University Press.

Labaree, D. F. (2008). An uneasy relationship: The history of teacher education in the university. In M. Cochran-Smith, S. Feiman-Nemser, J. McIntyre, & K. with Demers

(Eds.), *Handbook of research on teacher education* (3rd ed., pp. 290–306). New York: Routledge.

Lambert, D., & Totterdell, M. (1996). Crossing academic communities: Clarifying the conceptual landscape in initial teacher education. In D. Blake, V. Hanley, M. Jennings, & M. Lloyd (Eds.), *Researching school-based teacher education* (pp. 13–26). Abingdon: Avebury.

Loewenberg Ball, D. (2000). Bridging practices; intertwining content and pedagogy in teaching and learning to teach. *Journal of Teacher Education, 51*(3), 241–247.

MacDonald, M. (2019). Teacher supply goes from glut to scarcity in a few short years. *University Affairs*. Retrieved from https://www.universityaffairs.ca/news/news-article/teacher-supply-goes-from-glut-to-scarcity-in-a-few-short-years/

MacKinnon, K. (2019). *Re-Connecting* with the vision of convening spaces for scholarly work in teaching. *Master of Teaching Research Journal, 1*(2), 1–3.

McAleavy, T. (2016). *Teaching as a research-engaged profession: Problems and possibilities.* Reading: Education Development Trust.

McDougall, D., Hewitt, J., Montemurro, D., Kosnik, C., & Cuckovic, B. (2017). Graduate teacher education at OISE: Transition to a fiver-term program. In D. Petrarca & J. Kitchen (Eds.), *Initial teacher education in Ontario: The first year of four-semester teacher education programs* (pp. 155–172). Ottawa: Canadian Association for Teacher Education (CATE).

McIntyre, D. (1990). Ideas and principles guiding the internship scheme. In P. Benton (Ed.), *The Oxford internship scheme: Integration plus partnership in initial teacher education* (pp. 17–33). London: Calouste Gulbenkian Foundation.

McIntyre, D. (1995). Initial teacher education as practical theorising: A response to Paul Hirst. *British Journal of Educational Studies, 43*(4), 365–383. doi:10.1080/00071005.1995.9974045

Menter, I. (2017). Teacher education research. In *Oxford research Encyclopedia of education*. Oxford: Oxford University Press. https://doi.org/10.1093/acrefore/9780190264093.013.275

Menter, I., Hulme, M., Elliot, D., Lewin, J., Baumfield, V., Britton, A., ... McQueen, I. (2010). *Literature review on teacher education in the 21st century* (S. G. S. Reserach Ed.). Glasgow: University of Glasgow.

Nutley, S., Walter, I., & Davies, H. T. (2003). From knowing to doing: A framework for understanding the evidence-into-practice agenda. *Evaluation, 9*(2), 125–143.

Ofsted. (2018). Building great teachers? Initial teacher education curriculum research: Phase 2. Retrieved from https://www.gov.uk/government/publications/initial-teacher-education-curriculum-research/building-great-teachers

Olmedo, A., Bailey, P. L. J., & Ball, S. J. (2013). To infinity and beyond ...: Heterarchical governance, the teach for all network in europe and the making of profits and minds. *European Educational Research Journal, 12*(4), 492–512. doi:10.2304/eerj.2013.12.4.492

Pfeffer, A. (2018). Ontario teacher shortage looming, educators warn. *CBC News*. Retrieved from https://www.cbc.ca/news/canada/ottawa/ontario-quebec-teacher-shortage-1.4803517

Pring, R. (2017). Research and the undermining of teacher education. In M. A. Peters, B. Cowie, & I. Menter, (Eds.), *A companion to research in teacher education* (pp. 609–620). Dordrecht: Springer.

Puustinen, M., Säntti, J., Koski, A., & Tammi, T. (2018). Teaching: A practical or research-based profession? Teacher candidates' approaches to research-based teacher education. *Teaching and Teacher Education, 74*, 170–179. doi:10.1016/j.tate.2018.05.004

Sachs, J. (2003). *The activist teaching profession*. Maidenhead: Open University Press.

Tatto, M. T., & Hordern, J. (2017). The configuration of teacher education as a professional field of practice: A comparative study of mathematics education. In J. Furlong & G. Whitty (Eds.), *Knowledge and the study of education: An international exploration* (pp. 255–274). Oxford: Oxford Comparative Education.

Toom, A., Tiilikainen, M., Heikonen, L., Leijen, Ä., Mena, J., & Husu, J. (2019). Teacher candidate learning of action-oriented knowledge from triggering incidents in teaching practice. *Teachers and Teaching, 25*(5), 536–552. doi:10.1080/13540602.2019.1652162

Totterdell, M., & Lambert, D. (1998). The professional formation of teachers: A case study in reconceptualising initial teacher education through an evolving model of partnership in training and learning. *Teacher Development, 2*(3), 351–371. doi:10.1080/13664539800200066

Turvey, K. (2018). Humanising as innovation in a cold climate of [so-called-evidence-based] teacher education. *Journal of Education for Teaching, 45*(1), 15–30. doi:10.1080/02607476.2019.1550603

Turvey, K., & Pachler, N. (2020). Design principles for fostering pedagogical provenance through research in technology supported learning. *Computers & Education, 146*. doi:10.1016/j.compedu.2019.103736

Watson, D., Hollister, R., Stroud, S. E., & Babcock, E. (2011). *The engaged university: International perspectives on civic engagement*. London: Taylor & Francis.

White, S., Down, B., Mills, M., Shore, S., & Woods, A. (2020). Strengthening a research-rich teaching profession: An Australian study. *Teaching Education*, 1–15. doi: 10.1080/10476210.2020.1737666

Wieser, C. (2018). Evidence and its integration into teacher knowledge: Foucaultian perspectives to link research knowledge and teaching. *Journal of Education for Teaching, 44*(5), 637–650. doi:10.1080/02607476.2018.1516352

Winch, C., Oancea, A., & Orchard, J. (2015). The contribution of educational research to teachers' professional learning: Philosophical understandings. *Oxford Review of Education, 41*(2), 202–216. doi:10.1080/03054985.2015.1017406

Wisby, E., & Whitty, G. (2019). Maintaining (ecosystems for) a broad view of educational research and its relationship to practice. In D. Godfrey & C. Brown (Eds.), *An ecosystem for research-engaged schools: Reforming education through research* (p. 187). London: Routledge.

Young, M., & Muller, J. (2014). From the sociology of professions to the sociology of professional knowledge. In M. Young & J. Muller (Eds.), *Knowledge, expertise and the professions* (pp. 3–17). Abingdon: Routledge.

Zeichner, K. M. (2017). *The struggle for the soul of teacher education*. Abingdon: Routledge.

4
THE KNOWLEDGE QUALITY CONUNDRUM

In June 2020, there was a surge of protests in major cities as part of the Black Lives Matter movement, galvanised by the death of George Floyd. In Bristol, the statue of Edward Colston, a slave trader, was pulled down by the crowd and thrown into the docks. I grew up in Bristol. My secondary school had been created through a merger between a boys' school and a girls' school that had been funded by Colston. Whilst I was at the school, the pastoral Houses were named after "great" Bristolian men, one of whom was Edward Colston. However, I have no recollection of having ever been taught about Colston, slavery or about how Bristol's wealth was built on the back of slave traders, only learning about these subsequently. I recognise that it is an aspect of white privilege to be able to go through life ignorant of the suffering and discrimination caused by slavery and the subsequent way that wealth was created, distributed and maintained through white supremacy. As a white person growing up in Bristol, I was ignorant of this important history, and I regret not having been formally educated about this. Four of the countries I visited in this research are former British colonies; three of them remain part of the Commonwealth. Each of these countries has a history of slavery and oppression of Indigenous communities, and they all, including England, have a history of discrimination and prejudice against migrant communities and people of colour. Education is an important way of addressing and redressing systemic issues of racism and inequalities, but to do so, it needs to have a consciousness presence in teacher education. This chapter looks at how teacher education programmes seek to address these issues: how they can enable a flow of knowledge and ideas from a range of sources whilst being constrained through governance and accountability infrastructures.

Deciding what should be learnt is a fundamental question for any educational programme. In the case of teaching, this question is often broken down into questions of practice, and of what sorts of knowledge new teachers need and where that knowledge comes from. As with most enduring issues, the nature of the problem changes through time and gets reconstructed in relation to the prevailing context of teacher education, and in how teacher education pedagogy conceptualises the transformation necessary. For example, when teacher education was perceived as needing professionalisation, so many countries moved teacher education away from specialist Teachers' Colleges and Normal Schools into universities, reflecting a focus on academic or theoretical knowledge and higher entry requirements (see Chapter 3). When teacher education has been seen as overly theoretical, there have been calls to return to a more practice orientation and a focus on more time in schools and an emphasis on teaching skills (Furlong, 2013). Under either scenario, the important questions are: Where does the knowledge that teachers need come from? Whose knowledge is it? There is always a tension centred around the appropriate balance (or imbalance) between theory and practice in teacher education programmes, the role of research as a form of knowledge and who decides what teachers need to know, and by extension what is left out. These are fundamental questions about the role of knowledge in the transformation of new teachers.

For teacher educators, this presents a quality conundrum that has a strong spatial dimension, particularly around hierarchies and representation. As Murray (2017) notes, there are two movements related to this: the practice turn and the university turn happening concurrently in different parts of the world. Some countries are seeking to raise the status of teacher education through focusing on Masters-level and university-led provision, and others emphasise the technical aspects of teaching through emphasising school engagement and the importance of practice and core practices. However, both of these approaches make assumptions about what is wrong with teacher education and what needs to be "fixed". In either case, issues of justice, equity and, as Cochran-Smith and colleagues (2018) would argue, democracy can be forgotten.

These questions are inherently political. Sleeter (2019) highlights that we need to consider how what we teach sustains the power dynamic over who defines good teaching and expectations about compliance. Likewise, an overemphasis on theoretical knowledge can fail to engage new teachers in the challenges they may face by abstracting the realities of teaching for social justice and equity. For university-based teacher education programmes, there is a quality conundrum about what knowledge teacher education programmes should include, and the pedagogies necessary for new teachers to learn from them. This is a knowledge conundrum as the knowledges for teacher education are often laid down in compliance obligations around core or prescribed content in programmes. At the same time, teacher educators must ensure that new teachers have the practical, intellectual and ethical understandings they need to be able to teach all students effectively. The quality conundrum lies in what sort of knowledges should feature in teacher education programmes.

Knowledges for new teachers

In their report for the Donaldson Review in Scotland, Menter et al. (2010) identified four paradigms of teacher professionalism, each of which leads to a different emphasis within initial teacher education (ITE). To summarise their categories:

- The effective teacher: with an emphasis on meeting standards and competences;
- The reflective teacher: with an emphasis on individual professional development achieved through practice;
- The enquiring teacher: adopting an enquiry approach, which in some cases has veered towards a research orientation; and
- The transformative teacher: which adopts an activist stance in relation to enquiries in order to contribute to social change.

Menter and colleagues (ibid.) note that these models tend to build on each other and so run broadly chronologically. They each situate the teacher differently in relation to the knowledge and skills related to teaching (and in the latter ones to research). Approaches aligned with standards and competences and reflective practice tend to emphasise practical skills over a knowledge base for teaching, and in some cases, like in England, were developed in response to what was seen as an overly theoretical approach to teacher education focused on the so-called foundational disciplines of philosophy, psychology, sociology and history (Furlong, 2013).

There continues to be wide-spread debates about the sorts of knowledge that teachers need and the best ways for them to gain that knowledge. For example, Eraut (2007, 2010) highlights the importance of tacit knowledge in teaching and how challenging it can be to observe, articulate and develop tacit knowledge, particularly when observing a more experienced professional such as in an apprenticeship model of teacher education. Winch (2017) explores this question from a philosophical standpoint: looking at the different ways in which knowledge for teaching is understood and the extent to which it represents different forms of substantive and propositional knowledge, and in particular how "know-how" represents different forms of knowing. The distinction between know-how and know-that has been widely used to differentiate between technical or craft-based approaches to teaching (with a focus on practical skills and apprenticeship style pedagogies) and the view of teaching as a profession, requiring situational judgement and deeper knowledge. These views reflect different types of knowledges and ideas and how they might be key for the transformation of new teachers.

Debates on how to build teacher education programmes reflect this distinction, in what Kennedy (2015) has called parsing the practice of teaching, by breaking teaching down into a discrete set of topics or practices which can fail to recognise the nature of the issues as new teachers experience them. Kennedy's approach recognises the range of problems that the teacher education curriculum has tried to address, such as creating bridges between theory and practice, or content and practical experiences (Loewenberg Ball, 2000), linking theory and practice and integrating research effectively into practicum experiences (Flores, 2018, 2020a, 2020b; Ulvik, Helleve, & Smith, 2017). Whilst there are variations in how different countries respond to this issue (Jenset, Klette, & Hammerness, 2017), central to all is the challenge of ensuring that experience results in meaningful learning (such as from taught courses) particularly as students enter practicum (Chan, 2019; Cramp & Khan, 2018; Kostiainen et al., 2018).

There are however three further dimensions to this debate: first that education policy can seek to unite or further widen the divide between theory and practice (see, for example, the case in England's policy towards employment-based routes into teaching in Youens, Smethem & Simmons, 2018); that assessments are key in shaping what knowledge is taught and privileged by student teachers (Sjöberg, 2018); and that the transition from research or evidence into practice is not smooth or linear but requires judgement (Biesta, 2007; Nutley, Walter, & Davies, 2003). As Cochran Smith and Zeichner highlighted, this is not just a system of whether theory and/or practice are more important but the ontological issues of adopting one system over another (2005).

In the research area of teacher education pedagogy, there are two recent developments which are influencing programme design: the emphasis on core practices that has been developed from the work of Grossman and colleagues in the Core Practice Consortium, and the implications for both the content and pedagogy of programmes when they seek to focus on social justice and equity (see Grudnoff et al., 2017). These movements are not necessarily oppositional, and many teacher education programmes seek to incorporate both to some extent, but they do reflect different emphasis on the knowledge quality conundrum: what knowledge should be covered in an ITE programme, how is that knowledge conceptualised and how it should be introduced to new teachers.

Core practices and culturally relevant pedagogies

The need for a consensus about the form and process of teacher education has been made for some time (Cochran-Smith, 2004, 2005; Cochran-Smith & Zeichner, 2005; Hiebert, Gallimore, & Stigler, 2002). Grossman, Hammerness and McDonald (2009) argued that teacher education needed a common language around core practices that would help to address common issues such as the separation of methods and foundations courses which leads to a disconnection between theoretical and practical classroom work; the need to integrate practices throughout teacher education programmes; and the need to resituate practice at the core of the teacher education curriculum. Their work builds on the scholarship developed from subject-based investigations into pedagogical content knowledge, collated from TeachingWorks and other frameworks from University of Michigan, Core Practice Consortium, Center to Support Excellence in Teaching at Stanford and University of Washington's Ambitious

Science Teaching Project. They describe the findings of this work as comprising of high-leverage practices: research-based and effective practices that could be used frequently and widely to support novices' understanding and progress. This body of work has been developed into a series of approaches for teacher education which could be used to support the development of core practices through representations and approximations of practice, achieved through strategies such as modelling and rehearsal (Grossman, 2018), and supported by a range of research into the practices into how those core practices can be adopted and used (Anderson & Herr, 2011; Grossman, Kazemi, Kavanagh, Franke, & Dutro, 2019; Grossman & Pupik Dean, 2019; O'Flaherty & Beal, 2018; Van Der Schaaf, Slof, Boven, & De Jong, 2019).

However, this work has been criticised in particular for the ways in which an emphasis on identifying and centring core practices may risk peripheralising equity and justice issues (Philip et al., 2018; Souto-Manning, 2018; Souto-Manning & Stillman, 2020). Philip et al. (2018) also make the link with market-based solutions to education, and Souto-Manning (2018) illustrates that there are other ways to promote good practices for teaching that are more critical. Sleeter's (2019) argument is compelling: whilst she notes the value of identifying cohesive practices to support new teachers in practice-based learning, she is also critical of inquiry-based approaches which assume that teachers will constantly confront situations that require judgements and decision-making. She argues that a practice-based approach assumes a power dynamic "that occurs when some actors define good teaching and others are expected to comply" (ibid., p. 1). In contrast, she argues that:

> Inquiry-based approaches see learning to teach as learning to construct theory within practice, and learning to use judgment in complex and uncertain conditions. This view of teaching does not eschew learning basic practices, but rather complicates it.

Sleeter argues for a more relational approach, which:

> begins with the premise that students and their families are holders of knowledge that matters in the classroom, and that a problem in the professionalization of teaching is devaluation of that knowledge, especially when students and families occupy lower positions of social status.
>
> *(Ibid.)*

Sleeter's argument aligns with approaches centred around culturally responsive, culturally relevant, culturally appropriate or culturally sensitive pedagogy for teacher education (Kumashiro, 2015; Kumashiro, Neal, & Sleeter, 2015; Ladson-Billings, 2014; Villegas & Lucas, 2002). These approaches recognise that there are different forms of knowledges and knowing, which are attributable to different cultural traditions beyond that of the powerful white elite. Awareness and inclusion of such approaches can enable all children to engage with deep learning. For many teachers, particularly those that entered the profession because of their commitment to do good and to make society better, these values align with their own personal moral positions (although Starck, Riddle, Sinclair and Warikoo (2020) recognise that teachers' views are no less racist than others in society). However, countries with high levels of prescription in content and pedagogy and in accountability and oversight can constrain movements towards a culturally responsive pedagogy.

Payne and Zeichner (2017) have argued that teacher preparation must include a broader range of expertise from students' families and communities, but that this challenges the traditional hegemony of academic knowledge within university-based teacher education. They have described a "community knowledge" which is "contextualized or ecological knowledge" about children, families, educational norms and culture of a local community (Payne and Zeichner, 2017, p. 1107); elsewhere, this has been called "funds of knowledge": what teachers can learn from communities to construct theories of teaching and to shape their engagement in the practices and activities of teaching (González, Moll, & Amanti, 2005). Empirical work has explored ways in which this can be incorporated into teacher education programmes (see, for example, McDonald, Bowman, & Brayko, 2013), and there is a range of research that shows that culturally responsive pedagogy can have a positive impact on achievement (Abrahams & Troike, 1972; Foster, 1997; Gay, 2010). In whatever ways these knowledges are incorporated into teacher education programmes reflects a view on how they contribute to the flow of ideas that new teachers need.

However, there have been concerns summarised by Lim, Tan, and Saito (2019) as misconceptions and ambiguities over what culturally relevant pedagogy involves or looks like in classrooms (Gay, 2002; Young, 2010). This lack of clarity can result in difficulties related to its enactment (Foster & Peele, 1999; Seidl, 2016) particularly if it is over simplified and superficial (Kim & Pulido, 2015; Ladson-Billings, 2014), which can result in trivialised and static notions of culture (Morrison, Robbins, & Rose, 2008; Sleeter, 2012; Young, 2010). And so, there is a danger that culturally responsive pedagogy could represent culture as essentialised and fixed (Sleeter, 2012).

One of the issues facing many teacher education providers is that the majority of teacher education applicants are white, and bring little experience or knowledge of other cultural backgrounds (Barry & Lechner, 1995; Gilbert, 1995; Larke, 1990; McIntyre, 1997; Su, 1997; Valli, 1995). In addition, they may hold stereotypical beliefs about children from particular places or backgrounds, and have little awareness or understanding of discrimination, especially racism (Avery & Walker, 1993; Su, 1997). The strategies within teacher education, whilst full of good intensions, do little to address structural inequalities (Su, 1997) and may result in approaches described as colour blindness (McIntyre, 1997; Valli, 1995). In other words, there are still issues to be addressed in how knowledges are represented and incorporated into teacher education pedagogy.

Whilst there is no doubt that there is a need to diversify the groups of people who wish to become teachers, it is also paramount that teacher education programmes consider how they address issues of culturally relevant pedagogy, community knowledges and structural issues of white supremacy. These approaches may not be universal, as it is important to consider specific contexts (Alvunger & Wahlström, 2017), both in terms of the different people who are seeking to become teachers (Hamilton & O'Dwyer, 2018) and the ways in which practice is constructed and understood (Totterdell & Lambert, 1998), and the tensions that can be created when trying to address these issues in a highly regulated policy context (Ben-Peretz, 2001).

In all the sites I visited, equity and diversity were considered important issues for teacher education. Australia, Canada and New Zealand are all former British colonies and current members of the Commonwealth. Each has made important contributions to developing approaches to education to promote equity, particularly for Indigenous communities. Even so, the contexts of each of these nations are different, particularly around the relationship and status between European settlers and Indigenous communities, and levels of integration and exclusion, political and social power and influence. The US has its own history of colonialism and slavery and also shares a concern for equity, democracy and social justice. Education for all has a different connotation in Britain, as a former colonial power and aggressor, with a long-standing (and controversial) history of migration from around the world. London in particular is a hyper-diverse city, but with a somewhat different distribution pattern to some of the other contexts with high levels of integration (with some schools serving children who speak over 100 different languages). Recent political events, the obvious example of Brexit in the UK, and the events of June 2020 around the death of George Floyd and protests under the Black Lives Matter movement, have raised concerns about racism in British society, and by extension in its educational system and what knowledges are privileged within it.

In each of the countries studied there is a concern about the achievement or education gap experienced by students from different ethnic backgrounds, articulated by one of my interviewees as the shameful "brown tail" of students from marginalised groups whose assessment scores are significantly underperforming. In New Zealand, the government has funded research into how to address this issue through teacher education (Cochran-Smith et al., 2016; Grudnoff et al., 2017), resulting in a Masters-level ITE programme and the establishment of six facets of practice for equity (Grudnoff et al., 2017). It is important to note that in this project, practice was interpreted as principles of practice rather than specific teaching strategies or behaviours, and so sits in contrast with the core practice movement.

Research findings like the facets of practice for equity are valuable contributions to the field. However, there are still questions as to how teacher educators can fully integrate such pedagogical practices into all teacher education programmes, whilst still addressing dominant ideas about practice and knowledge that sustain power dominance and powerful voices. This is a quality conundrum; underpinning the core practice movement is an argument about social justice: that improving practice will benefit all students (and all student teachers). Culturally responsive pedagogy seeks to create conditions for learning that are effective for all, but particularly those that are marginalised by mainstream cultural groups. Both approaches to teacher education are affected by the overall accountability and governance structures that universities operate in, and the extent to which particular approaches and pedagogies are mandated in accreditation processes and specified ITE curriculum and privileged in assessment regimes and practices. In some countries, there is a recognition of the importance of community groups as partners in teacher education and of the contribution of community-based teacher educators (White, 2018), but not all partners equally value and promote this through their practices.

In addition, these issues are not simple; research conducted in New Zealand highlights a tension between supporting students to achieve well in terms of the mainstream parameters for academic success and achievement, alongside supporting cultural identity (Lynch & Rata, 2018). These observations raise the question as to what extent an education system can support cultural identity and community knowledges, whilst still preparing those from a minority background to be equipped to function successfully in a majority society (at least until that dominance and power gets disrupted). This can be a very challenging topic, as it gets at the heart of concerns about white supremacy and how the elite retain their power. However, this is further compounded when the conditions for teacher education curriculum and pedagogy are set externally and by powerful organisations, which limit the opportunities for alternative perspectives, and ultimately non-compliance could result in the withdrawal of the ability to provide teacher education.

As Sleeter points out, the quality conundrum here is dominated by who decides what achievement looks like, and how that affects practices. The challenge for teacher educators is how to address this quality conundrum within their programmes and how to best prepare new teachers to work in diverse settings. The rest of this chapter explores the practice of Queensland University of Technology (QUT) in this regard. Initially, New Zealand looked like the obvious case study for this theme; as a bicultural nation, many of the accountability and governance regimes are mindful of the diversity of New Zealand society and are particularly inclusive of Māori and Pasifika cultures. In addition, there has been investment in teaching for equity approaches in ITE. However, the QUT example has two distinct advantages: first, the challenge of working with rural and remote communities adds a spatial dimension to this problem, not addressed so explicitly elsewhere; and second, QUT, like most other ITE providers, is grappling with the challenge of having to meet university requirements around staffing, research and cost-cutting, an accountability system which is prescriptive in content and pedagogy (and not centred on culturally responsive approaches). In that sense, it has features of being both typical and atypical in relation to dealing with the conundrum around teacher education knowledge.

Queensland teacher recruitment problem: teachers for rural and remote communities

Most of the teacher education providers in this study are situated in large urban centres. Urban centres with large populations require more schools and more teachers. Urban centres also tend to be where universities are located. For many large-scale teacher education providers, one of their main roles is providing teachers for the large urban area they serve. QUT presents a rather different scenario. The State of Queensland covers a huge area of 1,852,642 square kilometres (715,309 square miles), and boasts being the world's sixth-largest subnational entity. Whilst Brisbane itself is Australia's third largest city, with a population of 2.28 million, Queensland is characterised by a very low population density (2.93 square kilometres or 7.6 square miles). Therefore, unlike many other urban-based teacher education providers, one of the issues that dominates the teacher education provision in Brisbane and for QUT is the need to supply teachers for rural and remote communities outside the city itself.

QUT is not the largest teacher education provider in Queensland. At the time of the data collection, QUT had 2,947 students (on both undergraduate and postgraduate programmes), whilst the Australian Catholic University had more students (10,333) these were not all based in Queensland. According to the Australian Good Universities Guide, QUT also received a higher satisfaction (89%) rating than the Australian Catholic University (81%). Within Queensland, other universities have satellite campuses, some closer to rural and remote communities, but these often have significantly lower numbers.

Rural and remote communities in Australia, and in Queensland in particular, suffer similar disadvantages to other marginalised communities (including in urban environments). The Australian Institute of Health and Welfare (a branch of the Australian Government) summarises the issue as:

> On average, Australians living in rural and remote areas have shorter lives, higher levels of disease and injury and poorer access to and use of health services, compared with people living in metropolitan areas. Poorer health outcomes in rural and remote areas may be due to multiple factors including lifestyle differences and a level of disadvantage related to education and employment opportunities, as well as access to health services.
>
> *https://www.aihw.gov.au/reports-data/population-groups/ rural-remote-australians/overview*

The term rural and remote is widely used to denote all areas outside Australia's major cities, and which can be further classified as *Inner regional, Outer regional, Remote* or *Very remote*. These remote areas can also face specific problems which the Australian Institute of Health and Welfare note are difficult to assess due to:

- the interactions between remoteness, low socio-economic position and the higher proportion of Indigenous Australians in many of these areas compared with Major cities;

- the variability in the distribution of disadvantage and of Indigenous Australians across all areas, for example, levels of disadvantage on the fringe of Major cities can be more akin to those in rural/remote areas than to inner-city areas;
- gaps in the availability and coverage of health data in rural and remote areas, and in the information available at the local area level.

> *https://www.aihw.gov.au/reports-data/population-groups
> /rural-remote-australians/links-other-information*

Teacher supply for rural and remote communities is a particular issue, and one in which the ethnic make-up of those areas is a key feature. Beutel and colleagues note that there are distinctive geographic and topological factors (Beutel, Adie, & Hudson, 2011), which stem from the low population density and isolated nature of the regions:

> The combination of large geographic distances, disproportionate population distribution along with significant contextual and cultural differences between urban and rural Australia contribute to an imbalance in the supply of teachers to rural areas (Lyons, 2009). Staffing schools in rural and remote Australia presents significant challenges with few teachers selecting to take up teaching appointments in non-urban communities.
>
> *(Ibid.)*

Preparing teachers to serve these communities is a clear challenge and one foregrounded by the Human Rights and Equal Opportunity Commission's inquiry into rural and remote education (HREOC, 2000), which:

> placed the responsibility squarely on teacher education institutions stating that "most teacher training does not equip new recruits with the skills and knowledge needed for teaching in rural and remote Australia" (p. 43). In Australia, the overwhelming majority of teachers are trained in universities in urban areas with less than a quarter of all practicum placements taking place in non-metropolitan schools (Halsey, 2005). Furthermore, the majority of preservice teachers taking up rural placements come from regional universities or live in rural areas (White, 2006). Thus, it is argued that metropolitan universities need to consider how they might encourage their preservice teachers to experience a rural practicum.
>
> *(Beutel, Adie, & Hudson, 2011 p. 379)*

The onus then on universities such as QUT, situated within urban centres, is to ensure that they support the need for teachers for rural and remote communities. In order to do this, the teacher educators require a high level of knowledge about those communities, including an understanding of the complex relationship between rural and remote communities, indicators of low socio-economic status and Indigenous communities. Whilst Indigenous communities in Australia are over-represented in low socio-economic areas, it does not automatically follow that all rural and remote communities are dominated by Indigenous populations. Some rural and remote communities are mining towns populated by former European settlers and fly in/fly out workers. Understanding the issues these communities face is key to providing them with an effective education.

Who are the new teachers?

One of the key ways of addressing issues of equity is through recruiting teachers from a broader range of backgrounds and experiences. An Australian Institute for Teaching and School Leadership (AITSL) report, published in 2019, highlighted the gender and ethnicity gap between the total population, the school population and teacher population. For example, while Aboriginal and Torres Strait Islander students accounted for close to 6% of Australia's students, they were represented by only 2% of teachers, with an even smaller percentage in leadership roles. Teacher educators at QUT remarked that recent trends indicate a changing demographic amongst prospective teachers, including a rise in career changers who were seeking access to teacher education.

QUT has two routes into teaching: an undergraduate four-year (Bachelors) programme and a postgraduate (Masters) programme. The student population on each tend to have different characteristics. Students on the Masters programme were more likely to feature career changers. For these students, the opportunity of a part-time programme that could be taken at a distance, alongside either full-time working or a family commitment, is key both financially and practically. Teacher educators at QUT cited this as a key reason for ensuring that the practice component of their programme was a four- to five-week placement rather than a longer internship (although this has now been extended to six weeks), as this was something that could be accommodated within the lives of career changers. This trend was also evident in the other sites of practice. For example, the University of Auckland teacher educators remarked on the impact on the so-called gig-economy making flexible working more attractive to potential teacher candidates, and accommodating career changers has been a recent development within the Teach First recruitment strategy for England.

The QUT undergraduate programme, however, has a rather different demographic. Policy advisory documents (Teacher Education Ministerial Advisory Group, 2014) make specific reference to the number of people who study teaching without any intention of becoming a teacher. Teacher educators at QUT explained that across the university, electing for (teacher) education modules was seen as a good way for a student to raise their grade point average, and so were sometimes selected by students from other majors who had no intention of becoming a teacher. They also reflected on the maturity of undergraduate students, some of who had little understanding of a teaching career until they had undertaken their first practicum placement; it was only when faced with the reality of teaching that they were able to commit to a career in teaching.

Both of these trends have been affected by the university-wide policy for "real world learning" which has emphasised opportunities for open, distance and blended learning, referred to by the people I spoke to as the "move to online" learning. This initiative was rolled out across the University through each Faculty sequentially and has been supported by a department of learning designers, working with the academics to ensure that all their modules were adapted for online learning. Each teaching session had to go through a process to make it suitable for distance learners: recording of lectures, practical tasks that could be replicated in "anyone's kitchen", online tutorials conducted via Zoom software and a range of real-time quizzes to ensure attendance. The lecturers noted that this had had a significant impact on their workload ("I can no-longer rock up and just teach a session") and had changed the teaching-learning relationship. For example, a number of teacher educators recounted that they no longer felt that they "knew" their students as well as they had previously, or that they only had access to their students' online persona, which they considered to be a partial reflection of who their students really were. They reported concerns that online students might not be fully engaged, and this could be seen when they were less well prepared (than campus-based students) for practicum. However, it was also noted that this "move to online" had enabled a number of students with "rich prior experiences" to become teachers (i.e., career changers); that it had diversified (and increased) the student body (particularly through international students studying at a distance); and had encouraged teacher educators to consider their pedagogy and practice in new ways. Importantly, it also enabled QUT to consider innovative ways to address the teacher recruitment issue in rural and remote areas of Queensland.

The "move to online", although university-wide and not specific to teacher education programmes, represents an opportunity to support people to become teachers beyond Brisbane. These changes have happened in the physical space of the university through the provision of technological infrastructure (material-economic arrangements), but are also reflected through university-wide initiatives (which affect both the social-political and cultural-discursive arrangements). They have spatial implications, allowing for a more flexible and footloose educational experience, but they also represent a shift in the way that knowledge in and around teacher education is parsed and presented pedagogically. Moves towards opening up university experiences and encouraging the participation of students from a wider (and more dispersed or online) community represents a shift in how students are perceived, influenced by student satisfaction metrics. However, it also raises questions about the importance of the relationship between a student teacher and their teacher educators or course instructors, and how students are supported to work in environments with which they are unfamiliar. It also reflects a view of the teacher education provision where the cultural identity of students can remain, to some extent, invisible as they learn online.

Preparing teachers for rural and remote communities

There are two key ways in which QUT has sought to prepare teachers for rural and remote communities in Queensland: one is through their partnership with the Kelvin Grove Teacher Education Centre of Excellence (KGTECE) and the other is through the design of their own teacher education programmes (discussed in the next section). Both represent different approaches to diversifying the teacher education experience: the former has a strong emphasis on preparing new teachers specifically for rural and remote communities, and the latter on the support offered for teachers who will teach in a range of settings. Each represents different takes on how teacher knowledge is constructed and developed.

At the time of my site visit, the continued funding of the Teacher Education Centres of Excellence (TECE) was under review, and the TECE situated at Kelvin Grove State College was described to me as the most successful (and was the only TECE which subsequently had their funding continued for a further year). A Queensland Government initiative, TECEs were allocated additional funds for the following purpose:

> To assist schools to lift teaching standards and give schools the support they need to provide a safe and supportive learning environment and the best educational outcomes for their students.
>
> The Teacher Education Centre of Excellence (TECE) program targets the recruitment of high performing preservice teachers to provide supportive professional learning and ensure classroom readiness. Programs are developed as a partnership between the department and a range of Higher Education Institutions (HEIs) to enhance and support the final year/s of preservice education. The program focuses on teaching excellence using the Australian Professional Standards for Teachers (APST) graduate level to provide a consistent application of excellence. There are currently 6 TECEs operating across Queensland.
>
> *Queensland Government website: https://education.qld.gov.au/about-us/ budgets-funding-grants/grants/state-schools/core-funding/teacher- education-centre-of-excellence accessed 03/02/2020*

Each TECE focused on a particular theme, and the one at Kelvin Grove State College, known as the KGTECE, focused specifically on preparing teachers for rural and remote communities. The KGTECE was run by Linda Eager, who was named as finalist in the Queensland College of Teachers Excellent Leadership in Teaching and Learning TEACHX Award. The 2019 Annual Report for KGTECE shows an impressive retention rate, with 98.2% of teachers still within the state system (out of 112 graduates over three years), and the two teachers no longer in the state system, currently teaching in the private system (of which the Catholic education system is considered part but separate to the independent sector). The Annual Report also shows how the number of applications and acceptances for the programme has increased (2020 cohort received 223 enquiries, 154 application and 140 acceptances).

The success of the KGTECE programme has to be understood on its own merits and also within the context of the incentivisation of teachers to teach in rural and remote communities. Supported by the Beyond the Range Professional Experience Grant[1] and the Rural and Remote STEM (science, technology, engineering or math) Graduate Teacher Scholarships,[2] student teachers are offered financial incentives to undertake a practicum experience in rural and remote communities. In addition, in this system where teachers are employed by the government rather than by the schools, teachers who work in rural and remote communities amass transfer points, which can then be used to transfer to a school deemed to be in a more desirable location.

Nevertheless, getting high-quality teachers to work in rural and remote communities is still a challenge, and rural schools often experience high turnover rates. The KGTECE seeks to ensure that new teachers are adequately prepared to work in rural and remote communities. The programme is centred around practical support and a long-term commitment to these communities: graduates of the KGTECE are offered a placement in a rural and remote school, where there is a high chance of a job vacancy, and of the KGTECE participant gaining employment. The programme is formulated in consultation with local representatives from these rural and remote communities who contribute to it in a variety of ways (through hosting, supporting and directly teaching on the programme). The programme also focuses on preparing new teachers in what to expect from these communities through the key features of the programme outlined below:

- **Myth-busting about teaching in rural and remote communities**: One of the barriers for individuals considering teaching in rural and remote communities is a number of myths about those communities, including the degree of isolation, lack of (internet) connectivity and concerns around safety. Linda described how she spent a lot of her time myth-busting these concerns. The programme promoted "straight talking" with their participants about the difference between the real and perceived dangers (and benefits) of working within these communities.
- **Teachers teaching teachers**: The programme offered by KGTECE is organised centrally, but is taught exclusively by current practitioners. Linda indicated that she felt this was important for both the credibility and contemporary nature of teaching but also as a counterpoint to some of the more theoretical and abstracted input student teachers received from their university providers (KGTECE works with a range of university-based providers based in Brisbane). She felt that credibility as a practitioner was important and practitioners could support the student teachers to connect theory and practice in a meaningful way. She also described initiatives focusing on how experienced teachers worked through problems with trainees such as dealing with a disruptive class and making that thinking transparent for the new teachers.

- **Mentoring**: A key feature of the programme is the availability of a teacher mentor for each participant. Whilst it is common practice for teacher education programmes to allocate school-based mentors, the KGTECE approach differs in that it promotes mentoring without judgement or assessment; mentors are encouraged to be supportive, to enable student teachers to make mistakes and are explicitly trained to adopt this approach and not to pass judgement on the student teacher's practice.
- **Targeted feedback**: Linda's latest concern was about the development of high-quality targeted feedback to student teachers. She showed me two examples of completed Professional Experience feedback forms, one with targeted feedback and one without, and how her focus for the coming year was to enable supervising teachers to offer more specific, targeted feedback which enables the student teachers to understand their achievement in relation to the Teacher Standards and what they need to do to improve.

KGTECE is a vibrant, respected programme of teacher education. The strategies outlined above are only part of the experience offered by KGTECE, and are used here as illustrative examples of the type of pedagogy and practitioner-orientated knowledge which underpins their practice. Specific responses have been designed from the perspective of what the new teacher needs in order to be able to be successful in a rural and remote environment. The strategies used are supported by the literature on good practice in professional (teacher) learning, but also, perhaps with the exception of myth-busting, are not particular to teaching in rural and remote communities but have wider applicability to new teachers in a number of contexts.

The KGTECE is driven by a clear sense of what their student teachers need: what the gaps in their knowledge are likely to be about rural and remote communities and what support they will need to address these gaps. The pedagogical features reflect a perspective of teacher education which respects the new teacher as a novice professional and emphasises their learning as part of a supportive community. It also has a particular approach to understanding what sort of knowledge-based practices are needed to support that learning: a focus on community, mentoring and creating spaces for experimentation whilst also emphasising and foregrounding practice; the approach is strongly community- and classroom-situated, whilst still addressing pertinent knowledge-related issues. In this sense, the programme does not necessarily address specific community-based knowledge issues, but it does feature community knowledge and engagement as an integral part of the overall approach.

It is important to recognise that the KGTECE is a complementary programme, running alongside the QUT programme, as an additional component for those successful applicants. The QUT programme also features community immersion programmes and specialist content on rural and remote communities, Indigenous communities and Indigenous ways of knowing and pedagogy, which are available to all students and not just those on KGTECE programmes. What the

KGTECE programme adds is the way that it seeks to change the representational nature of the practice of teacher education. Through the myth-busting approach, and the focus on developing a high-quality training environment (with the approach to mentoring, and the emphasis on up-to-date practice-based support), the programme is effectively seeking to change the narrative about teaching in rural and remote communities: to see that working in these communities is an opportunity to extend practice, to develop innovative approaches, to teach high-quality lessons, to make a real difference. The programme seeks to change the representation of rural and remote communities into a positive opportunity for committed professionals.

KGTECE is partly able to achieve this because it sits "outside" the teacher education system in Queensland. KGTECE works with three Brisbane-based universities: QUT, University of the Sunshine Coast and Griffith University. For the 2020 cohort, they also received requests from University of Queensland, Australian Catholic University and Christian Heritage College. But KGTECE is not a teacher education provider in its own right, and so has not had to work through the Queensland College of Teachers (QCT) accreditation system, although Linda has been a panel member and assessor for this system (more on the QCT accreditation system below). These arrangements make it easier for KGTECE to develop their teacher education provision along these lines: it gives them additional capacity for effective change.

Teacher education at QUT

At the time of my visit, the teacher education provision at QUT had been through significant change and upheaval. At the university level, the faculty have moved into a new building with state of the art teaching facilities and open-plan academic offices; a move which has been accompanied by a University-wide directive to move to open, distance and blended learning, a faculty and administrative staffing restructure and a new process of programme accreditation. The Faculty had undergone a process of "reimagining" their teacher education provision. This process appeared to combine both the move to online and blended learning as well as the reaccreditation requirements overseen by the QCT. Within the Australian system, it is the QCT which oversees and accredits teacher education provision for the state. Successful providers who pass the accreditation process are then enabled to go on and assess new teachers against the Teacher Standards. Both the Standards and the Accreditation principles are influenced by the national Standards (Australian Professional Standards for Teachers) and the AITSL Accreditation of ITE programmes in Australia Standards and Procedures (AITSL, 2019).

The process for accreditation was considered to be particularly challenging by the people I interviewed at QUT. Each document was reputed to be over 1,000 pages long, and that each version or specialism of the programme required a full and unique set of accreditation documents, and would be held by the QCT to robust scrutiny. However, at the time of my visit, the accreditation process was complete and the faculty were settling in to teach their new programmes.

The reimagining of the teacher education provision was partly necessitated by a new accreditation system introduced by AITSL as well as internal changes at QUT. The QUT programme design had been developed based on the following three interrelated teaching approaches respectively related to: teacher education pedagogy, learning from practical experiences and desirable graduate attributes. Alongside these design drivers, the new programmes had to be aligned with the ITE frameworks such as the teacher standards (APSTs) from AITSL, Australian Qualifications frameworks and templates developed by the QCT. These university and accreditation frameworks all privilege a certain set of ideas and knowledges to feature in teacher education programmes.

Primarily with regard to the teacher education pedagogy, the QUT programmes are based on the "realistic approach" formulated by Fred Korthagen (see, for example, Korthagen, 2001, 2010; Korthagen & Kessels, 1999) aimed to achieve a genuine integration of theory and practice through a deep process of professional change; reflections on concrete, recently experienced and relatively short teaching situations; an emphasis on student learning outcomes; and a development of personal practical theories drawn from formal theories and their own thinking.

The approach to learning from practical experiences is a research-based orientation on the notion of praxis defined by Groundwater-Smith, Mitchell, Mockler, Ponte and Rönnerman (2012) as "the concept we use to critically explore the facilitation of research in transformative partnerships. It is also used to explore the conditions in which these partnerships construct intersubjectively – practical knowledge about educational practice in the field" (p. 4). This occurs through professional experiences that are co-ordinated with on campus units, and features more prominently in the Masters-level programme which has a stronger emphasis on research.

Finally, the third approach is common to all programmes of study at QUT and is expressed as a commitment to "real world" learning (as outlined in the QUT Real World 2020 Vision Blueprint 6[3] document which outlines QUT's vision, goals and principles). For the QUT teacher education programme, this means that:

> graduates will not only be well prepared and classroom ready, they will be highly skilled, enterprising graduates well suited to 21st century employment and careers who, throughout their lives, will thrive in changing and complex working environments.

The learning experiences involved in this approach encompass technology, innovation, entrepreneurial thinking, work-integrated learning, authentic assessment and a focus on Aboriginal and Torres Strait Island knowledges. Related to QUT's move towards online learning, the design was based on a

Community of Inquiry model (see, for example, Swan, Garrison, and Richardson, 2009) to draw upon social, cognitive and teaching presences.

These approaches are evident in the teacher education pedagogy which emphasises practitioner research, the role of reflection and continuing research into the effectiveness of their practice. The programme seeks to ensure there is firm grounding in the foundational disciplines, including sociology, psychology, curriculum and professional practice, and to ensure there are no tensions among these different "traditions" and following the work of Gore (2001), quality pedagogy is placed at the core of learning and teaching.

Processing change

The "move to online", part of the QUT-wide initiative reflected in the university's Vision outlined above, has enabled a more diverse student body to enrol for teacher education, including part-time students, career changers and international students. The teacher educators explained that this shift had meant some adaptations in their teaching to cater for this changing student demographic, and that this had created additional workload. This additional workload was acknowledged at all areas of the leadership of the teacher education provision, and was partly seen as a by-product of the quality of the teacher educators involved in the system who "take their job really seriously, and always go the extra mile for their students". In other words, the practices of teacher educators and the culture of support and pastoral care were used to support the developing technological infrastructure used to mediate the teacher education provision. This was not necessarily seen as a bad thing, as two of the teacher educators reflected that this has caused them to rethink aspects of their teaching and alternative ways through which they could develop high-quality relationships with online students. However, as outlined above, some teacher educators described the challenge of getting to know their students beyond their online persona, a situation that was further exacerbated when they were unable to visit their students on practicum or watch them teach. This was partly due to the large numbers on the programme. As one teacher educator explained to me:

> I'm teaching them to teach [my subject], but I never get to see them do it, so I don't know how well they are understanding the content of my sessions. Because placements are allocated elsewhere I don't know where they are going, the quality of the host teacher who is supporting them, or even if they are getting the opportunity to teach [their subject]. When I teach them I either have to backward map (think about when you were at school) or forward map (imagine you are teaching this). It makes effective reflection really hard.
> *(Interview, QUT, 2019)*

As outlined above, the Korthagen cycle of reflection (1999) places professional action, reflection and adaption to action as a key part of the process of learning to teach: one that values the experience of teaching, and links it with theoretical knowledge. Whilst the teacher education programme was designed for this to take place, when there is a time lag between the practicum and the curriculum units, it is challenging to complete this cycle effectively. However, one teacher educator suggested that the students themselves felt they were being "over-reflective", which she explained as perhaps attributable to their lack of relevant experience to make reflection meaningful and to be used as an opportunity to learn.

Pedagogically then, disconnecting practicum from the taught components appears to have made developing a strong connection between theory and practice more challenging, disrupting the flow and influences of ideas, and potentially disconnected knowledge from the taught elements of the programmes from the experience of practice. This was being proactively addressed by the teacher educators who were adapting their online teaching to improve their contact and relationships with students. Knowledges in these taught components however come alive during the practicum experiences, a key part of any teacher education programme. The student teachers are still introduced to a range of ideas and knowledges in the programme, and the issue is how they are brought together.

Supervising "prac"

The allocation, supervision and monitoring of placements (or "prac", short for practicum) is undertaken in QUT by a specific department, known as Professional Experience (PEx). This department was responsible for allocating students to partnership schools, organised primarily on the basis of location. The department was adapting to the diversification of the student body and had recently accommodated some international placements (within the QCT guidelines), and were also working with KGTECE to secure and promote rural and remote placements across Queensland (not just for students on the TECE programme but others who wished to work in rural and remote communities too).

Although placements in the undergraduate and postgraduates programmes were of different lengths (averaging around four to five weeks), they were scheduled to take place at a similar time so that students were placed in a school with others from different programmes, year cohorts and specialisms. In Australia, teaching "out of field" or outside your specialism is not uncommon, and so student teachers (or pre-service teachers as they are known) would not necessarily gain experience of their key area, particularly if they had two subject areas (such as English and History) as is common practice.

Once on "prac", the PEx office, along with their team of teacher educators and University Partners, monitors the progress of the student teachers through an email reflective task and site visit. At the time of my visit, it was explained that these visits do not necessarily feature observing a taught lesson but are conducted along the lines of a Professional Learning Conversation, as introduced to QUT by Associate Professor Rosie LeCornu. The Professional Learning Conversation takes place during a site visit, with all the student teachers present and participating (site visits can take place online if necessary). The purpose of the Professional Learning Conversation is to:

- Foster personal professional reflection;
- Build links between school, teaching experience and university study; and
- Encourage student teachers to seek and provide support for each other.

A conversation is held in a group setting, and the student teachers are encouraged to discuss, reflect and question their own and others' methods of teaching to gain insight into their own teaching practice. Unless either the school or the student teacher reports significant concerns during the practicum, the professional learning conversation, email updates and progress report forms are the main form of communication between the university and the school during the practicum period.

School partners are responsible for the assessment of the student teachers on their "prac". This is made possible through a statewide approach to assessing the APST and the Queensland Professional experience framework, developed by the QCT. The QCT website hosts a range of frameworks, standards and support documents and reporting frameworks to standardise the understanding, assessment and judgement against the Teacher Standards and to support all teacher educators in their use.

Additionally, schools in Queensland are beholden to regular review, a feature of which is their association with local universities. Therefore, schools are motivated to take part in university-based teacher education, and through this statewide system are familiar with and, in the case of QUT, responsible for the assessment of individual student teachers. These practice arrangements affect the role of the university-based engagement with the school-based practicum. In other systems, where the assessment of the student teacher is the responsibility of the awarding university and where inappropriate assessment yields a high penalty under inspection, the visit of the university tutor has multiple purposes, including support (to the school and the student), development, quality assurance and judgement. In Queensland, judgement is undertaken by the school, and so the main focus of the visit is to monitor the progress of the student and their placement experience.

The PEx office had recently recruited a number of "university partners" or part-time staff to undertake some of the school visits. These appointments were classified as professional staff, removing the requirement for them to have higher or research degrees, but which also meant that QUT could recruit from a wider pool of applicants with recent and relevant school experience (and the appropriate teacher registration required by QCT): former head teachers, recent teachers with young families, those experiencing a career break and so forth. These university partners had a wide range of recent professional experience, highly valued by the student teachers and that could inform the site-based professional learning conversations. This arrangement, however, was unpopular with some teacher educators, as they felt it further distanced the practical experience from the taught components of the programme and affected their ability to provide all-around support for their students. Conversely, some teacher educators had allowed their teacher certification to lapse, preventing them from undertaking school visits.

But from the point of view of the knowledges evident on teacher education programmes, the QUT arrangements illustrate the knowledge quality conundrum well. There are three dimensions to the teacher education programme: the university-orientated taught and assessed components representing academic knowledge pedagogically aligned to reflection on practice, the knowledge gained through practicum and the professional learning conversations; and the sorts of knowledge developed through the kinds of community immersion and engagement activities outlined above. These aspects of the programme offer opportunities for a flow of ideas, which represent a range of opportunities for transformation to occur. However, there are questions as to how the structure of the programme enables these ideas to flow pedagogically.

Preparing teachers for diverse communities

Clearly the financial incentives and the work of the KGTECE are both instrumental in seeking to address the issue of finding teachers for rural and remote communities, and this is supported by a statewide mechanism to ensure the standards for new teachers are shared and widely understood and easily accessible. The processes and procedures at QUT, where practicum is scheduled alongside the teaching of units and modules which are made available online, enable the teacher education provision to stretch much wider than the city of Brisbane. But such arrangements have both knowledge and pedagogical implications, particularly when enacting a reflective pedagogical approach: they require a solid knowledge base that includes pedagogical and community knowledges in order to address questions around culturally responsive pedagogy and the diverse population of Queensland.

However, the difference between the approach of the KGTECE and the QUT programme reflects the wider constraints inherent to many teacher education programmes within prescriptive accountability systems. The quality discourse driving the KGTECE programme is one that privileges practice and community-based support. It has been formed by an analysis of the knowledge gaps or misconceptions held by student teachers, a deep knowledge of the context of rural and remote education and drivers to address those gaps authentically. Combined with taught courses in Indigenous knowledges, the programme provides a range of knowledges and ideas for teachers teaching in diverse settings. The approach has been influenced by the specific concerns raised by teachers preparing for rural and remote communities, and engagement and representation with the rural and remote communities themselves.

The quality discourse driving the infrastructural changes to the QUT programme is situated at both a university and at an accountability level: a desire to improve the student experience, to open up programmes to a more flexible and diverse student body unrestricted by location and also to ensure high-quality content and assessment practices through standardisation. These features are common to universities who see themselves as part of a global marketplace and to local and national accountability mechanisms. The practical approaches adopted by QUT, adapting the curriculum arrangements for the teacher education provision and establishing the role of university partners, has changed the ways that placement supervision is allocated across the programme. There are questions as to the extent to which such an approach moves teacher educators away from supporting students and school partners they know well and from the community-based knowledges prevalent in the communities to which the new teachers will serve. The institutional response to the knowledge quality conundrum is to focus the university's contribution to teacher education as rooted in research-based knowledges and developing specialised academic content. One of the most popular changes in the reimagining of the teacher education curriculum was a revamped and much improved unit that focused on Indigenous knowledges and perspectives.

Clearly location is a substantial factor in the presence of community-based knowledges in teacher education. Whilst both KGTECE and QUT have sought to improve the availability of community-based knowledges in their programme, whether this goes far enough and whether it has a substantial impact on the student teachers remains to be seen. In all the sites I visited, there was evidence of a recognition to address gaps in the understanding of new teachers and a desire to educate them to teach in diverse communities. These were particularly developed around Indigenous communities in Australia, Canada and New Zealand, where the active engagement in these communities were part of the programme validation and accreditation processes. One teacher educator (not based at QUT) described to me the challenge of addressing this effectively with large numbers of students: as specific taught components were common to all teacher education programmes, there was a temptation for the university to use an economy of scale to bring the students together, which prevented a pedagogical approach that sought to highlight, for example, white privilege and giving students a small (intimate) space with which to discuss their responses. The teacher educator commented that if all the students were brought together in a large lecture hall, pedagogically the only option is for someone to address them and to "tell them not to be racist", without giving them the space to understand the complexity around what racism and white supremacy means. This position was reflected in many of the university sites who were considering how reformations of this part of the programme were most successful when student teachers were given appropriate space and support to interrogate the ideas and consequences in depth.

Nevertheless, as Sleeter notes, there is a hierarchy of what knowledges are considered important. These are reinforced by official discourses of what is considered necessary in teacher preparation. The scope to challenge these discourses is limited when they can influence programme accreditation. As Ball (2003) has highlighted though, there is a distinction here between the expression and the text of policy (which recognises plurality of views, and in some cases the importance of community and Indigenous perspectives) and the enactment of policy (see also Maguire, Perryman, Ball, & Braun, 2011). The different sites of practice are key too: university programmes need to be matched by action taking place in school partnerships. Recognising the power and influence of such dominant discourses are important, as are active encounters that can create opportunities for student teachers to reflect, in an informed way, about the practices they observe.

The representational space here is important: the visibility of knowledge in teacher education programmes matters. Some teacher educators talked to me of their relief to see units on Indigenous communities given more space and front-loaded in the curriculum, as this signalled their importance and the institution's commitment in a visible way. Silence sends messages too, as it indicates what is not considered important and what is not valued. However, the representational is not sufficient: perspectives developed through taught sessions need to be reflected in all aspects of a programme, including those orientated to practice and partnership.

The focus in the KGTECE programme is deliberately balanced against the programme's content from the university-based provider. Whilst it may not yet be available to all QUT students, it presents an interesting example of how partnerships and alliances can support a range of knowledges across teacher education programmes.

Notes

1. https://teach.qld.gov.au/scholarships-and-grants/beyond-the-range-professional-experience-grant.
2. https://teach.qld.gov.au/scholarships-and-grants/rural-and-remote-graduate-teacher-scholarships.
3. https://cms.qut.edu.au/__data/assets/pdf_file/0006/894066/qut-blueprint-6-final.pdf.

References

Abrahams, R. D., & Troike, R. C. (1972). *Language and cultural diversity in American education*. Englewood Cliffs, NJ: Prentice-Hall.

AITSL. (2019). *Spotlight: Diversity in school leadership*. Retrieved from https://www.aitsl.edu.au/docs/default-source/research-evidence/spotlight/spotlight-diversity-in-school-leadership.pdf?sfvrsn=93effa3c_2

Alvunger, D., & Wahlström, N. (2017). Research-based teacher education? Exploring the meaning potentials of Swedish teacher education. *Teachers and Teaching, 24*(4), 332–349. doi:10.1080/13540602.2017.1403315

Anderson, G. L., & Herr, K. (2011). Scaling up "evidence-based" practices for teachers is a profitable but discredited paradigm. *Educational Researcher, 40*(6), 287–289. doi:10.3102/0013189X11417619

Avery, P. G., & Walker, C. (1993). Prospective teachers' perceptions of ethnic and gender differences in academic achievement. *Journal of Teacher Education, 44*(1), 27–37.

Ball, S. J. (2003). The teacher's soul and the terrors of performativity. *Journal of Education Policy, 18*(2), 215–228. doi:10.1080/0268093022000043065

Barry, N. H., & Lechner, J. V. (1995). Preservice teachers' attitudes about and awareness of multicultural teaching and learning. *Teaching and Teacher Education, 11*(2), 149–161.

Ben-Peretz, M. (2001). The impossible role of teacher educators in a changing world. *Journal of Teacher Education, 52*(1), 48–56. doi:10.1177/0022487101052001005

Beutel, D., Adie, L., & Hudson, S. (2011). Promoting rural and remote teacher education in Australia through the over the Hill project. *International Journal of Learning, 18*(2), 377–388.

Biesta, G. (2007). Why "what works" won't work: Evidence-based practice and the democratic deficit in educational research. *Educational Theory, 57*(1), 1–22. doi:10.1111/j.1741-5446.2006.00241.x

Chan, C. (2019). Crossing institutional borders: Exploring pre-service teacher education partnerships through the lens of border theory. *Teaching and Teacher Education, 86*, 102893. doi:10.1016/j.tate.2019.102893

Cochran-Smith, M. (2004). The problem of teacher education. *Journal of Teacher Education, 55*(4), 295–299. doi:10.1177/0022487104268057

Cochran-Smith, M. (2005). Studying teacher education: What we know and need to know. *Journal of Teacher Education, 56*(4), 301–306. doi: 10.1177/0022487105280116

Cochran-Smith, M., Carney, M. C., Keefe, E. S., Burton, S., Chang, W.-C., Fernández, M. B., … Baker, M. (2018). *Reclaiming accountability in teacher education*. New York: Teachers College Press.

Cochran-Smith, M., Ell, F., Grudnoff, L., Haigh, M., Hill, M., & Ludlow, L. (2016). Initial teacher education: What does it take to put equity at the center? *Teaching and Teacher Education, 57*, 67–78. doi:10.1016/j.tate.2016.03.006

Cochran-Smith, M., & Zeichner, K. M. (2005). *Studying teacher education: The report of the AERA panel on research and teacher education*. Mahwah, NJ: Lawrence Erlbaum Associates.

Cramp, A., & Khan, S. (2018). The convivial space – Exploring teacher learning through practitioner research. *Professional Development in Education, 45*(3), 344–355. doi:10.1080/19415257.2018.1431957

Eraut, M. (2007). *Theoretical and practical knowledge revisited*. Paper presented at the 12th Bienniel EARLI Conference 2007, Budapest, Hungary.

Eraut, M. (2010). Knowledge, working practices, and learning. In S. Billett (Ed.), *Learning through practice, professional and practice-based learning* (Vol. 1, pp. 37–58). Dordrecht: Springer.

Flores, M. A. (2018). Linking teaching and research in initial teacher education: Knowledge mobilisation and research-informed practice. *Journal of Education for Teaching, 44*(5), 621–636. doi:10.1080/02607476.2018.1516351

Flores, M. A. (2020a). Feeling like a student but thinking like a teacher: A study of the development of professional identity in initial teacher education. *Journal of Education for Teaching, 46*(2), 145–158. doi:10.1080/02607476.2020.1724659

Flores, M. A. (2020b). Learning to teach: Knowledge, competences and support in initial teacher education and in the early years of teaching. *European Journal of Teacher Education, 43*(2), 127–130. doi:10.1080/02619768.2020.1733828

Foster, M. (1997). *Black teachers on teaching*. New York: New Press.

Foster, M., & Peele, T. (1999). Teaching and learning in the contexts of African American English and culture. *Education and Urban Society, 31*(2), 177–189.

Furlong, J. (2013). *Education – An anatomy of the discipline: Rescuing the university project.* Abingdon: Routledge.

Gay, G. (2002). Preparing for culturally responsive teaching. *Journal of Teacher Education, 53*(2), 106–116.

Gay, G. (2010). *Culturally responsive teaching: Theory, research, and practice/Geneva Gay* (2nd ed.). New York: Teachers College Press.

Gilbert, S. L. (1995). Perspectives of rural prospective teachers toward teaching in urban schools. *Urban Education, 30*(3), 290–305.

González, M., Moll, L. C., & Amanti, C. (2005). Introduction: Theorizing practices. In M. González, L. C. Moll, & C. Amanti (Eds.), *Funds of knowledge: Theorizing practices in households, communities and classrooms* (pp. 1–25). New York: Routledge.

Gore, J. M. (2001). Disciplining bodies: On the continuity of power relations in pedagogy. In C. Paechter, R. Edwards, R. Harrison, & P. Twining (Eds.), *Learning, space and identity* (pp. 167–181). London: Sage.

Grossman, P. (2018). *Teaching core practices in teacher education.* Cambridge, MA: Harvard Education Publishing Group.

Grossman, P., Hammerness, K., & McDonald, M. (2009). Redefining teaching, re-imagining teacher education. *Teachers and Teaching, 15*(2), 273–289. doi:10.1080/13540600902875340

Grossman, P., Kazemi, E., Kavanagh, S. S., Franke, M., & Dutro, E. (2019). Learning to facilitate discussions: Collaborations in practice-based teacher education. *Teaching and teacher education, 81,* 97–99. doi:10.1016/j.tate.2019.02.002

Grossman, P., & Pupik Dean, C. G. (2019). Negotiating a common language and shared understanding about core practices: The case of discussion. *Teaching and Teacher Education, 80,* 157–166. doi:10.1016/j.tate.2019.01.009

Groundwater-Smith, S., Mitchell, J., Mockler, N., Ponte, P., & Ronnerman, K. (2012). *Facilitating practitioner research: Developing transformational partnerships.* London: Routledge.

Grudnoff, L., Haigh, M., Hill, M., Cochran-Smith, M., Ell, F., & Ludlow, L. (2017). Teaching for equity: Insights from international evidence with implications for a teacher education curriculum. *The Curriculum Journal, 28*(3), 305–326. doi:10.1080/09585176.2017.1292934

Halsey, R. J. (2005). *Submission to the inquiry into teacher education.* Rural education forum Australia. http://www.aph.gov.au/house/committee/evt/teachereduc/subs/sub045.pdf

Hamilton, M., & O'Dwyer, A. (2018). Exploring student learning approaches on an initial teacher education programme: A comparison of mature learners and direct entry third-level students. *Teaching and Teacher Education, 71,* 251–261. doi:10.1016/j.tate.2018.01.011

Hiebert, J., Gallimore, R., & Stigler, J. W. (2002). A knowledge base for the teaching profession: What would it look like and how can we get one? *Educational Researcher, 31*(5), 3–15.

HREOC. (2000). *"Education Access": National Inquiry into Rural and Remote Education.* Sydney: https://humanrights.gov.au/sites/default/files/content/pdf/human_rights/rural_remote/Access_final.pdf

Jenset, I. S., Klette, K., & Hammerness, K. (2017). Grounding teacher education in practice around the world: An examination of teacher education coursework in teacher education programs in Finland, Norway, and the United States. *Journal of Teacher Education, 69*(2), 184–197. doi:10.1177/0022487117728248

Kennedy, M. (2015). Parsing the practice of teaching. *Journal of Teacher Education, 67*(1), 6–17. doi:10.1177/0022487115614617

Kim, J., & Pulido, I. (2015). Examining hip-hop as culturally relevant pedagogy. *Journal of Curriculum and Pedagogy, 12*(1), 17–35. doi:10.1080/15505170.2015.1008077

Korthagen, F. (2001). *Linking practice and theory: The pedagogy of realistic teacher education*. Mahwah, NJ: Lawrence Erlbaum Associates Publishers.

Korthagen, F. (2010). Situated learning theory and the pedagogy of teacher education: Towards an integrative view of teacher behavior and teacher learning. *Teaching and Teacher Education, 26*(1), 98–106. doi:10.1016/j.tate.2009.05.001

Korthagen, F., & Kessels, J. (1999). Changing the pedagogy of teacher education. *Educational Researcher, 28*(4), 4–17.

Kostiainen, E., Ukskoski, T., Ruohotie-Lyhty, M., Kauppinen, M., Kainulainen, J., & Mäkinen, T. (2018). Meaningful learning in teacher education. *Teaching and Teacher Education, 71*, 66–77. doi:10.1016/j.tate.2017.12.009

Kumashiro, K. K. (2015). *Against common sense: Teaching and learning toward social justice* (3rd ed.). London: Routledge.

Kumashiro, K. K., Neal, L. V. I., & Sleeter, C. E. (2015). *Diversifying the teacher workforce: Preparing and retaining highly effective teachers*. London: Routledge.

Ladson-Billings, G. (2014). Culturally relevant pedagogy 2.0: a.k.a. the Remix. *Harvard Educational Review, 84*(1), 74–84. doi: 10.17763/haer.84.1.p2rj131485484751

Larke, P. J. (1990). Cultural diversity awareness inventory: Assessing the sensitivity of preservice teachers. *Action in Teacher Education, 12*(3), 23–30. doi:10.1080/01626620.1990.10734396

Lim, L., Tan, M., & Saito, E. (2019). Culturally relevant pedagogy: Developing principles of description and analysis. *Teaching and Teacher Education, 77*, 43–52. doi:10.1016/j.tate.2018.09.011

Loewenberg Ball, D. (2000). Bridging practices; intertwining content and pedagogy in teaching and learning to teach. *Journal of Teacher Education, 51*(3), 241–247.

Lyons, T. (2009). Teachers' motivations for working in rural schools. In T. Lyons, J-L Choi, & G. McPhan (Eds.), *Improving equity in rural education: Proceedings of the International Symposium for Innovation in Rural Education (ISFIRE) 2009* (pp. 167–177). Armidale, NSW: University of New England.

Lynch, C., & Rata, E. (2018). Culturally responsive pedagogy: A New Zealand case study. *International Studies in Sociology of Education, 27*(4), 391–408. doi:10.1080/09620214.2018.1468274

Maguire, M., Perryman, J., Ball, S., & Braun, A. (2011). The ordinary school – What is it? *British Journal of Sociology of Education, 32*(1), 1–16. doi:10.1080/01425692.2011.527718

McDonald, M. A., Bowman, M., & Brayko, K. (2013). Learning to see students: Opportunities to develop relational practices of teaching through community-based placements in teacher education. *Teachers College Record, 115*(4), 1–35.

McIntyre, A. (1997). *Making meaning of whiteness: Exploring racial identity with White teachers*. Albany: State University of New York Press.

Menter, I., Hulme, M., Elliot, D., Lewin, J., Baumfield, V., Britton, A., ... McQueen, I. (2010). *Literature review on teacher education in the 21st century* (S. G. S. Reserach Ed.). Glasgow: University of Glasgow.

Morrison, K. A., Robbins, H. H., & Rose, D. G. (2008). Operationalizing culturally relevant pedagogy: A synthesis of classroom-based research. *Equity & Excellence in Education, 41*(4), 433–452. doi:10.1080/10665680802400006

Murray, J. (2017). Defining teacher educators: International perspectives and contexts. In D. J. Clandinin & J. Husu (Eds.), *The Sage handbook of research on teacher education* (Vol. 2, pp. 1017–1032). London: SAGE Publishers.

Nutley, S., Walter, I., & Davies, H. T. (2003). From knowing to doing: A framework for understanding the evidence-into-practice agenda. *Evaluation, 9*(2), 125–143.

O'Flaherty, J., & Beal, E. M. (2018). Core competencies and high leverage practices of the beginning teacher: A synthesis of the literature. *Journal of Education for Teaching, 44*(4), 461–478. doi:10.1080/02607476.2018.1450826

Payne, K. A., & Zeichner, K. (2017). Multiple voices and participants in teacher education. In D. J. Clandinin & J. Husu (Eds.), *The Sage handbook of research on teacher education* (Vol. 2, pp. 1101–1116). Thousand Oaks, CA: Sage.

Philip, T. M., Souto-Manning, M., Anderson, L., Horn, I. J., Carter Andrews, D., Stillman, J., & Varghese, M. (2018). Making justice peripheral by constructing practice as "core": How the increasing prominence of core practices challenges teacher education. *Journal of Teacher Education, 70*(3), 251–264. doi:10.1177/0022487118798324

Seidl, B. (2016). Working with communities to explore and personalize culturally relevant pedagogies. *Journal of Teacher Education, 58*(2), 168–183. doi:10.1177/0022487106297845

Sjöberg, L. (2018). The shaping of pre-service teachers' professional knowledge base through assessments. *European Journal of Teacher Education, 41*(5), 604–619. doi:10.1080/02619768.2018.1529751

Sleeter, C. (2012). Confronting the marginalization of culturally responsive pedagogy. *Urban Education, 47*(3), 562–584. doi:10.1177/0042085911431472

Sleeter, C. (2019). Considering core assumptions about what it means to teach. *Teachers College Record, 121*, 1–4.

Souto-Manning, M. (2018). Toward praxically-just transformations: Interrupting racism in teacher education. *Journal of Education for Teaching, 45*(1), 97–113. doi:10.1080/02607476.2019.1550608

Souto-Manning, M., & Stillman, J. (2020). In the pursuit of transformative justice in the education of teacher educators. *The New Educator, 16*(1), 1–4. doi:10.1080/1547688x.2019.1698871

Starck, J. G., Riddle, T., Sinclair, S., & Warikoo, N. (2020). Teachers are people too: Examining the racial bias of teachers compared to other American adults. *Educational Researcher.* doi:10.3102/0013189x20912758

Su, Z. (1997). Teaching as a profession and as a career: Minority candidates' perspectives. *Teaching and Teacher Education, 13*(3), 325–340.

Swan, K. et al. (2009). "A Constructivist Approach to Online Learning: The Community of Inquiry Framework." *Information Technology and Constructivism in Higher Education: Progressive Learning Frameworks*, Carla R. Payne (Ed.) (pp. 43–57). IGI Global,. http://doi.org/10.4018/978-1-60566-654-9.ch004

Teacher Education Ministerial Advisory Group. (2014). *Action now: Classroom ready teachers.* Retrieved from http://www.studentsfirst.gov.au/teacher-education-ministerial-advisory-group

Totterdell, M., & Lambert, D. (1998). The professional formation of teachers: A case study in reconceptualising initial teacher education through an evolving model of partnership in training and learning. *Teacher Development, 2*(3), 351–371. doi:10.1080/13664539800200066

Ulvik, M., Helleve, I., & Smith, K. (2017). What and how student teachers learn during their practicum as a foundation for further professional development. *Professional Development in Education, 44*(5), 638–649. doi:10.1080/19415257.2017.1388271

Valli, L. (1995). The dilemma of race: Learning to be color blind and color conscious. *Journal of Teacher Education, 46*(2), 120–129.

Van Der Schaaf, M., Slof, B., Boven, L., & De Jong, A. (2019). Evidence for measuring teachers' core practices. *European Journal of Teacher Education, 42*(5), 675–694. doi:10.1080/02619768.2019.1652903

Villegas, A. M., & Lucas, T. (2002). *Educating culturally responsive teachers: A coherent approach*. New York: Suny Press.

White, S. (2006). Preparing preservice teachers for rural teaching: A new approach. *International Journal of Practical Experiences in Professional Education (PEPE)*, 9(1), 14–19.

White, S. (2018). Teacher educators for new times? Redefining an important occupational group. *Journal of Education for Teaching*, 45(2), 200–213. doi:10.1080/02607476.2018.1548174

Winch, C. (2017). *Teachers' know-how: A philosophical investigation*. Chichester: John Wiley & Sons.

Youens, B., Smethem, L., & Simmons, M. (2018). Move over Nelly: Lessons from 30 years of employment-based initial teacher education in England. *Teachers and Teaching*, 24(7), 854–869. doi:10.1080/13540602.2018.1481025

Young, E. (2010). Challenges to conceptualizing and actualizing culturally relevant pedagogy: How viable is the theory in classroom practice? *Journal of Teacher Education*, 61(3), 248–260. doi:10.1177/0022487109359775

5
THE TEACHER EDUCATOR QUALITY CONUNDRUM

This chapter was largely inspired by a brief instance that occurred during a lesson observation of a student teacher[1] in Arizona. The incident itself is quite commonplace, but within the context of the innovations that were happening at Mary Lou Fulton Teachers College (MLFTC) at Arizona State University (ASU), it caused me to pause and think about the changing nature of work of teacher educators, particularly when the programmes they work on are going through substantial change.

During a second-grade lesson (typically with children aged seven), the student teacher was leading the class through a series of activities, orientated around a set of worksheet-based tasks, which the teacher modelled, worked through collectively and then allowed the pupils to complete individually. She then went over the answers with the whole class. The format of the lesson episode was fairly straightforward. I sat towards the back of the class, near a group of four pupils. Two of the pupils participated in the teacher-directed activities as instructed, working at roughly the same pace as the rest of the class, completing the activities as they were instructed to do. The other two pupils worked differently. The girl next to me completed all the activities on the sheet before the student teacher had finished the instructions. She had completed them all accurately, neatly and seemingly effectively. She then sat still during the rest of the class. She was not disruptive. She did not attract the teacher's attention, did not indicate she had finished and she was not noticed by the teacher as she walked around checking the class's progress. As far as I could tell, the teacher was unaware the pupil had completed her work quickly or accurately. The other child in the group of four, a boy, was at a complete loss. He attempted some of the earlier tasks but had misunderstood the instructions, so he stopped. He put his head on the desk. He was not disruptive, but also did not call for the attention of the teacher. He sat quietly. As the teacher worked through the activities with the class so they could check their work – he diligently copied down the correct answers – the worksheet showed little evidence of this lack of engagement in class, nor did it indicate if or why he had not understood the work.

I introduced this chapter by saying that this vignette was fairly commonplace – and I am sure similar activities happen in the classrooms of many new and experienced teachers. After the lesson, I discussed what I had observed with the student teacher and she reflected, understandably, as to where her attention had been and considered what she would need to do in future lessons. I was not worried about the progress of those pupils or of the development of that new teacher. Instead, the incident made me think about the role of teacher educators.

The situation could be seen as was what Tatto and colleagues (2017) have described as an opportunity to learn for the new teacher (see also Blömeke, 2012; Cohen & Berlin, 2019). The teacher had planned and resourced her lesson diligently; it was well structured and overall well implemented. However, the execution of the lesson, whilst sound, did not work for all the pupils, or at least not for the group of pupils I was seated near. For any student teacher, noticing what happened, reflecting on why it happened, and considering the implications for future teaching is potentially a key learning moment, a point for reflection on how their teaching is being experienced by their class. An opportunity to learn is an incident, planned or not, which provides the student teacher with an opportunity to think about their practice differently. An opportunity to learn can stem from a taught element of the teacher education programme or through something that occurs in class. In this case, there was an opportunity to consider how the taught lesson is being experienced by the class, how the classroom monitoring could be more thorough and how to address the learning needs of the two individuals I have singled out. Such an opportunity to learn, I think, presents itself during the practice of many student teachers. The key question for me is how any new teacher becomes aware of that opportunity to learn and are given access to the knowledge they need to address it productively.

In this case, the student teacher (or teacher candidate, as final year clinical practice students are referred to) was part of a new teaming approach to teacher education (preparation) led by the MLFTC at ASU. Under this approach, a team of three teacher candidates are looking after one class under the supervision of the lead teacher who maintains responsibility for her own class in an adjoining classroom. They are part of a larger team of teachers working at the same grade level, and supported by a site lead, a teacher educator from MLFTC who works with the team and undertakes the requisite visits and observations. The teaming approach will be discussed in more detail later in this chapter.

Under this new approach, the student teacher (or teacher candidate) has two peers and various experienced and certified teachers who can support her practice; however, she was the only one teaching during this particular lesson (the others were either working with the Lead Teacher in another class or helping some pupils catch up with an assessment they had missed). Had any of the team been involved in the lesson, I wondered whether they would have noticed the two pupils and discussed the situation. I also considered what pre-placement preparation that new teacher could have been given to enable her to make the most of such opportunities to learn even when teaching alone.

In this chapter, the focus is on the work of teacher educators – those people who are dedicated to supporting new teachers as they go through their transformation. The teacher educator quality conundrum is strongly related to the practice quality conundrum outlined in Chapter 2, as there is an assumption that those teacher educators (school-based mentors and tutors) with recent, close-to-practice experience and expertise are the best people to support teachers through an apprenticeship type pedagogical model. However, practitioners who are so "close to practice" may focus too much on behavioural and procedural aspects of teaching, and so pay less attention to the knowledge and understanding of why situations occur, or the less observable aspects of practice that can make a significant difference in the developing understanding of new teachers. In other words, too much emphasis on teacher educators who focus on practice may have the intention of supporting new teachers well but can detract from giving them access to the complex knowledges they need for long-term success. This quality conundrum particularly comes to light in times of change when teacher educators' roles, responsibilities and pedagogies must adapt.

This chapter draws specifically on the site visit to MLFTC at ASU. The transition the College is making towards a teaming approach raises some interesting questions about the role of teacher educators, and the trends I observed in many contexts to compartmentalise part of the programme: to divide the role up between different actors and how that affects aspects of the teacher educator role. Traditionally teacher educators are divided into two groups: the experienced veteran classroom practitioner acting as Master to the apprentice, sharing their detailed knowledge of the school, students and "the ways we do things around here"; or the academic teacher educator, full of principles and theories but for whom classroom practice is a somewhat distant memory. Without a clear sense of the work of teacher educators, individuals in that role are left to act on instinct and experience. This chapter considers the role of the range of professionals who support new teachers, and how differing expertise can support their development or if too much emphasis on practical support can actually detract from developing high-quality understanding of practice.

Who are the teacher educators?

Teacher educators are not a homogenous group and can variously include those that work in universities, schools, communities and other third-sector organisations, in a variety of capacities (Kleinsasser, 2017; Murray, 2017; White, 2018). Even within universities, the role has increasingly been compartmentalised and diversified with divisions typically along the lines of supervision and teaching (Cochran-Smith, Grudnoff, Orland-Barak, & Smith, 2019). The categorisation offered in the Ducharme study conducted in the 1990s (E. R. Ducharme, 1993;

M. Ducharme, 1996) still has some resonance: that teacher educators tend to be white, female and former teachers, with a different demographic profile to other university faculty. Murray argues that the influence of the practice turn or practicum turn (Furlong, 2013; Mattsson, Eilertsen, & Rorrison, 2012), on the one hand, and the university turn (Murray, 2014), on the other, has further diversified and widened the group of people who identify as teacher educators.

White (2018) notes that as an occupational group, teacher educators have come under increasing scrutiny but are also becoming more diverse as a group. In her categorisation, she includes the important, but often under-recognised, group of community-based teacher educators (alongside those she categorises as university- or school-based). Community-based teacher educators are required to play a significant role in teacher education programme planning in both New Zealand and Australia, where consultation and authentic partnerships with community organisations were strongly encouraged through accreditation processes, particularly for cultural and social diversity. White (2018) also highlights that university-based teacher educators tend to come from two backgrounds: either having had previous experience as an academic researcher or from a teaching background; a characteristic that affects their identity as they adapt to new professional perspectives (Williams, 2014). For some then, teacher education is an accidental career (Mayer, Mitchell, Santoro, & White, 2011), commonly referred to as *second order* (Murray & Male, 2005). As a committed teacher educator, I find this distinction uncomfortable for its hierarchical distinction, which implies that teacher education is less important than other roles. However, the research is clear: teacher educators are under-inducted; lack professional development, and Holme, Robb and Berry (2016) suggest that the role is rarely the career goal of educators. There is little consensus as to their specialist knowledge base.

The diversity amongst teacher educators appears to be increasing. In the US, teacher educators might be students enrolled on a doctoral programme (Cochran-Smith et al., 2019). In other cases, they are typified as former teachers who transition into a new role, having to cross boundaries to do so (Trent, 2013). Smith (2005) notes the differences in their expertise, knowledge and experience that mark teacher educators out as different from teachers (and to academics), and indicating that the transition into teacher education requires much thought and reflection (Bullough, 2005; Zeichner, 2005). It is also important to recognise that teacher educators have different positionings and identities, depending on their phase or subject specialism (Vanassche & Kelchtermans, 2014), and whether they work in a university or school context (Andreasen, Bjørndal, & Kovač, 2019).

The changing nature and diversity of teacher educators would not be a problem if there was clarity as to their role, expectations and what particular or specialist knowledge they need. Unfortunately, there is a lack of clarity here too. Attention has been given to what teacher educators should know and be able to do (Goodwin & Kosnik, 2013; Goodwin et al., 2014; Murray & Male, 2005), and Koster, Brekelmans, Korthagen and Wubbels (2005) have sought to codify the list of knowledge and competencies that teacher educators need. However, the diversity and range of knowledges and ideas that teacher educators have are necessarily limited by the rather narrow range of people who become them. Goodwin and colleagues note that teacher educators tend to be white, a factor that has also received attention from those concerned with moral and equity issues (Willemse, Lunenberg, & Korthagen, 2005), and issues around justice or social justice (Goodwin & Darity, 2018), diversity and representation (Mitchem, Buffalo, Perez, & Rollins, 2019; Sleeter, 2008, 2019). In other words, who teacher educators are matters, not just for the effects on the new teachers they come into contact with and their repertoire of experiences, but also because of the status and development of the role itself.

Much of the work on teacher educators has focused on the growing division between the roles and responsibilities of university- and school-based teacher educators, illustrated through the different expectations they have of each other (Helleve & Ulvik, 2019; Mauri, Onrubia, Colomina, & Clarà, 2019). This is echoed in a large volume of work which focuses on mentoring of school-based teacher educators, and how theory and practice are understood (Mauri et al., 2019) and how practice can be differently evaluated by school- and university-based teacher educators (Barahona, 2019) as they emphasise different aspects of teacher development.

Teacher educators as members of the university faculty

Being part of a university faculty, teacher educators also need to address the expectations of being an academic and the precarious nature of academic contracts. These concerns are typified by what Grudnoff (Cochran-Smith et al., 2019) has called the bifurcation of their roles: as they juggle being both academics and teacher educators. Ellis and McNicholl (2015) have noted the heavy workload involved in university-based teacher education (particularly when they include time-consuming school visits), and the tensions that the teacher educators face in handling research expectations as a faculty member. At the same time, university-based teacher educators are criticised for being out of touch with schools. The dual expectations of teacher educators do not sit easily together. Cochran-Smith et al. (2019) highlight the challenges this presents for the teacher educators, including:

- Their ability to be recognised within their institution as researchers and academics;
- The induction and professional development they need in order to become high-quality teacher educators; and
- The dissonance between the dual expectations of them as teachers of teachers and as academics and researchers.

This is further complicated by the lack of status and respect offered to education faculty and the work they undertake in the academy (Labaree, 2006). Research conducted in teacher education by teacher educators is often hard to come by (Tack & Vanderlinde, 2019), undervalued and considered to be of low quality (as is often the criticism of self-study) (Vanassche & Kelchtermans, 2015a, 2015b).

However, living up to the expectations of the role and of being a university faculty member is not easy, as teacher educators experience a lack of induction, professional development and clarity over the specialist nature of their knowledge base (Goodwin & Darity, 2018; Ping, Schellings, & Beijaard, 2018). This lack of attention to their professional development needs is exacerbated by the changing working conditions offered to teacher educators in the faculty (Ellis & McNicholl, 2015; Furlong, 2013), as this group is also increasingly reliant on temporary and casualised employment contracts, making their work more and more precarious and reducing the opportunity for professional development and career advancement.

The casualisation of the contractual arrangements for teacher educators is a serious concern. In many universities, the precarious nature of recruitment to teacher education programmes can mean that numbers fluctuate each year. One solution for universities is to vary the contracts available to teacher educators. The availability of full-time, tenured academic contracts for teacher educators are decreasing, as the work becomes more diversified into sessional contracts, clinical contracts renewed on an annual basis or divided into non-academic roles such as university partners. These casualised contracts can have reduced status, reduced opportunities for research and are lacking in stability. The precarious nature can reduce the pool of people who are able to undertake causalised work of this nature, but also the capacity of teacher educators to become respected members of the academic community and to participate in research, professional development and programme innovation.

The challenge is that in many contexts, where teacher educators are still defined as academics, they are expected to be all things to all people: skilled up-to-date practitioners, empathetic mentors, and competent and prolific researchers. Here the analysis that Ellis and McNicholl (2015) make on advertisements for teacher education posts is revealing, as it shows that expectations for new teacher educators are impossibly high – to be skilled and expert practitioners as well as accomplished researchers. Their findings raise questions: who do we want our teacher educators to be, and what do we expect of them?

This is at the heart of the quality conundrum, as it reflects the tension over who are the best people to educate our teachers. Proponents of teaching-as-craft emphasise the importance of new teachers being supported by expert practitioners with practice-based knowledges, particularly in an apprenticeship-type, classroom-based model. This underplays the specific expertise of those that have developed knowledge expertise in teacher education, teacher development, professional learning or in a specific curriculum area (such as mathematics education). The teacher educator quality conundrum can overemphasise those teacher educators with practical experience, as they are well placed to help new teachers develop their practice, but in the long term, such emphasis can narrow the range of knowledges and ideas that new teachers are exposed to and could actually deny them an opportunity to this deeper specialist knowledge.

This quality conundrum becomes particularly acute in times of change. Whether changes come from inside or outside the programme community, any degree of change is likely to impact on the practice of teacher educators. But teacher educators are rarely seen as reformers: Cochran-Smith, Stringer Keefe and Carney (2018) note that they are often seen as the objects of reform rather than the agents. When they adopt reform work, it tends to be of a fairly narrow nature and related to narrow conceptions of how the "problem" of teacher education is constructed and therefore how the solution is formulated. Although others have also recognised the importance of the opportunity afforded to teacher educators as innovators such as through technological developments (Avidov-Ungar & Forkosh-Baruch, 2018) and the community around them (Hadar & Brody, 2018), teacher educators are often seen as passive or even resistant in periods of reform.

In every site I visited, change was an ever-present reality, and all the teacher educators I spoke with described adapting both proactively and reactively to reform either through the teacher education system, through university-wide initiatives, changes in the school communities or through seeking to enhance their own practice. These reforms can have implications for the recruitment of new teacher educators, and how those roles are defined and configured. However, these changes are often quiet, individual and, I would argue, largely unrecognised by others. But their impact could be significant, particularly if the changes to the role of teacher educators reduces the range of knowledges available to new teachers and focuses teacher education on a narrow set of practice-orientated behaviours. The changes being introduced at MLFTC is a good example of how changes to a programme will have implications for the work of teacher educators. But in order to understand these changes, it is key to understand the context of the teacher education programme and the nature of the changes being introduced.

Teacher shortages in Arizona

Teacher shortages across the US are widely reported. News reports highlight how schools in major urban areas like Chicago have had to close (Akhtar, 2019),[2] and a Learning Policy Institute report, published in 2019, estimated that in 2017/2018, there was a shortage of 110,000 teachers across the country. Unsurprisingly, the greatest shortages are found in the States where teachers pay is the lowest and where potential teacher candidates have a range of alternative career options. Arizona is one of those states experiencing severe teacher shortages. In 2019, there were an estimated 1,400 teaching vacancies in Arizona; the state ranks 45th out of 50 in teacher salaries, with a wide variation in pay between school districts (Lane, 2019).

In many ways, the situation in Arizona is exacerbated by the unprecedented growth of its capital city Phoenix. The US Census Bureau estimates that Phoenix is the fastest-growing city in the country (welcoming 25,288 new residents between 2017 and 2018), and is now the country's fifth most populous city with 1,660,272 residents. This is on the back of continuous growth: Phoenix has added 200,000 new residents since the 2010 census (to 2019), and both the state and Maricopa County (which is the home of metropolitan Phoenix) are recognised as the fastest growing across the US (Gallen, 2019).[3]

The population of Phoenix shows some interesting trends. As a hot, dry city, Phoenix has often attracted older people and temporary residents from colder parts of the US (known locally as snowbirds). Areas such as Sun City are designated as older communities where residents over the age of 55 live together sharing a high quality of life, without bearing the costs associated with a broad population base such as the local taxation needed to fund local school districts. Phoenix also has a large percentage of Hispanic or Latino residents (42.6% according to the US Census[4]) and a high number of foreign-born residents (19.5%). Further statistics suggest significant disadvantage: 19.4% of residents live in poverty, only 66.7% are employed and 16.1% have no health insurance. The new arrivals and most poverty-stricken areas tend to be located in the west part of the city, whilst the areas of greater wealth tend to be found in the north and east.

Whilst Phoenix has an overall shortage of teachers, the greatest need tends to be in the school districts with the most disadvantaged communities. These school districts, which are funded from local taxes and set their own pay scales, have to pay larger salaries to attract teachers, and yet still find themselves with a 25% shortage of teachers. Estimates indicate that the area is short of 7,500 teachers, with particular shortages in Mathematics and Science specialisms. Many school districts have resorted to a range of tactics, including importing qualified teachers from the Philippines (Lane, 2019; Sterling & Joffe-Block, 2018) and allowing emergency certification. Whilst emergency certification is not unusual in the US, in Arizona this option only requires a high school education, and some emergency certified teachers are not educated to degree level. In addition, Arizona suffers from high attrition rates, particularly amongst new teachers.

As with most areas of chronic need, the issue of dealing with teacher shortage is often beset with short-term solutions which can have a damaging effect on young people's education prospects. The lack of subject specialist teachers, particularly in middle schools, means that young people are often poorly prepared for high school classes and can miss out on entry to advanced courses in high school which can support university entrance. A conversation with an elementary school teacher in a school district of high need revealed that children were unlikely to be tested for special education needs unless they tested as being four grade levels below their actual age (the state average is two grade levels) – there is a lack of special education and counselling support – and most students were operating at one to two grade levels below their expected range.

These geographical and social factors make up a distinctive context for new teachers – one which is characterised by diversity, mobility, underfunding and high levels of poverty and educational needs and the corresponding knowledge demands that places on teachers – and indicate the high levels of support they are likely to need.

Teacher education in Arizona

As with most states across the US, there are a variety of ways to become a teacher in Arizona: through approved teacher education programmes, alternative and emergency certification routes. The Arizona Department for Education lists 16 alternative pathways to teacher certification,[5] which includes community college programmes, online programmes and programmes delivered through university providers. Phoenix also has a branch of Teach for America (taught through ASU).

MLFTC at ASU is the largest education faculty in the US, and has particular expertise in innovation and developing online learning. Among the top-ranked colleges in the US (it is ranked number 13), ASU is a (relatively) large provider of teacher education. The US News ranking of online programmes and under the category of Best Online Teacher Education and Professional Development, Specific Levels and Methods Programs, ASU ranked tied 13th in Education Programs but with an enrolment figure of 3,377, which is significantly more than any of its nearest rivals. For example, the largest online provider is The American College of Education (in Indianapolis, IN) had a higher number of 8,577, but was ranked at number 228–299.

MLFTC at ASU also has a particular emphasis on innovation: ranked the top in the US for five years in a row (Toshner, 2019[6]). As Dean Carol Basile remarked to me: "You're not here unless you want to do things at scale and move things quickly." To this end, MLFTC has been involved in a number of initiatives to support the supply of teachers in the state. MLFTC is the largest provider of participants in the Noyce Scholars programme, a programme designed specifically to support the recruitment of new teachers of STEM (Science Technology Engineering and Mathematics) subjects (MLFTC's programme has a particular emphasis on STEM specialist teachers in middle schools and supporting mentors for new STEM teachers). Recognising that middle schools have a dearth of suitably qualified mentors for STEM teachers, the MLFTC programme has been used to develop mentoring expertise in this area, alongside supporting the development of STEM teachers generally (and with a specific focus on problem-based learning).

Under the previous Dean, Dr Mari Koerner, ASU was recognised by the US Department of Education Office of Innovation and Improvement for its iTeachAZ programme, which sought to support the transition from student teaching to full employment by expanding the clinical experience (practicum) from a few weeks within the programme to a full year at the end of the programme. This programme emphasised more practical instruction and more time in front of a class, and can be seen as a forerunner to the latest innovation in teacher preparation outlined in the Next Education Workforce initiative.

Next Education Workforce initiative

MLFTC has used its understanding of the teacher supply situation in Arizona to both review how teacher education (or teacher preparation) is structured and how it relates to school-based practices. The new approach adopted by MLFTC is widely referred to as the new teaming model of teacher preparation developed through the Next Education Workforce Initiative. This initiative has been promoted and supported by Dean Carol Basile and is widely discussed in a range of YouTube videos, TV appearances and in her blog. The publicity literature quotes the following figures:

> A December 2018 survey by the Arizona School Personnel Administrators Association reported that 75.2% of teacher positions in the state remained "vacant or were filled by individuals not meeting standard teaching requirements."
> The 2019 PDK Poll of the Public's Attitudes Toward the Public Schools reports that 50% of teachers "say they've seriously considered leaving the profession in recent years."
> Simply certifying more people to perform jobs they are likely to leave in search of more money, status or professional stimulation is not a durable solution.

The MLFTC response is to argue:

> We're not facing a teacher supply problem. We're facing a workforce design problem.

This workforce design problem is typified by what they refer to as the "old normal":

> In the standard one teacher, one classroom model, we ask all teachers to be content experts and professional pedagogues; to assess children with learning disabilities and provide differentiated experiences to advanced students; to be role models and social workers; and much more.
> Too often, in too many schools, the job of being a teacher looks the same on day 5,000 as it did on day one.
> That's troubling on two fronts: first, it's hard for rookies and novices to meet the volume and variety of learning needs their students have; second, a profession that looks the same on day 5,000 as it does on day one isn't offering pathways for professional growth and advancement. That's a recipe for burnout and attrition.

The analysis of the "problem" of teacher education is not one that is uniquely Phoenician. In fact, there is little reference to the geographical or social factors outlined above, and the context is described in somewhat general and a-spatial terms. The arguments developed, however, will have specific resonance with School Districts in Arizona as they speak to the pertinent issues of retention and attrition and the growing complexity of student needs.

The MLFTC literature summarises the problem within the national context:

> Nationally, teacher preparation programs have long seen declining enrolment. Teachers switch careers or retire early. They receive less pay and enjoy less social status than many other professionals. We ask teachers to be all things to all people at all times. The job is hard in specific ways that inhibit success. As a result, our education system does not reliably deliver quality learning outcomes and experiences for nearly enough people and communities.

The Next Education Workforce initiative is based on two principles, each at a scale of the school workforce:

> The Next Education Workforce initiative starts with the conviction that, if we're not getting the workforce or the learning outcomes we want, we need to redesign the profession, the workplace and how we prepare people for both. We work with schools and other partners to 1) provide all students with deeper and personalized learning by building teams of educators with distributed expertise and 2) empower educators by developing new opportunities for role-based specialization and advancement.

These principles lead to a form of partnership working or "teaming" which is alluded to a more localised context:

> We work in deep, socially embedded collaboration with partner schools, districts and educators. Work in progress includes: providing team-based professional experiences for teacher candidates; fielding new roles and team structures for in-service educators; designing a prototype school of the future; conducting research into our own work; developing a robust array of professional resources that support individual educators, teams and organizational leaders.

Whilst the Dean and her leadership team are keen to point out that this initiative is based on the way that they believe that education workforce should be configured in the future (the "new normal"), the background of teacher shortages, particularly in Arizona, is a strong impetus and driver behind this initiative.

The teaming approach

At the time of my site visit, the teaming system was being developed in elementary and middle schools, with groups of teachers working at the same grade level. Whilst the vision is for an integrated team of community educators, professional educators and educational leaders to be working together, in some of the schools currently working with this system, the teams are established at grade levels, best described in the simple example of four classes (120 pupils) working with three certified teachers and three student teachers (or teacher candidates). One certified teacher takes lead responsibility for two classes (60 students) and the development of the three student teachers, and the wider team (of seven adults) work in rotation. In schools with a teacher shortage, both the lead teacher and the teacher candidates can be paid an additional stipend (sharing the salary of the vacant teaching position), and this prevents the teacher candidates from having to take additional work outside teaching to supplement their income. This approach also means that the teacher candidates become employees of the school district, and as such are more likely to stay in school districts which have a high need for new teachers.

The wider vision of the teaming model is that these teams will be even more flexible and supplemented by additional members, including specialist guidance, paraprofessionals and community support. However, schools are not yet designed for this approach, and so MLFTC are using teacher preparation as a way of encouraging school districts to adopt this model. The programme has been piloted with two school districts in Arizona, and subsequently expanded to a further 14 school districts and some 300–400 teacher candidates.

The responses to the "problems" identified in teaching have been constructed at a broader level of whole school reform through exercising the considerable influence MLFTC has through teacher preparation. Whilst the scheme is still in fairly early stages of development, the pitch from the team at MLFTC was well established. The Dean's presentation and the discussion with many of the interviewees used the same terminology, such as "the new normal" and describing teachers and students as "widgets" within the education system. Many of the offices featured Perspex table displays of the two key principles that underpin the programme.

This coherent approach to the rationale underpinning the initiative was somewhat in contrast with the people I met who were putting the programme into action: the school-based lead teachers, the student teachers (or teacher candidates) and the site leads (or supervising tutors) who all described a more fluid, developmental approach to "making the system work". It is important to stress the very early stage of development of this initiative. The team described how data was being collected retrospectively to show the impact on teacher candidates and schools (and by extension pupils). It appeared that the adaptations to the teacher education pedagogy and interventions were being developed, reviewed and enhanced by individual teacher educators as the year was unfolding.

In this respect, the most developed change has been in the cultural discursive arrangements of the programme: changing the narrative of how teacher preparation is seen as part of the education complex (Kemmis et al., 2014). This has led to some significant changes in the material economic arrangements of the programme, particularly around how the teacher placement is organised and supported (by the school and the university team). What has been somewhat left behind is the change in the practices expected of the teacher educators, and in particular the site leads and school-based mentors, and how this new approach will impact on the three years of curriculum instruction leading up to the practice teaching experience. These changes are in development and so reflect how the teacher educator quality conundrum gets played out, revealing how the work of teacher educators who focus on practice can take precedence over those who emphasise the knowledge needed for teacher understanding.

Changing teachers to educators

A key feature of the literature surrounding the Next Education Workforce initiative is the shift in use of terminology from teachers to educators. Also reflected in the Council for the Accreditation of Educator Preparation standards,[7] this change in terminology represents a reconceptualization of the education workforce to be more encompassing of other education professionals beyond those recognised as teachers. Specific mention is made of community educators. It also implies a shift in how the occupation of teaching is being conceptualised. Part of the marketing of Next Education Workforce refers to the 173 State Standards that apply to teachers in Arizona, the Dean argues:

> We have a set of standards in this State: we have one hundred and seventy three standards. We believe every single teacher candidate coming through our program needs to know very well those standards. We use the rubrics to make sure that they get at least a three on a scale of five. And this affects all those things that we do in teacher preparation, because we know that we want every one of them to be "day one ready". We want them to look more like a second year teacher than a first year teacher. And I believe that it is just not humanly possible today.
>
> *(ASU, Interview, 2020)*

This sentiment was also emphasised by other members of the leadership of the programme, who expanded this point:

> The number of things that we expect new candidates, any candidates, to be expert in, to be professional in, is staggering. But as a parent, I look at the list of things and I say to myself, "oh, my gosh, there's not a thing on this list really that I would cut", especially when you start to add up the diversity of kids with whom we're lucky enough to work.
>
> *(ASU, Interview A, 2020)*

Teaching has becoming increasingly complex, reflecting the diverse needs of children in the classroom, and the expanded understanding of the ways in which teachers can address those needs. By extension, expectations on new teachers have become more demanding. The leadership team at MLFTC argued that it is unreasonable to expect teachers to be expert in all those areas, but that a team of professionals are better placed to address those diverse needs. In the teaming approach, the classroom teacher becomes a lead educator working with a team of both specialist and community educators to address the needs of the students in their classroom. The teaming approach offers a range of adult educators with whom children may forge strong relationships. The education workforce is then seen as being made up of a continuum of educators with distributed expertise, as outlined in Table 5.1.

The programme leadership explained how this would work:

> So we started thinking about who are the professionals? Who are these community educators that could do all kinds of technical work, paid or unpaid? Now we're redefining paraprofessionals and teacher aides - and all of those well-intentioned people, good people, who want to do work in schools.
>
> *(ASU, Interview B, 2020)*

There is a dual narrative here of how classrooms are changing, simultaneously requiring different types of professional expertise, and so necessitating a changed teacher professionalism. However, within this argument, the exact nature of how teacher professionalism (and by extension teacher education – or preparation) needs to be adapted is less clear. I discussed with the programme leadership how this was changing the nature of teacher professionalism. It was acknowledged that the definition was changing:

> when we actually get out there and do the work, we start to realise that there are notions of "what does it mean to be a professional educator?". What are the things that count toward that? And what are the things that

TABLE 5.1 Continuum of educator roles (taken from ASU, n.d)

Community educators			Professional educators			Educational leaders	
Wraparound support	Content and instructional support	Teaching assistants	New teachers	Experienced teachers	Specialized teachers	Teacher leaders	Organizational leaders
Socio-emotional supports	Academic supports	Assessment	Assessment	Assessment analysis	Assessment & trend analysis	Roles of the experienced teachers ...AND...	Innovations around new instructional & staffing models
Mentoring	Connections to the "real world"	Some instruction	Short-term planning	Long- and short-term planning	Long-term planning	Strategic deployment of educators	Innovative budgeting
		Tutoring			Instructional intervention + modeling		
		Facilitation of digital learning	Small group instruction	Small & large group instruction	Academic, career, socio-economical support exerts	Team dynamics	Advocacy for new models & innovations

An adaptable model:
Specific job titles and responsibilities can and should vary among learning environments

Source: Taken from https://education.asu.edu/next-education-workforce/resources/elements-brief-specializationsand-advancement-pathways.

we hold up that maybe actually don't make sense? I think some of this work that we're doing is redefining the notion of "who is an educator?"

(ASU, Interview A, 2020)

In the elaboration, reference is made to the "incredibly important" role of people in the community who can "make life more grounded in actual real work examples", and to encourage such people to get more involved in education, acknowledging the training they would need to do so:

So you start to ask yourself: What are the knowledge, skills, dispositions that we think you need to be successful in all sorts of roles?

(ASU, Interview C, 2020)

The vision of a more distributed responsibility for education across the community necessitates a change in the role of the teacher, but also in the preparation afforded to that new teacher. Of course, as a new initiative, many of the effects of this initiative on schools, their workforce and teacher professionalism have yet to be realised, understood or theorised. It continues to be an aspect of the programme that the team are assessing and evaluating. In addition, such developments reflect substantial changes for how the work of teacher educators will need to adapt.

Changing teacher education practices

Such a changing context will no doubt have implications for the teacher educators (school-, university- and community-based) who contribute to the programme. Learning to teach as part of a team is substantially different for all aspects of the teacher education programme. At the time of the site visit, the changes had started to occur at an organisational level, but have yet to be fully embedded in the teacher education pedagogy across the whole programme. This is to be expected in a process of ongoing change and was recognised by those involved in the programme.

The experience of the individual teachers, the school-based mentors (called lead teachers in this scheme), the university-based mentors (called site leads) and the university-based tutors (which are made up of clinical faculty and academic faculty) will each require adjustment to the new set up. So far, the experience of the new teaming system has predominantly been located at the site of the practicum. This was made possible by the previous initiative, iTeachAZ, which placed all the practicum experiences in the final year of the undergraduate programme. Thereby, the transition to the new programme has involved changes to the organisation of the practicum experience, the relationship with partnership schools (and school districts) and those specific courses designed to support teacher candidates on their practicum (for example, the course on Professional Standards). The changes necessary for the remainder of the programme, including the taught curriculum content from the first three years of the undergraduate programme, had yet to be worked through in detail. The reasons for this are practical: initiatives have to start somewhere, and the growth of the programme appears to have been due to the popularity of the pilot scheme as a number of School Districts asked to be involved. However, there is a danger that focusing on the end point, the final year internship, without due consideration of the curriculum adaptation necessary to prepare the teacher candidates to work in teams, may mean that the teacher candidates are inadequately prepared to take up the new roles. The emphasis on the knowledge gained through experience comes at the end of the programme, disconnected from the ideas and alternative approaches encountered elsewhere.

The teacher educators and the adaptations they are making

For those lead teachers new to the teaming scheme, professional development has been valuable. The lead teacher I met on a site visit outlined how she had experienced a week's training in preparation for her role. Her description of the training was of a workshop where lead teachers worked collaboratively to forward plan how they might introduce, integrate and monitor the work of their team of teacher candidates, and how she had been able to adapt this model throughout her first year in this role. The interview with the site lead was similar, in that she described how she was aware that her role was changing. She described how the new arrangements were allowing her to spend more time in class with the teacher candidates and how this was (positively) affecting the mentoring support she could offer. Although the site lead was considerably more experienced (both as an educator and as a teacher educator) than the lead teacher, they both recounted in-programme adaption to their teacher education work: adaption that appeared to complement each other's changing roles. The developmental nature of the programme meant that they were given a lot of capacity to make these changes in-year and to use this experience to feedback to the programme team to inform further developments.

The teaming approach appears to be changing the funds of knowledge the teacher educators are drawing on to adapt to those changes. Under a traditional practicum model, the school-based mentor or lead teacher would be acting in what might be described as a mentoring capacity. Depending on the programme, mentoring could be conceived of as a process of coaching, apprenticeship or combined with some responsibility for the assessment of the programme (or *judgmentoring*, as described by Hobson and Malderez, 2013). Under the teaming approach, many of those roles could still apply; however, the changes to the programme arrangements also place the lead teacher in a range of different roles: as the leader of a team, with three teacher candidates and 60 students under her direct control and all the associated responsibility for planning, assessment, welfare and family liaison. In addition, the lead teacher is also a colleague of the teacher candidates (who are in some cases employees of the School District).

These new roles provide the lead teacher with valuable professional development, but require a different skill set to the role of mentoring alone, and indeed tensions could arise between the potentially conflicting roles of colleague, mentor and leader. There is also a shift in the balance of those roles over time: the lead teacher described modelling more at the beginning of the year, and as the new teachers developed, moving into a more collaborative approach.

Similarly, the site lead discussed how her role had shifted to one that was more of a "team member", working with the lead teacher as well as with taking on some of the mentoring of the teacher candidates. The site lead still held responsibility for the completion of lesson observation paperwork and other assessment documentation, but the role had become more akin with mentoring, and working on the individual development of the teacher candidates. In this sense, and as someone with extensive previous experience as a mentor, she was comfortable with this shift in roles, and described drawing on her extensive mentoring experience to enable her to shift these roles accordingly. So, within this scheme, the traditional division between university- and school-based teacher educators is sustained. Internationally, there are different expectations about the roles and responsibilities of a teacher educator, particularly if they are defined as clinical or academic faculty, to use the local terminology. Within this context, the role of the clinical faculty would appear to be shifting and reforming, developing alongside the experience of working within the team. However, the impact on those teacher educators classified as academic faculty was less clear.

A particular example of this shifting and reforming was recounted to me from the early stages of the academic year, when the lead teacher was responsible for two classes and three new teacher candidates, and she described a process of modelling and setting out classroom routines and shared procedures (such as call-outs and call-backs) which were shared between the two classes; this would enable all four teachers to move freely between the two classes with all the children familiar with the calls and responses. As the teacher candidates grew in experience, so they became more capable of taking on their own planning and resourcing of lessons. Whilst it was recognised that not all lead teachers would do this in the same way, the sharing of classroom practices and protocols is a clear way of ensuring ease of movement between the four teachers, and reflects the lead teacher's understanding of an adaptation needed to support these new teachers. It does, however, raise some interesting questions about the breaking down of the former model of one teacher to 30 students and one mentor to one teacher candidate model: a model criticised for creating clone-teachers or "widgets". In the pedagogical approach described above, the "clone" of the lead teacher could be extended to three teachers (rather than just one). In a situation like this, the quality of the lead teacher as a mentor and leader, and the support they received from the site leads, is of increasing importance. In this case, the mentor appeared to be outstanding in her role and was incredibly well supported. However, as the scheme expands, it would help to clarify the knowledge bases that teacher educators need to draw upon to support them in these changing roles.

The role of the site lead was also under construction. The experienced site lead discussed how she was spending much more time with the teacher candidates working with them on their practice. The number of formal and informal visits was being amended in the light of the new scheme, but the nature of those visits was also changing. The programme leadership described how the site leaders were being asked to undertake new roles:

> We have asked the site leaders to step in and say, why don't you watch the model [lesson] and then go next door when that teacher actually implements the lesson. And you can be the eyes of that teacher. That's the kind of the structure we wanted to happen at the beginning of the year.
> (ASU, Interview D, 2020)

In a programme experiencing rapid change, both the school and university-based teacher educators were adapting to their new roles, and there was evidence of some degree of blurring between these roles. This is partly due to the new nature of the programme: the conceptual approach to the programme is well-formed and clearly articulated, but the practice of teacher education and how it is being affected by this macro-change is still a work in progress, and in the example described above the site lead and lead teachers appear to be working collaboratively to work through those new roles. The impact on the taught provision, on how new teachers are prepared for their practicum experience and how the way in which the ideas from the taught elements of their programme and their practical experiences are allowed to flow together, has yet to be considered.

Teacher education curriculum

So far, the teacher educators discussed have been those with specific responsibility for the practicum, both from the school and from the university. However, teacher education provision also includes what I call a taught component, sometimes referred to as courses or units that focus on methods, theoretical perspectives and other areas of knowledge for teachers. Those courses may be taught by members of the teacher education faculty or have been assigned teaching assignments from other parts of the university (Craig, 2016), and make up a considerable component of the teacher education programme. In a new approach to teacher education, such as that of teaming, it is necessary to consider the changes to the "taught" curriculum required to prepare student teachers for their practical teaching experience.

This was an aspect of the programme that was still under some development. In a discussion with a curriculum specialist at MLFTC, the teaming initiative was described as "top down", and to this point had involved little conversation with faculty instructors. The scheme had been introduced first for primary-phase teachers, and was mostly orientated around clinical faculty who were on temporary annual contracts and, it was suggested, were keen to support the initiative. Tenured faculty who were often teaching the "taught" component of the programme, were more likely to be critical of the initiative: and it was acknowledged from the leadership team that pushback from faculty had been around the evidence base and the theoretical model of professional learning which underpinned the scheme, aspects which were still under development as the scheme matured.

The leadership team was enthusiastic about the success of the scheme and keen to generate data that revealed what the scheme had been able to achieve:

> Without data, without research to say, yes, this is the best thing for kids, all you have to stand on is your confidence that it feels right. Yeah, it looks right. When you go in, you're seeing kids being treated differently. You're seeing kids interacting differently. So right now, we have a lot of anecdotal reasons to be confident.
>
> (ASU, Interview D, 2020)

Reports suggested that the teacher candidates were taking more responsibility for their teaching and making quicker progress (often several months quicker) than expected on the previous programmes (an assertion that was likely to borne out as the data around the programme was processed). These learning gains were attributed to the authenticity of the experience:

> I look at transferable skills. The reality is that most of our teacher candidates, when they graduate, they'll go to a place that does not have teams as part of the teaching structure. They will be a single classroom teacher. So for me, I ask what would make that person successful coming from a team based environment? It would be those transferable skills: like data analysis, how to get to know my students. How do I bring in content experts when I'm not the content expert? If I know how to leverage educators and how to leverage expertise, I can bring in experts who do content boosters to provide assistance. We want students to advocate to be a part of a team.
>
> (ASU, Interview D, 2020)

The quotation above situates the programme firmly within the practice-turn tradition (see Chapter 2): emphasising the interactions that student teachers have with other educators as the main focus of teaching expertise. Conversely, the emphasis on content expertise as external to the teacher, as something that can be brought in, reflects the view that the full range of expertise required of teachers is unattainable. It also implies that teaching content is somehow external to that teaching relationship: that pedagogy and relationships are implicit to classroom interactions, whereas content is external to it. This viewpoint is also echoed in how the orientation of the programme has been around the practicum experience. It also speaks to concerns raised by the curriculum-based faculty:

> There has also been a little push back in terms like curriculum because we've had to change the way we deliver content. So now we've had to go

> from having classes all day to having classes in two hours in the evening. And so the faculty are worried about loss of content, loss of seat time … we're asking faculty to think about things differently, and sometimes that's difficult for them to do. The biggest area of pushback is where our school districts use scripted curriculum; the faculty are teaching theory based on best practices, and there is a disconnect with the districts which are using scripted lessons. And so there's a little bit of disconnect. And so the faculty are asking: who's driving the curriculum? Is it districts or is it faculty? … So there is this balancing act of teaching [them] best practices, but yet teaching them the risks they are going to be faced with: how can I use that score to inform my teaching? How can I differentiate?
>
> (ASU, Interview A, 2020)

Most of the interviewees emphasised the importance of practice, making comments such as "I am a firm believer that practice is everything". This focus on practice seems to be distanced from the curriculum aspects of the programme.

The model of teacher learning that underpins this programme is described in the programme website and handbook as clinical practice, but the introduction of team working will necessitate a re-evaluation of that clinical practice, and in particular how the knowledge base of new teachers needs to be developed to support their practical experience. The current iteration of clinical practice is grounded in the development of a specific skill set:

> But the actual practice is in the field. With residency, the clinical experience, which does more for teacher prep: content classes or the methods classes, right? I am a firm believer that practice is everything … What skills are we actually teaching teacher candidates? Because right now, as in elementary ed major, I may have my clinical experience in first grade, but my job that I get is maybe in seventh grade. So, while I may have been gotten really, really good at teaching phonics; teaching how to analyse a text in a seventh-grade level is a whole different skill. And so, if we are focussing on transferable skills that I can then carry from first grade to seventh grade. The clinical practice that we're trying to put in place now, the idea of teaming, is putting the students first versus content first.
>
> (ASU, Interview D, 2020)

If we return briefly to the vignette which opened this chapter, it is interesting to consider the under-engagement of two pupils (for different reasons) and whether these were related to the pedagogical or practical interventions of the teacher or whether they were related to the lesson content, and how that influenced the format of the lesson. What sort of intervention would have alerted the teacher candidate to the situation? The lesson observed was a mathematics lesson: opportunities to learn are a key feature of the literature in mathematics and in particular around pedagogical content knowledge in mathematics. Exposure to these ideas may have enabled the novice teacher to identity, be sensitised to and plan to address the issue. In other words, it is important to consider how the "taught" element of the programme could have contributed to the new teacher's development to have enabled them to become more aware of what was going on in their classroom. For example, specific awareness of the types of problems that pupils experience when learning mathematics may have given the student teacher an indication of particular warning signs that might indicate lack of challenge or confusion, or awareness of class-based formative assessment techniques may have alerted the teacher to variances in the pupils' learning and understanding. This is not to suggest that these elements were not covered in the programme of study; the point is to illustrate that for new teachers, opportunities to learn may occur through a variety of stimulus and so may be attributed to the contribution of teacher educators with a variety of expertise.

There is a significant opportunity to support the new teaming approach by drawing upon the expertise of content-specialist teacher educators to think deeply, theoretically and empirically about how a shift in the context of practicum necessitates changes in the taught provision. This may need to veer away from a core practice model (see Chapter 4) into a more content-rich approach designed to support new teachers' awareness of their classroom during periods of teaching.

Professionalism and quality discourses

It is not my intention to be critical of this new approach to teacher education, particularly when it is in development and under construction. The demand for teachers in Arizona presents a very real need, and the Next Education Workforce initiative is a well-thought-out approach to tackle that problem in a genuinely constructive and supportive way. This is not in question. However, it is important to consider how any new initiative, through the way in which it defines practice, changes our understanding of teacher professionalism, teacher development and the role of teacher educators. This question boils down to how teacher education pedagogy is designed for transformation to take place, and the role that teacher educators play to make that happen. Focusing on the development of knowledge and understanding at the expense of skills, or vice versa, is unproductive. It is important to recognise the complementary nature of both specialist knowledge of teacher education and practical experience of teaching. New teachers require both. The challenge is how to balance them in the most effective way.

The Next Education Workforce initiative at MLFTC is a great example of how universities are well placed to innovate and support change when they are given the opportunity to do so, and the capacity to leverage. The MLFTC programme also shows that universities are well placed to innovate as they have wide social reach and influence; in this case, working with a range of school districts in the Phoenix metropolitan region. This is an advantage of scale: universities serve broad communities and are often trusted partners within those communities.

This example of university practice also reveals the stratified way in which changes in teacher education can occur and how the work of teacher educators is changing. At MLFTC, the Next Education Workforce initiative was driven from the college leadership, and change was initially implemented in the partnership arrangements: focusing on the shape and form of the practicum in the final year of study. This has been facilitated by the structure of the programme: had the practicum been spread throughout the four-year degree, it would not have been possible. The implications for the partnership: the work of the school-based support team and the practicum support team (site and regional leads) are being worked through as the programme develops. The curriculum implications, and particularly how amendments will be needed in the taught components of the programme (in the first three years of the undergraduate degree), have yet to be considered. These courses will require adaptation too. Potentially, this initiative could provide a new wave of understanding of clinical practice, or indeed a new form of teacher education, perhaps offering new insights into how teacher education can be effective when divided into "theory now, practice later". Models that have adopted this approach previously, have experienced significant issues combining theory and practice in teacher education effectively (Menter, 2017). However, as this part of the programme develops, it will need teacher education expertise across the faculty: as teacher educators think through how the contribution of their taught courses will need to change in the light of the teaming initiative.

The challenge of defining the work of teacher educators within changing contracts, accountability frameworks and changing school practices is not to be underestimated. As roles are redefined and shifted, this raises questions about the knowledge that teacher educators need. The quality conundrum here is about the role and expertise of teacher educators and getting the balance right to ensure that new teachers are supported in the development of practical experience alongside their knowledge and understanding of practice. The example in this chapter shows how school-based and supervisory colleagues can work together as their roles shift to ensure that student teachers are well supported. However, the focus thus far has been overtly on practicum. A key element in responding to the quality conundrum has to focus on the entirety of the experience and the role that a strong, theoretically informed and robust content can provide.

The issue of recruiting appropriate teacher educators was common to all the research sites I visited. In each of the locations, there were varying factors as to what universities looked for in a teacher educator: whether there was an emphasis on academic credentials, research experience or practical experience of working in local schools. In some locations, teacher educators were expected to be both academic and close to practice (as echoed by Ellis and McNicholl (2015)). Recruitment of teacher educators, who are not expected to have a research profile (such as the clinical faculty at MLFTC), places a stronger emphasis on their school experience and ability to support student teachers.

However, this quality conundrum is about more than just the provision of support available for new teachers. As outlined at the start of this chapter, there are concerns about the status of teacher educators as members of the university faculty. Where teacher educators are only being offered casualised contracts, particularly if they are temporary renewable or sessional contracts, this can reduce their capacity to contribute to the field. Unless these approaches are supported by tenured, academic faculty, then there is a danger of a reduced presence of teacher education with the academy. On the other hand, by broadening out teacher education to what White (2018) called community-based teacher educators or other members of the community who can contribute to teacher education, the diversification of the teacher education workforce can more widely replicate the expertise in local communities. However, it is important to recognise that these roles have variable status, both within school communities and within the university infrastructure. There is a need to recognise the complementarity of these roles: the distinctive contribution they each bring to the experience of transformation for new teachers.

This notion of relative status also applies to the representational space; how the attributes of different teacher educators are valued will reflect the relative importance afforded to their experience and contribution. When considering how teacher educators contribute to the quality of a programme, it is important to reflect on how the variety of different expertise from the range of teacher educators can work together to support the development of teachers. Where an overemphasis is placed on either the practical or the theoretical aspects of learning to teach, balance needs to be restored through affirming and clarifying the importance of all aspects of the programme.

Does an approach that places teachers as part of a team of educators require fundamentally new ways of learning to teach? To what extent is this programme preparing teachers to be ready on "day one" or to be lifelong practitioners? To what extent will evidence show that the shift will be effective or that it has a chance to succeed? The answers to these questions have yet to be worked through. The anecdotal experience of those on the programme at MLFTC is incredibly positive and honest in terms of what work still needs to be done. The programme has been scaled up quickly and is clearly making an impact in Arizona now. For me, the question is one to do with sustainability and equity, not just in terms of how are the teachers ready and prepared for a career in teaching, but also in how this development changes the nature of teachers work, perhaps making it less (or more) desirable in the long term.

Notes

1 Or teacher candidates as they are referred to locally.
2 https://www.businessinsider.com/american-teacher-shortage-underpaid-overworked-teacher-strike?r=US&IR=T.
3 https://www.bizjournals.com/phoenix/news/2019/05/23/phoenix-leads-us-in-population-growth-new-census.html.
4 https://www.census.gov/quickfacts/fact/table/phoenixcityarizona/PST040219.
5 (https://cms.azed.gov/home/GetDocumentFile?id=5d5edaeb03e2b30ca0699205).

6 https://www.statepress.com/article/2019/09/spcommunity-number-one-in-innovation.
7 http://www.ncate.org/about/history.

References

Andreasen, J. K., Bjørndal, C. R. P., & Kovač, V. B. (2019). Being a teacher and teacher educator: The antecedents of teacher educator identity among mentor teachers. *Teaching and Teacher Education, 85*, 281–291. doi:10.1016/j.tate.2019.05.011

Avidov-Ungar, O., & Forkosh-Baruch, A. (2018). Professional identity of teacher educators in the digital era in light of demands of pedagogical innovation. *Teaching and Teacher Education, 73*, 183–191. doi:10.1016/j.tate.2018.03.017

Barahona, M. (2019). What matters to supervisors and is this reflected in what they do? Analysing the work of university supervisors of the practicum. *Journal of Education for Teaching, 45*(3), 262–276. doi:10.1080/09589236.2019.1599509

Blömeke, S. (2012). Content, preparation, and teaching methods: How diverse is teacher education across countries? *Comparative Education Review, 56*(4), 684–714. doi:0010-4086/2012/5604-0006

Bullough, R. V. (2005). Being and becoming a mentor: school-based teacher educators and teacher educator identity. *Teaching and Teacher Education, 21*(2), 143–155. doi:10.1016/j.tate.2004.12.002

Cochran-Smith, M., Grudnoff, L., Orland-Barak, L., & Smith, K. (2019). Educating teacher educators: International perspectives. *The New Educator*, 1–20. doi:10.1080/1547688x.2019.1670309

Cochran-Smith, M., Stringer Keefe, E., & Carney, M. C. (2018). Teacher educators as reformers: Competing agendas. *European Journal of Teacher Education, 41*(5), 572–590. doi:10.1080/02619768.2018.1523391

Cohen, J., & Berlin, R. (2019). What constitutes an "opportunity to learn" in teacher preparation? *Journal of Teacher Education, 71*(4), 434–448. doi:10.1177/0022487119879893

Craig, C. J. (2016). Structure of teacher education. In J. Loughran & M. L. Hamilton (Eds.), *International handbook of teacher education* (Vol. 1, pp. 69–135). Dordrecht: Springer.

Ducharme, E. R. (1993). *The lives of teacher educators*. New York: Teachers College Press.

Ducharme, M. (1996). A study of teacher educators: Research from the USA. *Journal of Education for Teaching, 22*(1), 57–70.

Ellis, V., & McNicholl, J. (2015). *Transforming teacher education: Reconfiguring the academic work*. London: Bloomsbury Publishing.

Furlong, J. (2013). *Education – An anatomy of the discipline: Rescuing the university project*. Abingdon: Routledge.

Goodwin, A. L., & Darity, K. (2018). Social justice teacher educators: What kind of knowing is needed? *Journal of Education for Teaching, 45*(1), 63–81. doi:10.1080/02607476.2019.1550606

Goodwin, A. L., & Kosnik, C. (2013). Quality teacher educators = quality teachers? Conceptualizing essential domains of knowledge for those who teach teachers. *Teacher Development, 17*(3), 334–346. doi:10.1080/13664530.2013.813766

Goodwin, A. L., Smith, L., Souto-Manning, M., Cheruvu, R., Tan, M. Y., Reed, R., & Taveras, L. (2014). What should teacher educators know and be able to do? Perspectives from practicing teacher educators. *Journal of Teacher Education, 65*(4), 284–302. doi:10.1177/0022487114535266

Hadar, L. L., & Brody, D. L. (2018). Individual growth and institutional advancement: The in-house model for teacher educators' professional learning. *Teaching and Teacher Education, 75*, 105–115. doi:10.1016/j.tate.2018.06.007

Helleve, I., & Ulvik, M. (2019). Tutors seen through the eyes of mentors assumptions for participation in third space in teacher education. *European Journal of Teacher Education, 42*(2), 228–242. doi:10.1080/02619768.2019.1570495

Hobson, A. J., & Malderez, A. (2013). Judgementoring and other threats to realizing the potential of school-based mentoring in teacher education. *International Journal of Mentoring and Coaching in Education, 2*(2), 89–108. doi:10.1108/IJMCE-03-2013-0019

Holme, R., Robb, A., & Berry, W. (2016). Becoming a teacher educator – the motivational factors. *European Journal of Teacher Education, 39*(3), 340–354. doi:10.1080/02619768.2016.1194391

Kemmis, S., Wilkinson, J., Edwards-Groves, C., Hardy, I., Grootenboer, P., & Bristol, L. (2014). *Changing practices, changing education.* Bristol: Springer Science & Business Media.

Kleinsasser, R. (2017). A quest for teacher educator work. In D. J. Clandinin & J. Husu (Eds.), *The Sage handbook of research on teacher education* (Vol. 2, pp. 1033–1048). London: Sage Publishing.

Koster, B., Brekelmans, M., Korthagen, F., & Wubbels, T. (2005). Quality requirements for teacher educators. *Teaching and Teacher Education, 21*(2), 157–176. doi:10.1016/j.tate.2004.12.004

Labaree, D. F. (2006). *The trouble with ed schools.* New Haven, CT: Yale University Press.

Lane, H. (2019, October 30, 2019). There's a teacher shortage in Arizona – And teachers from overseas are filling the gap. *CBS News.* Retrieved from https://www.cbsnews.com/news/arizona-schools-hiring-teaches-from-the-philippines-amid-fight-for-more-pay/

Mattsson, M., Eilertsen, T. V., & Rorrison, D. (2012). *A practicum turn in teacher education* (Vol. 6). Dordrecht: Springer Science & Business Media.

Mauri, T., Onrubia, J., Colomina, R., & Clarà, M. (2019). Sharing initial teacher education between school and university: Participants' perceptions of their roles and learning. *Teachers and Teaching, 25*(4), 469–485. doi:10.1080/13540602.2019.1601076

Mayer, D., Mitchell, J., Santoro, N., & White, S. (2011). Teacher educators and 'accidental' careers in academe: An Australian perspective. *Journal of Education for Teaching, 37*(3), 247–260. doi:10.1080/02607476.2011.588011

Menter, I. (2017). *The role and contribution of higher education in contemporary teacher education.* Retrieved from http://www.scde.ac.uk/wp-content/uploads/2017/05/Report-Ian-Menter-2017-05-25.pdf

Mitchem, M. C., Buffalo, G. R., Perez, A., & Rollins, E. R. (2019). Tales of existing and resisting as female teacher educators in neoliberal times. *The New Educator, 16*(1), 70–85. doi:10.1080/1547688x.2019.1681570

Murray, J. (2014). Teacher educators' constructions of professionalism: A case study. *Asia-Pacific Journal of Teacher Education, 42*(1), 7–21. doi:10.1080/1359866X.2013.870971

Murray, J. (2017). Defining teacher educators: International perspectives and contexts. In D. J. Clandinin & J. Husu (Eds.), *The Sage handbook of research on teacher education* (Vol. 2, pp. 1017–1032). London: SAGE Publishers.

Murray, J., & Male, T. (2005). Becoming a teacher educator: Evidence from the field. *Teaching and Teacher Education, 21*(2), 125–142. doi:10.1016/j.tate.2004.12.006

Ping, C., Schellings, G., & Beijaard, D. (2018). Teacher educators' professional learning: A literature review. *Teaching and Teacher Education, 75*, 93–104. doi:10.1016/j.tate.2018.06.003

Sleeter, C. (2008). Equity, democracy, and neoliberal assaults on teacher education. *Teaching and Teacher Education, 24*(8), 1947–1957. doi:10.1016/j.tate.2008.04.003

Sleeter, C. (2019). Considering core assumptions about what it means to teach. *Teachers College Record, 121*, 1–4.

Smith, K. (2005). Teacher educators' expertise: What do novice teachers and teacher educators say? *Teaching and Teacher Education, 21*(2), 177–192. doi:10.1016/j.tate.2004.12.008

Sterling, T. G., & Joffe-Block, J. (2018, Wed 5 Sep 2018). The job Americans won't take: Arizona looks to Philippines to fill teacher shortage. *The Guardian*. Retrieved from https://www.theguardian.com/us-news/2018/sep/05/arizona-teachers-filipino-schools-low-pay

Tack, H., & Vanderlinde, R. (2019). Capturing the relations between teacher educators' opportunities for professional growth, work pressure, work related basic needs satisfaction, and teacher educators' researcherly disposition. *European Journal of Teacher Education*, 1–19. doi:10.1080/02619768.2019.1628212

Tatto, M. T., Burn, K., Menter, I., Mutton, T., & Thompson, I. (2017). *Learning to teach in England and the United States: The evolution of policy and practice*. Abingdon: Routledge.

Trent, J. (2013). Becoming a teacher educator. *Journal of Teacher Education, 64*(3), 262–275. doi:10.1177/0022487112471998

Vanassche, E., & Kelchtermans, G. (2014). Teacher educators' professionalism in practice: Positioning theory and personal interpretative framework. *Teaching and Teacher Education, 44*, 117–127. doi:10.1016/j.tate.2014.08.006

Vanassche, E., & Kelchtermans, G. (2015a). Facilitating self-study of teacher education practices: Toward a pedagogy of teacher educator professional development. *Professional Development in Education, 42*(1), 100–122. doi:10.1080/19415257.2014.986813

Vanassche, E., & Kelchtermans, G. (2015b). The state of the art in self-study of teacher education practices: A systematic literature review. *Journal of Curriculum Studies, 47*(4), 508–528. doi:10.1080/00220272.2014.995712

White, S. (2018). Teacher educators for new times? Redefining an important occupational group. *Journal of Education for Teaching, 45*(2), 200–213. doi:10.1080/02607476.2018.1548174

Willemse, M., Lunenberg, M., & Korthagen, F. (2005). Values in education: A challenge for teacher educators. *Teaching and Teacher Education, 21*(2), 205–217. doi:10.1016/j.tate.2004.12.009

Williams, J. (2014). Teacher educator professional learning in the third space. *Journal of Teacher Education, 65*(4), 315–326. doi:10.1177/0022487114533128

Zeichner, K. (2005). Becoming a teacher educator: A personal perspective. *Teaching and Teacher Education, 21*(2), 117–124. doi:10.1016/j.tate.2004.12.001

6
THE GOVERNANCE QUALITY CONUNDRUM

Chapter 1 argued that Harvey's categorisation of different ways of understanding quality in higher education (HE) (Table 1.1) distinguishes between standards, quality assurance and quality (2007). Stakeholders may come to an activity with different definitions of quality, and by extension a different set of values, beliefs and principles by which they think an activity should change or be developed. We have already seen this in the preceding chapters where different expectations of quality are reflected in the quality conundrums affecting initial teacher education (ITE). In this chapter, we turn our attention to competing interpretations of quality from different stakeholders in ITE, in particular those of policymakers, universities, schools and individual teacher educators. These interpretations of quality are played out spatially: influenced by global policy trends around what is good practice in ITE, national issues of concern, individual priorities about employment and the local educational needs and expert opinions on what constitutes best practice. These interpretations influence the practice of teacher education, sometimes deliberately so, with stakeholders setting down parameters of quality, sometimes in the form of quality indicators or standards as a way of ensuring that teacher education fulfils their definition of quality. As argued in Chapter 1, one of the problems with these indicators is that they tend to focus on proxies of quality rather than indicators of how the programme provides a transformative educational experience (having adopted a definition of quality as transformation). Teacher education can become dominated by initiatives around accountability and governance which focus attention on specific indicators (such as an applicant's previous educational attainment or whether they are successful in gaining employment); these indicators are intended to emphasis aspects of a programme which can be measured and to use these as proxy indicators of standards or quality assurance, but which are unlikely to improve the educational practice. Indeed, as these measures often come from authoritative and powerful sources such as the awarding institution (the university) or the accrediting institution (local government or professional association), they can dominate attention, detracting teacher educators from what is important: the transformation of people into teachers. They are governance measures because they influence the infrastructure within which teacher education happens. These proxies for quality can have enormous power, as they can effectively control how teacher educators go about their work. In some cases, the imposition of an accountability or governance regime can limit the flow of ideas and knowledges in teacher education pedagogy which are key to the transformation needed to become a teacher. This can particularly occur in university-based ITE which is beholden to governance measures from HE as well as from those associated with teacher education, and is also susceptible to the changes that occur within schools.

Many of the issues explored in this chapter are common across international contexts. In very general terms, their motivations and access to policy technologies vary (Ball, 2003). For example, policymakers often seek to improve ITE through increased accountability regimes, universities strive for efficiency and value for money, teacher educators are concerned with enhancing the learning experience, school partners place a high store on the readiness of new teachers and stability for their classes and student teachers generally want to pass and get a good job. This is a narrative that I observed in nearly all the sites I visited and can also been seen across much of the ITE literature. However, it is further complicated by localised concerns often absent in the literature that introduce further considerations: teacher educators can be found trying to juggle a range of performance and accountability measures from different stakeholders, each seeking to improve quality but pulling in different directions. However, the governance infrastructure is often defended as a way of improving quality: ensuring that programmes are accountable; that they cover important areas of curriculum or experience; and that they focus attention on key strategic drivers. Indeed, inclusion of a topic or strategic priority in a governance system will have the impact of changing practice; however, it does not automatically follow that it would improve the transformational potential of a programme. This is at the heart of the governance quality conundrum: whether measures introduced (by authorities that oversee teacher education or by universities) that are intended to improve the quality of a programme will actually make a transformative difference. To explore this conundrum, this chapter will draw upon the example of the University of Auckland.

Growing accountability in ITE

Globally, teacher education has become a "policy problem" (Cochran-Smith & Fries, 2005), to which policymakers are turning more and more to narrow range of policies which are then "borrowed" in order to find a solution (Mayer, 2017). Many of these policy solutions are orientated around patterns of governance and oversight, seeking to control or at least to limit the work of teacher educators. This has occurred through what Cochran Smith and colleagues (2018) have described as teacher education's "era of accountability", an international trend they attribute to five broad developments:

1   Unprecedented global attention to teacher quality, tied to neoliberal economics;
2   A continuous public narrative asserting that "traditional" university-sponsored teacher education was failing to produce effective teachers who were prepared to respond to the demands of contemporary classrooms;
3   The conceptualization of teacher education as a public policy problem, wherein it was assumed that getting the right policies in place would boost teacher quality and the national economy;
4   The teacher education establishment's turn towards accountability, which was consistent with a conception of teacher quality defined as effectiveness and linked to the human capital paradigm; and
5   The belief that the reform of public education rather than other social policies was the major tool for redressing inequality and eradicating poverty in the US.

As discussed in Chapter 1, the indicators that are often used to judge teacher education vary between input, process, output and perspectival data. In each case, the indicators rarely reflect quality as a form of transformation, but are indicators that reflect standards taken as proxies for quality. Chapter 1 presented the argument that these indicators are orientated around standards and quality assurance. However, it is also important to note that policymakers and organisations focused on teacher professional development may have different drivers or motivations to the organisations where teacher education takes place, in this case, universities.

University pressures

Acknowledging that universities are the dominant but not the only institution involved in teacher education and that they do so in partnership with schools, it is important to recognise that professional education or training is only a very small part of what universities are set out to do. As argued by Connell (2019), research and the teaching of undergraduates have long been the remit of universities (although not always from their inception) and professional education or training is a new dimension to their work, and often not part of their core mission. This is particularly evident in historical accounts of the relationship between universities and teacher education.

Whilst it is now common internationally for teacher education to be based in universities, this has not always been the case, with teacher education having variously been situated in Colleges of Education, so-called Normal schools or teacher training colleges and through religious colleges of instruction (Furlong, 2013; Furlong & Whitty, 2017, Labaree, 2006, 2008). The move into universities occurred variously around the world across the latter part of the twentieth century. This transition has not always been a comfortable one, as education has been seen as the lowest status academic area with poor quality research and low status students (Labaree, 2006, 2008). This lack of status in the academy has been exacerbated by the cadre of teacher educators, who tend to either be postdoctorate education students with little or no experience of teaching (as can be found across the US) or former teachers without significant research training or experience (more typical in the UK, Australia and New Zealand), although there is some evidence that recruitment practices in these locations are changing (see Gunn, Berg, Haigh, & Hill, 2016). Whilst Pollard has argued that in the recent research assessment experience in the UK (Research Excellence Framework [REF]), the quality of education was comparable with other disciplines, education research is still viewed as having little intellectual or practical significance.

Consequently, there is the important question as to why locate teacher education in universities and what distinctive contribution they can bring. Chapter 3 highlighted the contribution that universities make to education as a discipline through their work to generate, validate and disseminate the findings of relevant research, and Chapter 5 explored the complexities experienced by teacher educators based in university settings. Furlong (2013) argues that ITE should not forget the fundamental purpose of universities: the quest for knowledge imbued since the days of John Henry Newman and Adam Smith. As Furlong puts it, the essential purpose of HE in the modern world is a concern for what he calls the "the maximisation of reason":

> It is this principle ... that is still at the heart of the idea of the university; it is this principle that can and should be applied to all of our research and to all forms of teaching, be they general or, as is more often the case in education, vocational.
>
> *(Furlong, 2013, p. 181)*

These notions are reflected in other accounts about teacher education and its relationship with research (see Chapter 3) and the importance attributed to teachers' right to develop "research literacy", through being "familiar with a range of research methods, with the latest research findings and with the implications of this research for their day-to-day practice, the flow of knowledge and ideas, and for education policy and practice more broadly" (BERA-RSA, 2014, p. 40).

Menter's (2017) report for the Scottish Council of Deans of Education into the role and contribution of HE in teacher education makes the case that universities offer an important complementary expertise to teacher education, concluding that:

> high quality teacher education is dependent on close and effective ('integrated') partnership between schools and universities, involving well-structured clinical experience for the beginning teachers and the availability to them of both research and teaching expertise.
>
> *(Ibid., p. 7)*

In 1996, Pring suggested that the role of universities in ITE could also be seen as more than the training of teachers and should be orientated around the analysis, development and critique of the intellectual component of teaching, all within centres of expertise (Pring, 1996, pp. 19–20). Menter (ibid.) also suggested that this concern for the intellectual component of teacher education should be extended to new teachers and other partners through:

- Models of ITE which enable beginning teachers to experience the theorising of practice – this entails fully integrated models of teacher education, which may well have clinical elements;
- From the outset, provision needs to be planned in partnership jointly by staff in universities and schools; and
- The partnership provision should extend beyond ITE to include shared approaches to continuing professional development and educational research, thus creating an extended professional community of practice and enquiry.

However, each of these arguments is taken from the viewpoint of teacher education and what universities contribute to that endeavour. Consequently, these arguments do not consider how well ITE fits within the remit and purpose of universities, particularly within a heightened period of accountability. Labaree (2006) has provided a fulsome account of the problems that education schools or faculties of education experience as low status members of the academy. This is a view supported by Bullough Jr., who, in his analysis of the US education system, highlights the precarious status of teacher education in university faculties, as teachers are seen as born and not made and therefore issues of teacher formation are not taken seriously (2014). Bullough Jr. argues that this is reflected in the calibre and experience of those that do teacher education (often graduate students) and who may not have requisite experience or expertise to do so.

In contrast, the League of European Research Universities has recently published an Advice Paper (de Graef, Busse, Cahill, Hansen, & Manon Kluijtmans, 2020) on what universities can do for the teaching profession. Their recommendations emphasise the role that teachers play in preparing students for university, the employment opportunities for doctoral graduates and the important connections between school subjects and university disciplines. They encourage further collaboration between university disciplines of the Arts, Humanities and Sciences with the Education faculty and that one of the ways to do this is through engagement in initial and continuing teacher education. However, this argument is predominantly orientated in how teacher education could directly or indirectly benefit other (non-Education) faculties of the university.

The proliferation of neoliberal new managerialism, widely referred to as New Policy Management, across the university sector increasingly marginalises ITE as a complex and costly activity. Moreover, universities are complex institutions with their own accountability regimes and governance structures that affect those that work in them (Ball, 2012; Jarvis, 2014). As an illustrative example, in England, academic standards are overseen by the Office for Students who can remove the degree-awarding powers of a university. Universities are also being subjected to assessment in research (REF), teaching (Teaching Excellence Framework) and knowledge exchange (Knowledge Exchange Framework). Student experience and satisfaction surveys contribute to these assessments, and results are widely publicised and combined into a range of international university-ranking league tables. At the time of the study, UCL, my own institution, had around 43,000 students, of which approximately 2,000 were in ITE. Institution-wide policies and practices are often designed with large undergraduate numbers in mind and may not sit well alongside the particular needs (such as safeguarding or stringent entry requirements) for teacher education. In other words, universities, whilst key to teacher education provision, are not always set up to facilitate teacher education, and can introduce standards, accountability or governance measures (such as staff-student ratios or contact-time expectations) which can create barriers to effective and even transformative learning for teachers.

The idea of transformative learning itself can cause tension between different stakeholders. For example, the focus from policymakers and teacher organisations on service standards and accountability measures may clash with university priorities around governance, quality assurance and value for money. Each of these initiatives is intended to "improve" teacher education but is orientated to a different vision of what improvement looks like. Moreover, efforts to "improve" teacher education, for example, through standardisation, have been criticised for stifling innovation and reducing teacher educators' capacity to enact transformative learning (Ellis, Steadman, & Trippestad, 2018). Conversely, others see standardisation as a feature of high-performing systems and an important way of improving their quality (Ingvarson et al., 2014). These competing discourses are at the heart of the governance quality conundrum for teacher educators: that attempts to improve teacher education through increased governance and quality assurance can actually detract from improving the transformative experience of learning to teach. Teacher educators need to navigate this complex landscape. The remainder of this chapter explores the example of the University of Auckland, a competitive and successful university (by international benchmark standards) situated within New Zealand, a country with a strong discourse about its priorities for education.

ITE concerns specific to New Zealand

One of the key features of the New Zealand context is the bicultural nation status, formalised by the 1840 Treaty of Waitangi between Indigenous Māori peoples and British colonisers. Although the treaty was imperfect and led to many injustices and misunderstandings (Orange, 1987), a key aspect of its realisation is access to high-quality education, a significant challenge for New Zealand, a country with intersectional inequalities, characterised broadly by the large number of Māori and Pasifika students who are over-represented in low socio-economic groups.

The University of Auckland is situated in the city of Auckland, the largest city in New Zealand with a population of 1.675 million (making up almost one-third of the 4.794 million population of New Zealand). New Zealand is not a densely populated country and features a largely rural and dispersed population. Auckland is not the capital city, but is the largest and most sprawling, covering a similar area to Los Angeles. One of Auckland's key features is the large multicultural mix of population, welcoming many migrants from across New Zealand and from other parts of the globe. Auckland is a hub for new migrants. The city of Auckland is arguably the largest Polynesian city in the world with a high level of diversity, including Māori, Pākehā (i.e. New Zealanders of European descent), many people from Pacific Islands, such as Samoa, Tonga, the Cook Islands and Fiji, and immigrants from Asian nations including China, Korea and India (according to 2018 census data: https://www.stats.govt.nz/2018-census/).

The diversity of both New Zealand and Auckland are widely celebrated, but present a particular educational concern characterised as an "achievement gap" (a phrase which has been criticised by Ladson-Billings and more accurately described as an education debt). Whilst students appear to do well overall, aggregate results mask one of the largest gaps between high- and low-achieving students among Organisation for Economic Co-operation and Development (OECD) countries (New Zealand Ministry of Education, 2011). Low-income and poor students, who are often Māori and Pacific Islanders, are over-represented in the low-achieving group, while Pākehā (European settlers) and Asians are over-represented in the high-achieving group (Snook & O'Neill, 2014). In response to disappointing results on international tests, such as Trends in International Mathematics and Science Study and Program for International Student Assessment, OECD designated New Zealand as a "high achievement, low equity" country (New Zealand Ministry of Education, 2011; OECD, 2011). The New Zealand Ministry of Education have sought to address this issue through their strategy for Māori Education ("Ka Hikitia") (New Zealand Ministry of Education, 2007) and a Pasifika Education Plan (New Zealand Ministry of Education, 2012). The challenges of social inequality based on income, ethnicity and language combine intersectionally to make structural disadvantage difficult to address (Boston, 2013).

However, the commitment to equity and in particular to honouring the Treaty of Waitangi is not just reflected in policy. For example, in 2013, in response to the New Zealand Ministry of Education call for proposals for "exemplary teacher education programs" that were more intellectually demanding (i.e. used higher entrance criteria, Masters programmes) and more practice-focused, the University of Auckland established a Masters of Teaching (MTchg) programme, with a strong emphasis on understanding Research Teaching for Equity (RITE) (Cochran-Smith et al., 2016; Grudnoff et al., 2017). Whilst, at the time of my site visit, this programme was being phased out due to lack of funding and difficulties recruiting sufficient numbers of students, the commitment of the Auckland teacher educators to the principles of equity and learning from and working with schools across the (economic) spectrum was strongly evident. It was also evident in some of the accountability measures pertinent to teacher education.

New Zealand teacher standards and code of responsibility

A key difference between the New Zealand Teacher Standards and those from other countries featured in this research is the inclusion of Māori language, culture and knowledge and its influences on educational practice, a key feature in the New Zealand Code and Standards for Teachers, published following a review in 2017. The language and tone of these documents are quite different to policy documents from other countries studied, reflecting a different orientation to policy formation which appears to speak directly to and attempt to be more inclusive of the voice of the profession. For example, the document features headings such as "We're in this together", specific recognition of the voices from the profession that emerged from the consultation, "We heard that the profession wants a registration policy that …", and also specific recognition of Māori language and culture, "Promotes our commitment to the Code and Standards, and in particular, te reo me ngā tikanga Māori".

This is most evident in the expression of values that underpin the Teacher Standards, which are articulated not just in the Māori language, but also through emphasising Māori cultural perspective and priorities:

WHAKAMANA: empowering all learners to reach their highest potential by providing high-quality teaching and leadership.
MANAAKITANGA: creating a welcoming, caring and creative learning environment that treats everyone with respect and dignity.
PONO: showing integrity by acting in ways that are fair, honest, ethical and just.
WHANAUNGATANGA: engaging in positive and collaborative relationships with our learners, their families and whanau, our colleagues and the wider community.

These perspectives are reflected also in the Code of Professional Responsibility which echoes a commitment to Society, to the Teaching Profession, to Families and Whanau (a Māori term for extended family or community) and to learners; this is then broken down into a range of behaviours that go towards meeting that code. The Teacher Standards also reflect these perspectives, emphasising Te Tiriti o Waitangi partnership, professional learning alongside professional relationships. The Standards are accompanied by a Quality Practice template and a website which elaborates on other details and exemplars (https://teachingcouncil.nz/content/our-code-our-standards) (see also Tātaiako and Tapasā which articulate what practice for Māori and Pasifika students should look like at different stages of a teachers' career, beginning with entry to teacher education). Therefore, the commitment to equity and recognising Māori culture are reflected not just in the expression of the Teacher Standards, but also in the resources made available to support the use of the standards for different teachers at different levels. The strong emphasis on equity and community engagement would appear to be deliberately positioned in opposition to the more common neoliberal expressions about achievement, attainment and progress. Whilst the motivations behind the policy may still be motivated by international comparisons, the articulation would appear to be clearly orientated to a focus on equity and honouring the bicultural context of New Zealand.

The discourse around quality is located in the representational space of teaching as valuing different cultural perspectives. Inclusion of Māori language and ideas of Māori pedagogy are signifiers as to their importance. However, these cultural signifiers alone are not sufficient. The distribution of high-quality education provision for low-income families, particularly those from Māori or Pasifika backgrounds, is an issue around equity which is a shared concern of most stakeholders within the education community, who argue that educational equity is needed to break the cycle of poverty and lack of opportunity.

The bi-language expression of these values, their inclusion within authoritative policy documents and their wide availability, along with support materials, are also reflected in ITE's practice architecture. This is emphasised, or indeed mandated, through the governance measures pertinent to teacher education such as the programme accreditation system.

Teacher education programme accreditation

The focus on equity and bicultural awareness is enshrined in the teacher education programme accreditation documentation, which was introduced in 2019. The team at the University of Auckland emphasised three significant changes in the new accreditation procedures from previous versions. The first difference was a shift from input to output measures, with an emphasis on the way in which teacher education was being assessed, including specifying key tasks for student teachers to undertake. The second difference was a requirement to have consulted with local community groups, in particular Māori iwi, in the areas where teacher education is taking place. The third was an emphasis on partnership consultation and involvement in programme planning.

Local community involvement

A key aspect of the new accreditation process was the requirement to have actively consulted with local community groups, which within the New Zealand context specifically means local Māori iwi (tribal groupings) and Pasifika peoples. This is encapsulated in ITE requirements which require "authentic partnerships" that are "strengthened and expanded over the following two to three years". Authenticity is defined as:

> Authenticity in partnerships occurs through arrangements and negotiations to ensure all partners have a shared understanding of their respective roles and responsibilities ... Such partnerships ultimately reflect an

enduring relationship that takes into account the aspirations, wellbeing, and success of all learners. The notion of partnership is different from a consultation model, where in partnership mutual benefits are explicit and interdependent, structured, with a shared responsibility for success.

This is encapsulated in Item 1.3 of the ITE Requirements document: Design and Delivery Based on Authentic Partnerships, which states that:

> Programme design and delivery must be based on authentic consultation and partnership with relevant key partners.
>
> There must be a plan to show how authentic partnerships with key partners (with mutual benefits that are explicit and interdependent, structured, and with a shared responsibility for success) will be strengthened and expanded over the following two to three years.

The documentation goes on to list the evidence that would be needed to support meeting this requirement:

- Details of which schools/centres/kura are key partners;
- Details of which Māori iwi are key partners;
- Details of which other groups or organisations with an interest in ITE, such as PLD providers, healthcare organisations, industry-employers, are key partners (if any);
- Evidence of authentic consultation;
- An outline of what aspects of the programme key partners have helped to develop; and
- A plan for how authentic partnerships with key partners will be strengthened and expanded over the following two to three years.

Details are also required about the exact nature of this involvement in all aspects of the programme design, delivery and assessment and review.

All the teacher educators I interviewed were supportive of this approach, although there were clearly some issues in meeting this requirement. The benefits of partnership for the ITE institution were clear at one level (to meet the requirements for accreditation), while the benefits for Māori were less clear. Seeking partnership just to meet requirements was felt to be inappropriate, and there were struggles to understand how to share power and decision-making with iwi and community groups in a space that had traditionally been dominated by consultation with schools and early childhood centres only. This requirement opened a space for new practices in ITE that could benefit Māori student teachers and students in schools, but it seemed to be difficult for the institution to move forward and begin these partnerships.

The principle of local community involvement is aligned to the values shared by the teacher educators at the University of Auckland. For example, a teacher educator described a number of projects she had recently been involved with which were all focused around increasing partnership and partner engagement in teacher education. She described herself as a strong advocate of partnership working, and was motivated to maintain authentic partnerships which sought to recognise and value the respective contributions and knowledges of both school- and university-based teacher educators. In this discussion, however, she noted that across the university more emphasis was placed on research partnerships than those grounded in partnership engagement. This was also reflected in recruitment criteria which focused on academic credentials (specifically Masters and PhD levels of education, publications and research profile) rather than looking towards recent or current school partners who had a good understanding of ITE, of recent policy and its impacts on teachers and the practical dimension of teacher education.

With respect to the former, in the accreditation criteria, the engagement of community groups is about changing the nature of teacher education provision, taking into account community interests and perspectives and respecting a plurality of perspectives on learning, inclusive of a range of ideas and knowledges. The articulation is a more expansive notion of the role of knowledges and ideas within transformative teacher education pedagogy. Along with concerns about teacher educators (discussed fully in Chapter 5), this debate is orientated around attendant discourses of what is required for a transformative experience in New Zealand.

The New Zealand pedagogical approach

New Zealand is recognised for having a long-term commitment to progressive educational ideas, often cited as originating in the 1937 conference and subsequently developed through New Education Fellowship (Couch, 2011). These principles, whilst challenged and developed through subsequent educational movements, are still a dominant feature of New Zealand's educational tradition. Combined with feminist and Māori cultural resurgence ideals (Mutch, 2013), this tradition is characterised by the famous and influential early years' curriculum *Te Whāriki*:

> Following a 1993 draft, the final curriculum, Te Whāriki, Early childhood curriculum (Ministry of Education, 1996) presented a holistic, child-centred, bicultural early childhood approach. While the early influences of naturalistic and progressive ideas can be seen, it also makes use of socio-cultural (Vygotsky, 1962) and socio-ecological (Bronfenbrenner, 1979) theories and Kaupapa Māori (indigenous) concepts. Te Whāriki has received international acclaim. Germany, Norway and Denmark (Fleer, 2003) and the United Kingdom (Siraj-Blatchford & Clarke, 2000) are countries that have taken inspiration from Te Whāriki when developing their own early childhood curricula.

> The title Te Whāriki was chosen with care. Literally translated it means a woven flax mat. This metaphor works at several levels. First, at a national level, it represents all the early childhood services as a coherent whole and, in particular, acknowledges the place of Māori culture and language in New Zealand society. Second, in relation to the curriculum itself, it is an interlocking of the four underpinning principles (empowerment, holistic development, family and community, and relationships) and the five strands (well-being, belonging, contribution, communication, and exploration). Third, it represents the curriculum (or course of learning) that each child will undertake – not as a linear and structured progression but as a complex interweaving of experiences and developments.
>
> *(Ibid., p. 107)*

Whilst Mutch recognises that more recent developments and international influences (around curriculum reform) have incorporated reforms and accountability regimes recognisable as stemming from the Global Education Reform Movement (GERM), since the 2000s, New Zealand has adopted an inquiry pedagogical model, but this has been criticised by the OECD judgement of the performance of New Zealand in international comparisons. In her paper, Mutch describes the New Zealand pedagogical approach:

> New Zealand's liberal-progressive education tradition has served it well. It was a tangible expression of New Zealand's developing identity which aimed to foster an egalitarian ethos within a bi-cultural society. From the early days of New Zealand's formal education system, forward-thinking educators and policy makers have sought to make classrooms and early childhood centres more child-centred, relevant, engaging and inclusive.
>
> *(Ibid.)*

The OECD has also recognised the specific nature of this approach and its features:

> Since the establishment of self-managing schools in 1989, New Zealand has one of the most devolved school systems in the world. Average student learning outcomes are very good by international comparison even though there are concerns about the proportion of students that are not performing well. ... As part of the national strategy to achieve [their] goals, New Zealand has developed its own distinctive model of evaluation and assessment characterised by a high level of trust in schools and school professionals. There are no full-cohort national tests and teachers are given prime responsibility to assess their students' learning. Teachers also have a good degree of ownership of their own appraisal and are involved in school self-review.
>
> *(Nusche, Laveault, MacBeath, & Santiago, 2012, p. 9)*

This approach has been under considerable threat by the sorts of reform movements experienced by many other countries, but the approach is popular with parents in New Zealand. This is borne out in both Mutch's review and in recent government surveys of parents (as reported by the Minister of Education, Chris Hipkins at the Normal and Model Schools Association [NAMSA] conference, September 2019). During my site visit, many colleagues took time to explain to me (with some sense of pride) of the unique and respected progressive pedagogical tradition in New Zealand, and how this was embedded in the practices of schools and across the various approaches to teacher education. It was driven, as far as I could ascertain, by a shared commitment to quality and equity, which foregrounded student voice, community engagement and plurality of ideas; this approach therefore acts as a backdrop to the understanding of transformation across the New Zealand context, recognising a strong values position as integral to how teacher education was understood. Unusually, these values are evident in some of the accountability and governance measures (such as the Teacher Standards), but putting them into practice is challenging within a university context.

Pedagogical initiatives: Mahi Tahi days

The neoliberal imperatives which widely influence universities and the dominant narratives evident in the GERM do not sit easily alongside this commitment to high-quality teacher education in New Zealand. An illustrative example of where they can come into conflict is through one initiative described by several of the interviewees around the establishment of Mahi Tahi days.

Mahi Tahi (working together as one) days brought together student teachers with school-based colleagues and university-based teacher educators to work together and to combine theory and practice in a meaningful way. A Mahi Tahi day involved using a 360 degree recording of an expert teacher working with students along with copies of the lesson plan and paperwork, and targeted observation techniques for different groups of student teachers. Then the students, mentors and teacher educators were brought together with the expert teacher to discuss the lesson, the reflections, the observations, examples of students work and what the next steps might be for that class.

From a pedagogical perspective, this approach offers many distinct advantages, including collaborative working across and between the university and school partners, on a specific teaching event and through authentic dialogue and feedback. The approach appeared to have the support and backing of the teacher educators and school partners and had been positively piloted. The plan was to expand this model into the new programme. This, however, ran into some logistical difficulties at the university level. These included concerns about the timetabling of these events (as they were not connected to a specific course or module), how they would be "counted" in the workload of teacher educators and seeking permission for what appeared to be taking a "day out" of the course.

These constraints meant that the original plan for six Mahi Tahi days was reduced to three with concerns that they could be reduced further.

The teacher educators, who discussed this initiative with me, saw the administrative barriers they encountered with the university as symptomatic of the challenges of working within a multi-faculty university where university-wide service standards (such as staff to student ratios, class sizes thresholds and workload calculations) did not take into account the specific requirements of ITE. This example reflects the accountability quality conundrum: university processes and procedures are designed to ensure equity and equal access amongst students and staff in an efficient way. The structures put in place to achieve this do not correspond to an attempt to improve the learning experience from the perspective of the teacher educators. Although the university policies are designed with equity between students, and service standards in mind, their implementation could prevent attempts to improve the ITE educational experience.

The practice tradition: the role of normal schools

Partnership is a key site of practice for ITE, and schools as sites of practice are central to the transformative experience of teacher education. One of the practice traditions within the New Zealand teacher education infrastructure is the role of Normal and Model Schools. Continued government support for Normal Schools reflects an acknowledgement of the important role that schools play in the teacher education partnership. However, as a group of schools, concerned about their own status and direct funding from government, the Normal Schools are also seeking to support the transformation of student teachers perhaps with a different agenda.

The NAMSA has been involved in teacher education in New Zealand since 1876, and Normal Schools are part of the teacher education national provision landscape. Normal Schools receive additional government funding to support teacher education and for that funding provide specialist advice and support for new teachers; in that sense, they are significant sites of practice not only for the student teachers who are located placements within Normal Schools, but also as NAMSA acts as an influential lobbying group in this field (for example, the Minister of Education spoke at their 2019 conference in Wellington).

The origins of the Normal Schools are described on the NAMSA website:

> Normal Schools have been in existence since the 16th Century when a group of schools in France became interested in preparing people for teaching. The French concept of "école normale" was to establish schools to model best teaching practices thereby setting a standard or norm for student teachers. ... The 22 Normal schools in New Zealand appointed by the Government provide a major teaching practicum facility for five universities nationwide.

During the year Normal Schools have a number of students on placement. Placement provides opportunities for student teachers and their pupils to get to know each other over a long-term basis and enables student teachers and classroom teachers to form stronger collegial relationships. In their second and third years, student teachers also spend time teaching small groups in various curriculum areas and other full time practicum blocks. Student teachers bring another valued perspective to our schools.

Normal and Model Schools are proud to be given this status as an exemplary school. We have a long history of school-based teacher education in New Zealand and our teachers are chosen for their expert knowledge and experience. We also share our quality teaching and experiences with many visiting educators from around New Zealand as well as internationally. We take our close association with the universities of New Zealand seriously and know that this relationship benefits our children in many ways, with the learning of our children of the utmost priority.

(http://www.namsa.ac.nz/1/pages/3-history-of-normal-schools)

Whilst Normal Schools are an influential part of the teacher education landscape and national practice architecture, they still rely on additional government funding, an increasing concern as the government was reviewing its education provision. It was not surprising therefore that one of the main themes of the NAMSA conference was on how to evidence the impact of the Normal Schools. A key feature of this conference was a series of presentations followed by round table discussions from recently graduated teachers about their experiences on placement or employment in Normal Schools, with a strong emphasis on sharing the particular contribution that the Normal Schools made to an individual's development as a new teacher.

Whilst it was clear that many university-based providers (who also attended the conference) valued their partnership with Normal Schools, the contribution of Normal Schools to the national infrastructure appeared to be the provision of high-quality placements with specialist support (at the financial burden of the state rather than the university). Several Normal School Principals had become involved in the teacher education accreditation process and, due to their commitment to teacher education, were actively involved in the consultation and programme planning developed around reaccreditation at the University of Auckland, activities that one might expect from very committed school-based partners. Discussions were also taking place as to other ways that the Normal Schools could support universities in the provision of high-quality school-based experiences.

In my discussion with a local Normal School leadership team, they noted the competing priorities for their university-based colleagues. They noted that the reduction in applications for teacher education raised financial issues for the university and were concerned about the quality of entrants to the profession. They also noted that it was difficult for teacher educators to maintain their obligations to the university as well as remaining up to date with developments in schools.

Whilst many of these observations about teacher education partnerships are quite common, they reflect a frustration in the conception of partnership on the programmes, and an awareness of the sometimes contradictory pressures facing teacher education situated within universities, namely a reliance on the funding from adequate recruitment and pressures on teacher educators to undertake full academic duties (over and above recent school experience). The indicators of quality adopted by the university do not translate easily into high-quality teacher education.

Teacher education is a partnership-orientated activity, and the engagement of stakeholders is crucial. However, this does not mean that all stakeholders view the activity in the same way, or share the same priorities for development. One of the unifying dimensions between the Normal Schools and their university partners was a shared concern for how teacher education could play a role in addressing New Zealand's issues around equity. However, the capacity for Normal Schools to be adaptive in their teacher education expertise differed to the larger and more complex infrastructure of the university partner.

University considerations

I have identified that the emphasis on bicultural practices is a key feature of the teacher education provision that I observed at the University of Auckland. It can be seen as a dominant theme or feature of the practice architecture that underpins the teacher education provision, prioritised and sanctioned through official discourses of the ITE Requirements and Teacher Standards (the material economic arrangements), and supported and prioritised through the intersubjectivities of the teacher educators I spoke to at the University.

At the time of my visit, the university had been through a number of restructures, which had resulted in a loss of staff. Accounts of this varied amongst the interviewees and the number of staff lost differed from 28 to 45; but what is clear is that a substantial number of staff had left and that this had had a huge impact on the people who remained, described by one interviewee as suffering from intense "survivor guilt". Various reasons were offered for these restructures, including a change in senior leadership, a decline in enrolments and a university-mandated staff:student ratio which was over-reached in teacher education. There was a sense amongst the interviewees that the staff with research profiles had been prioritised or "saved" and taken out of the assessment, and teacher education staff without strong research profiles had been targeted and adversely affected. A number of interviewees explained that this left the teacher education activity with a number of challenges: modules (or courses) without an identified leader or someone with the appropriate expertise, elective modules had been cut, some areas of specialism (such as English) had lost all their specialist lecturers and some modules were now shared across programmes. The sense of frustration was further compounded by the halting of some developmental work and the additional workload picked up by remaining staff.

There appeared to be a tension between the interpretations of quality adopted by the university leadership through their governance structures, which were focused on standards, accountability and value for money, and research benchmarks and the idea of education as transformation expressed by the teacher educators. The accountability measures of the university were orientated around student evaluations of individual modules, so teacher educators felt they were held accountable through the evaluations of their teaching. Employability rates were also highly valued by the institution, a metric that has less comparative value during a period of high teacher demand. However, there was also a feeling that the universities were unaware of the complexities of teacher education and in how transformation in a practice-based programme needed to be developed.

The focus of the university's governance and oversight of accountability do not contain any qualities distinctive to ITE: student course evaluations are centred on the individual lecturer (reflecting individualised performance common with neoliberal accountability regimes); school engagement is not seen as the shared responsibility of the teacher education provision, but as the remit of the programme director or placements office. This is additionally compounded by the regulation that teacher educators can only visit if they are certified teachers, and many university-based teacher educators have enabled their certification to lapse thus preventing them from undertaking school visits. Similarly, employment statistics are not a valid measure of success when situated within a recruitment space of high demand for teachers, ensuring high levels of employability (presumably unrelated to quality). In other words, accountability and governance measures intended to indicate quality across the university may not enhance quality for teacher education.

Different interpretations of quality

In much of the literature, education policy is situated as a threat to university-based teacher education, as the drivers are placed in tension with high-quality teacher education practices. This is not the case in New Zealand. The motivation for a more equitable education system is at the heart of both the education policy context and the motivations of teacher educators (even though this may be perhaps for different reasons). The government has even invested in university-based teacher education provision.

At the University of Auckland, the actions of the university have been prompted by concerns about the financial viability of the programme, but have had a substantial impact on the practice architecture for teacher education. Interestingly this tension does not appear to stem from the governance regime (although there are some challenges here) but from the university-based infrastructure in which the teacher education system is based. The moves towards further developing and realising the ambition of a teacher education system motivated by the idea of an equitable education system which values cultural diversity appear to be in tension with a neoliberal management system employed by the university within a climate of cost-cutting, efficiency measures and falling recruitment.

The failure of the national accountability regime to tackle the university infrastructure effectively leaves teacher educators powerless to enact their (and the government's) vision of high-quality teacher education, and to use their teacher education expertise to the best effect for their students. In this sense, then national education policy does not appear to be the main constraint to high-quality teacher education.

Of course, this is not to suggest that the university is somehow at fault. There are several constraints that the university itself needs to contend with. The University of Auckland is a prestigious institution, the highest ranked university in New Zealand, according to the QS World University Rankings, and within the Education subject rankings of the same system was ranked number 17 in the world and the best in New Zealand (according to the University Subject Rankings, 2018). It is traditionally the largest teacher education provider in New Zealand, after merging with the Auckland Teacher Training College, and is well located in Auckland, the city with the highest demand for new teachers.

However, the University of Auckland is increasingly finding itself in an ITE competitive market. Teacher training is also provided in Auckland by a number of other providers, in particular the Auckland University of Technology University (known as AUT) is situated in the north of the city and tends to cater for schools and applicants in that region. Other providers from across New Zealand (such as Massey University, University of Canterbury in Christchurch and University of Waikato) all provide some teacher education in Auckland. More recently, additional competition has been introduced by Teach First New Zealand, originally a small-scale programme in partnership with University of Auckland, but more recently expanded in collaboration with Mindlab, part of UniTech, and rumoured to have become a private training establishment.

The location of University of Auckland appears to be a significant factor for the students I spoke to as to why they chose to do their teacher training here. The undergraduate and postgraduate students all indicated that location in Auckland, and proximity to their home, was a key if not the primary reason for choosing the University of Auckland. However, recent changes in the recruitment of teachers have reduced the University of Auckland's position as the largest teacher education provider, as the nearest rival, AUT, was growing due to a "funky and more impressive recruitment strategy".

The reduction in students is not just attributable to the marketing efforts of AUT, as there has been a reduction in applications across the board. But there was also some concern expressed that the main marketing efforts of the University of Auckland were targeted at their international status, ranking and research success. Some of the teacher educators I spoke to considered this as an example of the disconnect between the values of the university (orientated around research and high academic achievement) and the reality of the teacher education market (more orientated to usefulness and practical experience). This disconnect was also exemplified by other university-based strategies that failed to recognise the different teaching loads of teacher educators, the lack of available research funding and the recruitment of researchers over school-based colleagues with experience of teacher education and the areas of specialism needed for teacher education programs. This was further exacerbated by the closure of the Masters of Teaching programme with its specific focus on Teaching for Equity. In other words, there is a case to be made that the lack of university engagement with teacher education as a part of the repertoire of activity has created a context that makes it difficult for teacher educators to enact transformative learning effectively.

There appears to be some significant constraints in enacting the national and local drivers towards a highly equitable teacher education system. The actions of the university are aligned to their own constraints and concerns: the demand for international competitiveness, the increased emphasis on high-quality research and the expensive nature of teacher education programmes. Therefore, to attribute this dissonance to a difference in values would be disingenuous. But these indicators are part of the university's definition of quality, which focuses on standards through foregrounding value for money, and service standards and that this emphasis differs to the concept of quality as transformation as adopted by the teacher educators.

As noted in Chapter 1, teacher education is a practice that happens in a range of sites: the university and the practicum school in particular. These sites are connected to their communities and are often well positioned to draw upon and develop strong partnerships with those communities. They are also part of global networks, international communities and a footloose community of shared interests. Increasingly this community is working in virtual spaces. However, as teaching is a profoundly relational (rather than transactional) activity, so the site of practice matters.

But teacher education is also situated in a hierarchical arrangement of educational organisations each with their own set of governance arrangements: the practice authority that is embedded across schools and the academic authority often escribed to universities. Status and prestige are even more dominant in high-ranking institutions. This status is differently expressed to that of policymakers, whose elected status, national power and decision-making authority sets them within a different sphere of influence. Within the practice of teacher education, universities and schools are both stakeholders which have to come together. The university-based teacher educator has to enable that coming together to work offering due credit and consideration to the differing perspectives, but also being mindful of the context of governance regimes within which they are working, which make up their capacity to act.

The task of creating the conditions for transformation in teacher education is then shared amongst these partners and stakeholders, but can be challenging to enact when they have different conceptions of quality and when they occupy a different representational space. When there is a tension between the university governance infrastructure and the practice needed for transformation to take place, a perspective shared by the teacher educators in Auckland, then this creates challenging tensions to resolve. At the heart lies differing interpretations of what quality looks like.

References

Ball, S. J. (2003). The teacher's soul and the terrors of performativity. *Journal of Education Policy, 18*(2), 215–228. doi:10.1080/0268093022000043065

Ball, S. J. (2012). Performativity, commodification and commitment: An I-spy guide to the neoliberal university. *British Journal of Educational Studies, 60*(1), 17–28. doi:10.1080/00071005.2011.650940

BERA-RSA. (2014). *Research and the teaching profession: Building the capacity for a self-improving education system. Final Report of the BERA-RSA Inquiry into the Role of Research in Teacher Education.* Retrieved from London: https://www.bera.ac.uk/project/research-and-teacher-education

Boston, J. (2013). *Improving educational performance: Why tackling child poverty must be part of the solution.* Paper presented at the Symposium on the Poverty Impacts on Learning, Wellington, New Zealand.

Bronfenbrenner, U. (1979). *The ecology of human development: Experiments by nature and design.* Cambridge, MA: Harvard University Press.

Bullough, R. V. (2014). Toward reconstructing the narrative of teacher education. *Journal of Teacher Education, 65*(3), 185–194. doi:10.1177/0022487113519131

Cochran-Smith, M., Carney, M. C., Keefe, E. S., Burton, S., Chang, W.-C., Fernández, M. B., ... Baker, M. (2018). *Reclaiming accountability in teacher education.* New York: Teachers College Press.

Cochran-Smith, M., Ell, F., Grudnoff, L., Haigh, M., Hill, M., & Ludlow, L. (2016). Initial teacher education: What does it take to put equity at the center? *Teaching and Teacher Education, 57,* 67–78. doi:10.1016/j.tate.2016.03.006

Cochran-Smith, M., & Fries, K. (2005). Researching teacher education in changing times: Politics and paradigms. In M. Cochran-Smith & K. Zeichner (Eds.), *Studying teacher education: The report of the AERA Panel on Research and Teacher Education* (pp. 69–109). Mahwah, NJ: Lawrence Erlbaum.

Connell, R. (2019). *The good university: What universities actually do and why its time for radical change.* London: Zed Books Ltd.

Couch, D. J. (2011). *New Zealand education's progressive origin: 1937 to 1944- the seven years from idea to orthodoxy.* Master of Education, University of Auckland, Unpublished.

de Graef, O., Busse, B., Cahill, V., Hansen, J. R., & Manon Kluijtmans, M. (2020). *Tomorrow's teachers today: What universities can do for the teaching profession.* Retrieved from Leuven, Belgium: https://www.leru.org/publications/tomorrows-teachers-today-what-universities-can-do-for-the-teaching-profession

Ellis, V., Steadman, S., & Trippestad, T. A. (2018). Teacher education and the GERM: Policy entrepreneurship, disruptive innovation and the rhetorics of reform. *Educational Review, 71*(1), 101–121. doi:10.1080/00131911.2019.1522040

Fleer, M. (2003). Early childhood education as an evolving 'community of practice' or as lived 'social reproduction': Researching the 'taken-for-granted'. *Contemporary Issues in Early Childhood, 4*(1), 64–79.

Furlong, J. (2013). *Education – An anatomy of the discipline: Rescuing the university project.* Abingdon: Routledge.

Furlong, J., & Whitty, G. (2017). Knowledge traditions in the study of education. In G. Whitty & J. Furlong (Eds.), *Knowledge and the study of education: An international exploration* (pp. 13–57). Oxford: Symposium.

Gunn, A., Berg, D., Haigh, M., & Hill, M. (2016). *Work of teacher educators: Teaching and learning in New Zealand University-based initial teacher education.* Retrieved from New Zealand: http://www.tlri.org.nz/sites/default/files/projects/TLRI%20Gunn%20End%20of%20project%20report%20-%20web%20ready.pdf

Grudnoff, L., Haigh, M., Hill, M., Cochran-Smith, M., Ell, F., & Ludlow, L. (2017). Teaching for equity: Insights from international evidence with implications for a teacher education curriculum. *The Curriculum Journal, 28*(3), 305–326. doi:10.1080/09585176.2017.1292934

Harvey, L. (2007). The epistemology of quality. *Perspectives in Education, 25*(3), 1–13.

Ingvarson, L., Reid, K., Buckley, S., Kleinhenz, E., Masters, G., & Rowley, G. (2014). *Best practice teacher education programs and Australia's own programs.* Canberra: Department of Education.

Jarvis, D. S. L. (2014). Regulating higher education: Quality assurance and neo-liberal managerialism in higher education—A critical introduction. *Policy & society, 33*(3), 155–166. doi:10.1016/j.polsoc.2014.09.005

Labaree, D. F. (2006). *The trouble with ed schools.* New Haven, CT: Yale University Press.

Labaree, D. F. (2008). An uneasy relationship: The history of teacher education in the university. In M. Cochran-Smith, S. Feiman-Nemser, J. McIntyre, & K. with Demers (Eds.), *Handbook of research on teacher education* (3rd ed., pp. 290–306), Melbourne: SAGE.

Mayer, D. (2017). Professionalizing teacher education. In *Oxford research Encyclopedia of education* (Vol. 1). Oxford: Oxford University Press.

Menter, I. (2017). *The role and contribution of higher education in contemporary teacher education.* Retrieved from http://www.scde.ac.uk/wp-content/uploads/2017/05/Report-Ian-Menter-2017-05-25.pdf

Mutch, C. (2013). Progressive education in New Zealand: A revered past, a contested present and an uncertain future *International Journal of Progressive Education, 9*(2), 98–116.

New Zealand Ministry of Education. (2007). *Ka hikitea e Managing for success. The Maori education strategy 2008–2012.* Retrieved from http://www.minedu.govt.nz/theMinistry/PolicyAndStrategy/KaHikitia/PublicationsAndResources-EnglishLanguageVersions.aspx

New Zealand Ministry of Education. (2011). *Reading literacy achievement: Primary schooling.* Retrieved from http://www.educationcounts.govt.nz/indicators/main/educationand-learning-outcomes/748.

New Zealand Ministry of Education. (2012). *Pasifika education plan.* Retrieved from http://www.education.govt.nz/ministry-of-education/overall-strategies-and-policies/pasifika-education-plan-2013-2017

Nusche, D., Laveault, D., MacBeath, J., & Santiago, P. (2012). *OECD reviews of evaluation and assessment in education.* New Zealand 2011. Retrieved from http://www.oecd.org/education/school/49681441.pdf

OECD. (2011). *Society at a glance: Key findings New Zealand.* Retrieved from http://www.oecd.org/dataoecd/38/35/47573309.pdf

Orange, C. (1987). *The treaty of Waitangi.* Wellington: Bridget Williams Books.

Pring, R. (1996). 'Just desert'. In J. Furlong & R. Smith (Eds.), *The role of higher education in initial teacher education* (pp. 8–22). Abingdon: Kogan Page.

Siraj-Blatchford, I., & Clarke, P. (2000). *Supporting identity, diversity and language in the early years*. London: McGraw-Hill Education (UK).

Snook, I., & O'Neill, J. (2014). Poverty and inequality of educational achievement. In V. M. Carpenter & S. Osborne (Eds.), *Twelve thousand hours: Education and poverty in Aotearoa New Zealand* (pp. 19–43). Auckland: Dunmore Publishing.

University Subject Rankings. (2018). The University of Auckland Rankings. Retrieved from https://www.topuniversities.com/node/2191/ranking-details/university-subject-rankings/2018

Vygotsky, L. S. (1962). *Thought and Language*. Cambridge, MA: The MIT Press.

7
THE CONTEXTS FOR TRANSFORMATION

Practice architectures

In Chapter 1, I argued that education is an important part of the production and reproduction of spatial inequalities. Teacher education is an important tool that can go some way to addressing these inequalities. However, poor teacher education could have the opposite effect and could perpetuate a polarisation of educational and social opportunity between the affluent and less advantaged. In the previous chapters, I outlined how five universities from different countries each tackled a quality conundrum. These quality conundrums are presented as criticisms or ideas around teacher education, which are designed to improve its quality but have the potential to reproduce or exacerbate inequalities further. In the analysis, I've argued that these conundrums can disrupt the flow of knowledge and ideas which can then act as a barrier to supporting transformation, a key goal in teacher education pedagogy. In the preceding chapters, we have seen teacher educators negotiate these conundrums in a range of ways: adopting value positions, counter narratives or developing integrated approaches. We have also seen how context can act as an enabler and a constraint in what universities can do, both in terms of setting the problems out and in offering opportunities to address them. In this chapter, the findings from across those practices are drawn together. The aim is to demonstrate how the university infrastructure can enable or constrain the practice of teacher education.

Teacher education has been described as "unforgivingly complex" (Cochran-Smith, 2003, p. 4); so, synthesising the teacher education practice across five different institutions is a challenging task and requires some compartmentalisation. The practices have therefore been divided into four main categories which were themes from across each of the sites visited:

- How teacher education partnerships are configured;
- How the three message systems of schooling (curriculum, pedagogy and assessment) are structured;

- How teacher educators' roles are changing; and
- How accountability drives practices.

These aspects of teacher education practices interweave and intersect. Changes in any of these categories are likely to have a knock-on effect on the others. The theory of practice and practice architectures (Kemmis et al., 2014) is an effective way of laying out the practice of initial teacher education (ITE) into a series of arrangements and practice traditions which can show how they enable and constrain ITE practices. These arrangements are categorised in their cultural-discursive, material-economic and social-political nature, or the sayings, doings and relatings of the practice, and situates these arrangements within the spatial and temporal context, so that gaps, omissions and tensions between the arrangements can be observed and subsequently addressed. It is not the intention of this work to critique the practices or to suggest how the practices should be changed, but the findings are laid out here to lead to a deeper understanding of the common drivers which can influence ITE practices across a range of contexts and how university-based teacher educators and their institutions have responded to those drivers.

Theory of practice and practice architectures

Many studies of teacher education, and in particular the Studying Effectiveness in Teacher Education (SETE) (Mayer et al., 2015) and Research in Teaching for Equity (Cochran-Smith et al., 2016; Grudnoff et al., 2017) projects, have noted that teacher education is a complex activity and consequently draw upon complexity theory as an appropriate way to explore that complexity. As the SETE project elaborates:

> Questions about the quality of teachers and teacher education are therefore met at every turn with evidence of complexity: teaching is complex. Students are complex. Education is complex.
>
> *(Mayer et al., 2015, p. 16)*

There are many ways and approaches to viewing and deconstructing this complex activity. Communities of practice (Lave & Wenger, 1991; Wenger, 1998), cultural historical activity theory and policy studies are all popular approaches which can reveal trends, patterns and influences over teacher education. However, these approaches tend to focus on the conditions around teacher education rather than its attendant pedagogy and practice. This is not to suggest that these accounts are not useful or informative; they undoubtedly are and have contributed valuable understandings to the field. However, they do not get at the heart of the practice of teacher education. Whilst the conditions, policies and actors in and around teacher education will all influence the practice to some extent, they are partial – and cast (an albeit valuable) light on only one dimension of the activity. In order to understand the impact of the public debates and the changing landscape affecting university-based teacher education in a broader sense, it is important to view teacher education holistically, as a practice of itself but also comprising of a range of practices undertaken by a number of people (teacher educators, school-based mentors and others). It is for this reason that the theory of practice and practice architectures provides a useful anchor for this work.

Ecologies of practices

As the previous chapters have demonstrated, teacher education is a complex activity with a number of stakeholders: student teachers, universities and university-based teacher educators, schools and school-based teacher educators, community groups, as well as stakeholders with vested interests such as local and national governments, professional associations, unions and agencies with governance and oversight responsibilities. Universities and schools also engage with a number of other practice-based activities such as research, consultancy and the teaching of students and pupils. Changes in these practice-based activities are likely to have a knock-on effect on the practice of teacher education. It is useful then to see teacher education as part of this rich ecology of practices, with various interdependencies, influential relationships and flows of energy and ideas.

Although looking at education in a broader sense, Kemmis et al. (2014) adopt an ecologies of practices approach in order to understand how schools, teachers, students, leaders and communities respond to the current conditions of education. Adopting a philosophical-empirical inquiry, and based on the work of Schatzki (2012), they developed a theory of *ecologies of practices*. Within this theory, they see practices as making up a series of *projects* (that which is the answer to the question: what are you doing?) and which are situated in ecological relationships with each other. They identified the following practices:

- Educational research and evaluation practices;
- Educational leadership practices;
- Initial and continuing teacher education practices;
- Educational practices (planning, teaching, assessing);
- Students' academic (learning) and social practices; and
- Cultural, material and social practices in the society.

These practices make up what Kemmis and colleagues describe as the Education Complex. Their theory demonstrates that each practice is formed through its *practice architecture*, but must be seen as part of this complex, connected to the other inter-related practices. ITE is part of and influenced by this broader Education Complex, and the theory of practice and practice architectures enables a way of exploring this practice whilst recognising the influences others have upon it.

The idea of an ecology or ecologies of practices is particularly significant for teacher education, being made up of a range of stakeholders with sometimes competing agendas. Drawing from the natural sciences, ecologies have a range of concepts that helps to explain how ecologies work, such as through cycles, flows, networks and nested systems. Ecologies have a range of interdependencies and networks through which energies flow and cycles emerge (such as food chains). When productive, ecologies can work in dynamic balance with all elements receiving and providing the energy flow necessary to sustain the ecology. But this balance can be disrupted by the introduction of an invasive species, which can seek to disrupt the energy flows and the established networked relationships. Ecologies are formed through succession, adaptation and in some cases extinction. As outlined in Chapter 1, transformation in ITE is achieved through a flow of ideas and knowledges enacted through teacher education pedagogy. An ecology exists through its flow of energy, and effective teacher education similarly exists through its flow of ideas.

For example, one could argue that the introduction of alternative providers to the teacher education ecosystem (a subset of an ecology) mirrors the introduction of an invasive species: it consumes resources or energy flow previously made available to established species. If those established species are unable to respond quickly, they can be cut out of the energy cycle; they need to either adapt or head towards extinction. In a similar vein, teacher education is vulnerable to invasion; for example, changes in school funding arrangements could enhance or detract from their ability to provide high-quality placements, or changes in the economic superstructure could affect the supply of new applicants for teacher training placements. In the previous chapters, I have tried to show how teacher education in the places I visited were responding to changes in the ecologies of practices around them, and how this was affecting the flow of ideas. However, to fully understand what is happening across and between different stakeholders in the ecology, it is important to consider how their various practices intersect and get played out.

The practice of teacher education

There are three premises to the Kemmis et al.'s (2014) theory of practice and practice architectures, which make it particularly appropriate for the study of teacher education:

- Pedagogy is seen as a collective social practice made up of individual practices which take place in social contexts, and are influenced by and, in turn, influence those social contexts;
- It is not possible to understand a practice, or indeed a pedagogy of a project such as teacher education, without taking into account the collective nature of those practices, the specific location in which they occur and the impact this has on the social actors (both teachers and students) who take part in the practice; and
- The site of practice is an important part of understanding that practice and needs to be understood in the context of its history and influences.

Practice architectures 165

The quality conundrums are directed at different aspects of the practice of teacher education and come from a range of sources, thereby reflecting these principles of collective social practice, the significance of the sites of practice and the hinterland of practice-based histories and influences. The conundrums themselves are such precisely because they disrupt the flow of energy (or ideas) through the ecology. By viewing teacher education pedagogy as a constellation of practices, the theory of practice architectures enables a laying out of those practices. For example, should a programme adopt a particular pedagogical approach, such as clinical practice, this has to be enacted through a range of practices conducted by university-based teacher educators, school-based mentors and a range of site-based architectures and arrangements in order to make the practice happen. The theory of practice and practice architectures enables those arrangements and the relationships between them to be laid out for analysis by exploring how they happen in intersubjective spaces (Figure 7.1).

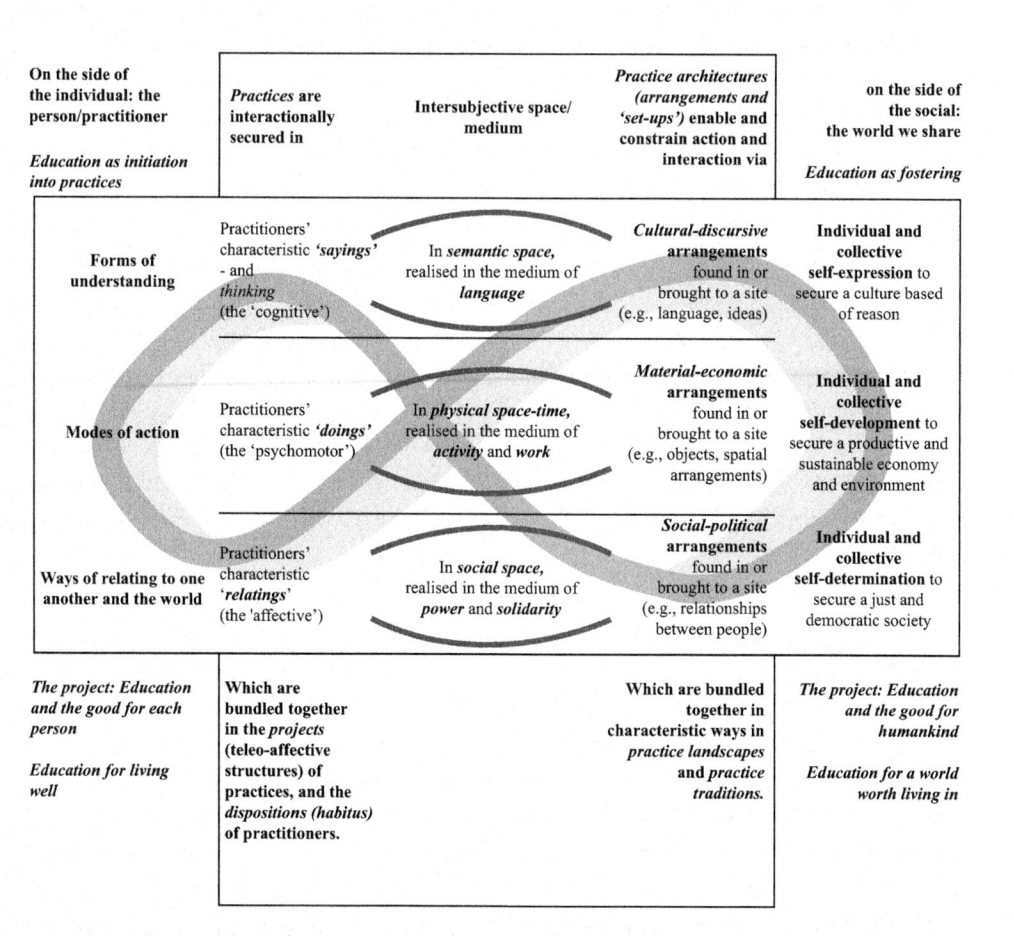

On the side of the individual: the person/practitioner	Practices are interactionally secured in	Intersubjective space/ medium	Practice architectures (arrangements and 'set-ups') enable and constrain action and interaction via	on the side of the social: the world we share
Education as initiation into practices				*Education as fostering*
Forms of understanding	Practitioners' characteristic *'sayings'* - and *thinking* (the 'cognitive')	In *semantic space*, realised in the medium of *language*	*Cultural-discursive* arrangements found in or brought to a site (e.g., language, ideas)	Individual and collective self-expression to secure a culture based of reason
Modes of action	Practitioners' characteristic *'doings'* (the 'psychomotor')	In *physical space-time*, realised in the medium of *activity* and *work*	*Material-economic* arrangements found in or brought to a site (e.g., objects, spatial arrangements)	Individual and collective self-development to secure a productive and sustainable economy and environment
Ways of relating to one another and the world	Practitioners' characteristic *'relatings'* (the 'affective')	In *social space*, realised in the medium of *power* and *solidarity*	*Social-political* arrangements found in or brought to a site (e.g., relationships between people)	Individual and collective self-determination to secure a just and democratic society
The project: Education and the good for each person *Education for living well*	Which are bundled together in the *projects* (teleo-affective structures) of practices, and the dispositions (habitus) of practitioners.		Which are bundled together in characteristic ways in practice landscapes and *practice traditions*.	*The project: Education and the good for humankind* *Education for a world worth living in*

FIGURE 7.1 A theory of education (from Kemmis and Mahon, 2017).
Reprinted with permission from Springer Nature: *Coming to 'Practice Architectures': A Genealogy of the Theory* by Kemmis, S. and Mahon, K, 2017.

The diagram illustrates three key aspects to this theory:

- The dual nature of a practice as both being experienced by the individual (on the left of the diagram) and of the infrastructure needed for it to occur (on the right);
- The different arrangements necessary to make up the practice architecture which can "enable and constrain action and interaction" (as listed on the right-hand side); and
- The significance of the intersubjective spaces (or medium) through which those arrangements and practices come together (the centre of the diagram).

The theory of practices and practice architecture has been used to examine specific educational practices (Edwards-Groves & Grootenboer, 2015; Kemmis et al., 2014). Whilst, as Kemmis and colleagues note, teacher education makes up a significant part of the education complex, it is made up of distinct practices of its own. Across teacher education, the word practice is often used in a somewhat loose way, often confusing a range of different elements of practice, including:

- The work of university-based teacher educators in the practice of teacher education;
- The work of school-based mentors as they work with and support student teachers in their contexts, often reflecting on their own practice as teachers;
- The work of the student teachers themselves as they undertake their practice of learning and their "practice" or practicum school-based practical experience; and
- The practice of teaching both in schools and in university settings.

The use of the term practice in all these contexts is appropriate, as they reflect that practice can be understood as the individual application of a way of doing things and customary or habitual procedures. For Kemmis and colleagues, practice is defined as:

> A practice is a form of socially established cooperative human activity in which characteristic arrangements of actions and activities (doings) are comprehensible in terms of arrangements of relevant ideas in characteristic discourses (sayings), and when the people and objects involved are distributed in characteristics arrangements of relationships (relatings), and when this complex of sayings, doings and relatings 'hangs together' in a distinctive project.
>
> (Kemmis et al., 2014, p. 27)

The recognition of the discursive and political dimensions of practices is key to ensure that a view of practice does not become trivialised and over-instrumentalised. This point is made in Hordern's (2020) critique of the British

Educational Research Association's close-to-practice research (Wyse, 2020; Wyse, Brown, Oliver, & Poblete, 2020). Drawing on a research project with the same name, Wyse argues that being "close to practice" is a defining feature of education research and can be viewed as a strength, so long as it is conducted with rigour. However, Hordern argues that practice in this context is defined too loosely as any form of "action", which omits consideration of whether the practice itself is indeed *educational*. Hordern's (ibid.) notion of educational is similar to the concept of transformation adopted here, as it relates to the formation of the individual with an educational intent. Consequently, practice can be used reductively to refer to what is needed to fulfil policy or managerial objectives, and as such becomes normative. The theory of practice and practice architectures avoids this by explicitly opening up both the discursive and political dimensions of the arrangements which form the practice architecture.

This approach does not seek to identify "best practices". The nominalisation of something as "best practice" regards pedagogical practice in a bounded and solitary way, sitting alongside a culture of performativity and testing which fails to recognise the site-based needs and circumstances of schools, students and communities (Edwards-Groves, 2018). Instead, Edwards-Groves argues for a view of pedagogy which acknowledges that it takes place within sites of practice and that recognises the social dimensions that form pedagogy in those particular places.

It is this categorisation of practices as being influenced socially (within the company of others), dialogically (through talk and interaction), ontologically (in particular places) and temporally (in and through time) which is particularly useful for teacher education, as rather than categorising practices by those who undertake them or what they are intended to achieve, the theory sees these elements as combined and inter-related. The key distinction is between the types of practice arrangements:

- *Cultural-discursive arrangements* (in the medium of language and in the dimension of *semantic space*) that are the resources that make possible the *language and discourses* used in and about this practice; these arrangements enable and constrain the *sayings* characteristic of the practice (for example, constraining what it is relevant to say, or – especially – what language or specialist discourse is appropriate for describing, interpreting and justifying the practice);
- *Material-economic arrangements* (in the medium of *activity and work*, in the dimension of *physical space-time*) that are the resources that make possible the *activities* undertaken in the course of the practice; these arrangements enable and constrain the *doings* characteristic of the practice (for example, by constraining what can be done amid the physical set-ups of various kinds of rooms and indoor and outdoor spaces in a school); and
- *Social-political arrangements* (in the medium of *power and solidarity* and in the dimension of *social space*) that are the resources that make possible *the relationships between people and non-human objects* that occur in the practice; these

arrangements enable and constrain the *relatings* of the practice (for example by the organizational functions, rules and roles in an organisation, or by the communicative requirements of the lifeworld processes of reaching shared understandings, practical arrangements about what to do, and social solidarities; Habermas, 1987a).

(Kemmis et al., 2014, p. 32, italics in original)

Recognising then that practices are the product of their spatial and historical context, the theory of practice and practice architectures offers a way to examine teacher education which is strongly spatially located, drawing heavily on Schatzki's theory of timespace of human activity, which sees time and space not as containers or contexts of human activity but as constituent of it. In other words, human activity (in this case, the practice of teacher education) can be seen as an indeterminate timespatial event: a happening that is not pinned down by what precedes it or by the particular spatial location it occupies, but that is nevertheless influenced by the site ontologies of where the practice occurs and the practice traditions at work there.

Quality conundrums within the practice architecture

In the previous chapters, I have laid out the teacher education practices in relation to five quality conundrums, revealing:

- How the role of student teachers' practical experience is differently situated between the UCL Institute of Education's (IOE) Post Graduate Certificate in Education (PGCE) programme and the Teach First Leadership Development programme. This chapter argues that this is, in some part, attributable to the different arrangements of the programme such as the difference between an employment-place programme that seeks to prepare "classroom-ready teachers" and gradual-immersion programmes that focuses on the development of specialist expertise. These differences are reflected in the practice arrangements: the relative importance given to developing practice over specialist knowledge (cultural-discursive arrangements); the selection and foregrounding of generic support in the form of Participant Development Leads or tutors with a specialist background (material-economic arrangements); and the political- and community-based networks and associations the new teachers are inducted into (the social-political arrangements). The formation of these architectures directly influences the flow of ideas available for student teachers.
- The different ways in which research can contribute to teacher education. In the case of Ontario Institute for Studies in Education (OISE), research is seen as central to teacher education both in terms of the curriculum, pedagogy and assessment of the programme (the practice arrangements), but also in the status and tradition of the institution itself. The site ontology of the

university intersects with the programme practice arrangements, and as such sets out an environment that privileges the idea of research as a key pedagogy and source for ideas pertinent for new teachers.
- The ways in which certain knowledges are privileged and made visible through the practice arrangements of the teacher education programme at Queensland University of Technology (QUT). Here, the combination of the practice arrangements of Kelvin Grove Teacher Education Centre of Excellence and those of QUT have been used to foreground knowledges needed to support teachers working in rural and remote communities. These arrangements work when their cultural-discursive, material-economic and social-political arrangements are aligned and orientated to the same goal and enable the flow of ideas which new teachers need in order to be able to be successful, particularly in communities they may be unfamiliar with.
- The chapter exploring the changes under the Next Education Workforce initiative developed by Mary Lou Fulton Teachers College at Arizona State University (ASU), also highlights how changes in a practice architecture will affect the practices of individual teacher educators, depending on their role and contribution to the programme as a whole. Here the programme change orientated currently in the social-political and material-economic arrangements has yet to filter into all aspects of the cultural-discursive arrangements, and has the potential to privilege some ideas over others; the visibility of knowledge is key.
- And finally, examination of the practice arrangements, of the University of Auckland and its partners, shows how governance structures (attendant to teacher education and other university practices) can influence the practice architecture and affect the flow of ideas. This chapter also illustrates how dominant material-economic arrangements can be in a market-based activity.

Each of the quality conundrums outlined is different, but they share similar features. In particular, they all stem from an idea about focusing on an aspect of teacher education that will make it "better" in some way: through a focus on practice, research and alternative knowledges or through emphasising the experience of teacher educators or the institutional arrangements. The ideas themselves are often linked to coherent logic or evidence about what teachers need, and can be formulated in response to a perceived deficit in the current practice. The conundrum comes when this idea gets taken to a point where it becomes problematic or detrimental to quality. Such an imbalance can occur when it takes on additional power, such as when it gets adopted by an accountability regime, and as such can start to limit other activities or influences and so limit the flow of alternative ideas.

The concept of a quality conundrum is grounded in Harvey's distinction between standards, quality assurance and quality (2007). When an idea becomes part of the standards regime or a focus of quality assurance measures, then its transformative potential is reduced. This is not because the idea in itself changes, but the rationale and motivation for its use starts to change. For example, an institution placing more emphasis on practical experience because it addresses a need they have identified in their student teachers is very different to an institution doing this because it is mandated through a change in accreditation requirements. This distinction is at the heart of a discussion about quality, and the difference between adaptations made through authoritative and informed expertise and compliance. A really high-quality programme will seek to make adjustments because it improves its transformative potential.

In each example outlined, there is both a time and space relationship between practices and how they respond to changes, emerging from various institutions with their attendant traditions. The examples reveal how the teacher educators, through adapting their practices account for these changes, can seek to ameliorate any negative impacts and seek to maximise the quality of the learning experience. In other words, they constitute live examples of how teacher educators have sought to handle a quality conundrum to ensure that their programmes continue to be transformative for their students. Chapter 8 explores how they are able to do this within their spatial context. The remainder of this chapter draws together the trends across the universities studied to show how the practice arrangements affect different aspects of the programmes and the teacher educators' capacity to make change happen.

Curriculum, pedagogy and assessment

Planning any educational programme requires consideration of what Bernstein described as the three message systems of education: curriculum, pedagogy and assessment. With teacher education, this is further complicated by the role of practice, research and knowledge in the formation of new teachers, and what is necessary to transform a layperson into a new teacher. This requires what Mary Kennedy (2015) has called the parsing of practice: consideration of the best ways to organise and structure the necessary learning experiences.

Darling-Hammond and colleagues have identified the key components of highly successful teacher education programmes (see Chapter 1). In the universities I visited, due consideration was given to how each programme reflected these elements, in order to create opportunities for student teachers to learn. The process of developing and designing these programmes were often extremely complicated: involving consultation with a number of stakeholders and a deep understanding of legislative and regulatory infrastructure pertinent to each context. As an indicative list, teacher educators discussed having to consider:

- Entry requirements to the programme, and in particular, access to modules and units to other students outside teacher education;
- Timetabling requirements, including access to suitable classrooms such as laboratory or gymnasium space and access issues for international and part-time students;

- Scheduling requirements for practicum and preferences of partnership schools and school districts/boards as well as university schedules;
- Assessment scheduling and limitations on the timing of assessments relative to periods of practicum;
- Availability and expertise of individual staff; and
- Meaningful engagement with community groups and partnerships.

In nearly all cases these considerations required problem-solving and compromise. Typically, the pattern was that teacher educators would need to compromise their approach or their pedagogy in order to fit in with technical or operational requirements. This sometimes would mean that alternative and additional support mechanisms would need to be put in place, often unrecognised by the formal institutional structures. For example, in one university, the teacher educators felt the new programme arrangements did not offer sufficient in-practicum support, and so provided this informally and unofficially to their students, often in the evenings and on weekends.

A significant disruptor was the need to segment the programme in order for it to fit with modularisation. In all the universities studied, the programme of teacher education was divided into modules, units or courses (hitherto referred to as modules). Sometimes these modules would include the practicum component, sometimes practicums were assessed externally to the taught elements. Where the award was at a recognised level, such as at Bachelors or Masters level, so the assessments had to fulfil other requirements, such as knowledge of the literature, application of theory to practice and critical engagement. The formation of modules was essential to university infrastructures and fed into other programme arrangements around timetabling, student assessment and progression and staff workload. Each programme "parsed" the programme into components which were subsequently assessed individually. Units, modules and courses were not of an equal size between the institutions, nor were they divided up in the same way: some through subject or phase specialism, some through specialist themes. Some identified topics such as educating Indigenous communities as discrete topics, for others they were themes that ran through other courses. Some elements of the programme were optional or electives. In some cases, a specific module route was prescribed, and in others, modules could be selected or studied in any order. The programme compartmentalisation had to comply with university infrastructures often not designed for ITE: unit size, number of credit hours and so forth. In addition, in some cases, accreditation requirements outlined minimum requirements for taught or practical components, including their duration and scheduling. These arrangements happened in the intersubjective space between the material economic arrangements and the cultural discursive: between the stated intentions of the programme and the university requirements to which they are beholden. A good example of this would be the Mahi Tahi days described in Chapter 6, which were limited due to the non-standard way they aligned with university timetabling scheduling and workload monitoring, and required special dispensation. Similarly, the scheduling of the taught units alongside the practicum experience at QUT raised some concerns about how reflection, the main pedagogical approach of the programme, could be enacted successfully. These logistical arrangements can have very real effects on the learning on a programme.

There were two programmes that appeared to have more flexibility than others. As the IOE's PGCE programmes were designed before the IOE merged with University College London, the attendant structure of long-thin modules was only very loosely connected to specific assessment pieces, allowing the programmes to reflect a holistic view of learning to teach, characterised through a gradual immersion approach based on a spiral curriculum, deepening knowledge as the student teacher's experience grew (see Chapter 2). Similarly at OISE, the development of site-based cohort groups were seen as a way of offering a unified structure, facilitated by a group of teacher educators assigned to each cohort, sharing the teaching of their courses (modules). This creates an opportunity for greater coherence between modules and a more coherent learning experience for the student teachers.

Where taught elements were scheduled as discrete modules, there were concerns about how scheduling of those courses would allow student teachers to progress and deepen their understanding and make connections between them. For example, I asked where in the taught programme students teachers were taught how to plan a lesson; in some cases, this occurred through a generic placement module, through a generic pedagogy module, a subject- or phase-specific module or through a particular thematic emphasis (such as part of a module on teaching phonics). In each case, teacher educators reflected that there may be some repetition in how planning a lesson was taught, some contradictory advice and some frustration when schools and students reported that student teachers were confused and did not know how to plan a lesson! In some cases, where scheduling of modules was undertaken through a centralised university department, the teaching of lesson planning could come after practicum experiences or scheduled towards the end of the programme (although when this did happen, teacher educators campaigned heavily to prevent it).

The curriculum and pedagogical implications of these logistical concerns are significant. Teacher educators highlighted how the content of a taught session needs to be amended when teaching a specialist group of teachers with a focus on a particular subject or age group, or when teaching a large cohort covering various specialisms. Modules and programmes were continually being adapted to ensure that student teachers got the right content at the right time in relation to their development; but these were often less than optimal, and teacher educators reflected that they felt the student experience and learning opportunities suffered as a result.

These concerns were also reflected in assessment regimes, where logistical arrangements often left teacher educators to think creatively about where and how practice was assessed and by whom. This programme planning required teacher educators to consider the attendant assumptions of the relationship between the taught elements of the programme and proficiency in practicum (as discussed in Chapter 6). Assessment becomes a strong driver as to what is prioritised, particularly for those being assessed – students will focus their attention on where they will be judged. However, teacher educators also discussed the challenge of how to ensure all the components of the teacher Standards were aligned with the assessment requirements for a Bachelors or Masters degree or the award of a certificate. As a holistic integrated activity, dividing up teaching into elements can feel artificial and can lead to inauthentic assessment practices, such as generating assignments for fictional classes, creating imaginative reflections on practice that did not actually occur. In the case of New Zealand, where the accreditation regime emphasises outputs over inputs, the design of assessment pieces became central to programme planning.

Parsing content into modules, units or courses can create artificial divisions. For example, if we focus on planning in one area, curriculum content in another and assessment elsewhere, then, as one programme leader suggested to me, "it is the students that need to make the programme coherent" as they seek to bring together these seemingly separate entities. In the act of teaching, teachers do not compartmentalise their actions ("now I'm doing curriculum, now I'm doing pedagogy") but think holistically about their interactions with students, making what Orchard and Winch (2015) have called situational judgements. Compartmentalising aspects of the teaching knowledge base can detract from student teachers being able to integrate theory and practice. This acts as a barrier to their learning, as it can hamper progression in their understanding and also creates an unnecessary barrier between the taught components of the course (artificially divided into chunks) and the practical experience.

This issue has been discussed by Biesta (2019) in his argument for the importance of a spiral curriculum in teacher education. Biesta argues that teaching is about communication and interpretation that always requires judgement about "what" and "what for", and as such a spiral curriculum would enable students to "encounter the 'essence' of the practice of education" so that their understanding deepens as they gain more experience. He deliberately places such an approach as counter to compartmentalising teaching into chunks that "starts with the practical and factual and brings normative judgement in at a later stage". Biesta argues that such compartmentalisation is part of the age of measurement, which redefines teaching:

> in terms of input-output logic of interventions and effects which is not just influencing the practice of teaching but also seems to be key in contemporary efforts to make teaching evidence-based or evidence informed.
> *(Ibid., p. 269)*

The parsing of practice into artificial divisions between curriculum, pedagogy and assessment is not how most of the teacher educators I spoke to wanted their courses to be structured, but were necessitated through needing to comply with university and regulatory frameworks: to fit in with the material economic arrangements of the university infrastructure, and to ensure compliance with the list of content sometimes prescribed to be "covered" in teacher education programmes or assessed through a range of Standards. This is not to say that teacher educators felt that important areas should not be covered, but that they needed to be *seen to be covered*. In other words, the performance of teacher education needed to be made visible for accountability requirements. Such aspects of performativity have been widely recognised, and analysed through Foucauldian ideas elsewhere in the education system (Ball, 2003; Ball, Maguire, & Braun, 2012; Perryman, 2006), and results in what Ball (2003) has called an opacity rather than transparency. Ironically, rather than supporting student teachers to develop their own understanding of teaching, making the programme coherent through their own understanding, the teacher educators often reflected that the programme structure arrangements can stand in the way of generating a flow of ideas, making it challenging for such understanding to occur.

Partnerships

Partnerships are central to the work of teacher education, and a persistent concern as teacher educators try to work out the best way for schools and universities to work together in ITE. Much of the literature argues for a less hierarchical partnership arrangement, recognising schools as more than a site of practice, but as an equal partner in the provision of teacher education. Such proclamations are difficult to enact. Educational institutions are hierarchical by nature (Labaree, 2006), and the work of universities (being more research-orientated and abstract) can be seen as having higher status compared to the practice of teaching that happens in schools (Bullough Jr., 2014). Conversely, being grounded in practice is often seen as more relevant to the practice of learning to teach than abstract or theoretical knowledge. As such, much of the literature suggests that teacher education should be focussed on collaborative partnerships, but as Smith, Brisard and Menter (2007) suggest, most ITE partnerships are not of this collaborative nature, as there are a number of barriers to the formation of such partnerships, including conflicting policy environments for both schools and universities. In the site visits, I was able to witness a range of different partnership formations, made possible through different funding models, and levels of accountability for involvement in teacher education and universities afforded directly to schools. For example, in the case of schools in Queensland and the Normal Schools in New Zealand, schools have a vested interest in being involved in ITE and are remunerated directly for it. In Arizona, involvement in teacher education was seen as a key strategy to ensure future teachers for school districts. Where teacher education is not part of the accountability or financial regime for schools, then partnering in teacher education may not be a priority for individual schools.

During my site visits, I noted several initiatives developed to build and sustain productive ITE partnerships. In some cases, these were included in programme validation and accreditation requirements, such as outlined in Chapter 6, in terms of developing authentic partnerships and engaging community groups. Moreover, considerable effort goes into working with school partners to consider the sorts of support that new teachers need as they enter the profession. However, within this work there are tensions in all three aspects of the arrangements:

- Concerns around how schools are remunerated for the additional work that placements entail – the material-economic arrangements;
- Differences in perceptions between schools and universities as to what is required within teacher education – the cultural-discursive arrangements; and
- Differences between who holds the power within teacher education, particularly in relation to entry to the profession, and the distribution of (potential) new teachers in areas of need – the social-political arrangements.

In the preceding chapters, we have seen how these tensions play out in the resolution of the quality conundrums. In New Zealand, Normal Schools are paid directly by central funding for the teacher education work they undertake. In Queensland, my site visit coincided with a renegotiation with teacher unions about the direct payment to teachers for student teacher supervision. The form of renumeration, whether it comes out of programme fees or central funding and whether it goes directly to the school, teacher or is overseen by the School Board or District, has implications for the financial viability of teacher education as an activity within the university and also for the participation of schools.

Similarly, there can be a tension between universities and their partners as to what should be privileged in teacher education: the benefit of experience gained on practicum, the development of transferable skills and the relevance of theoretical or academic knowledge. In several sites, teacher educators I spoke to emphasised how practice was central to learning to teach, and many of the schools I visited declared how important they felt the university's contribution and expertise was. However, there were also tensions expressed: teacher educators being out of touch with the rapid pace of change in schools, a disconnect between theory and practice and a tension between what student teachers needed and what the course provided. These tensions were often located within the cultural discursive arrangements: different perceptions of what being a teacher meant, what was important and what was being prioritised.

However, it was in the social-political arrangements that the challenges to partnership seemed to be the most difficult. In many cases, the responsibility, and so the liability, of teacher education was held by the university. Whilst schools were partners, there was little long-term impact for them if their participation was weak (perhaps other than recruitment of future teachers). Schools wanted to be fully consulted and involved, and in some incidences were fully integrated into accreditation panels. However, in some cases, schools were distant from the challenges facing universities and unaware of why changes were being made. For example, as partnerships reviewed arrangements around placements and practicums, school preferences for timing and duration might not fit in with university schedules or the needs of a changing student population (including a shift to part-time students and career changers). In some cases, such as with ASU, changes have been made which are in line with the needs of schools as well as the university. In the Next Education Workforce initiative, practicum is undertaken as a year-long internship where the student teachers become part of the school district (sometimes as employees). In other places, where student teachers are career changers, placements blocks are four-week-long intensive and targeted placements. These decisions have been attributed to a variety of factors: the demographics of the student teachers (can they devote time and resources for an unpaid practicum?); regulatory frameworks; ability and capacity of schools to host; and cost to universities that pay for placements. However, the responsibility for the quality of the experience that ensues is often beholden specifically by the university alone.

Universities are consistently in favour of strong partnerships but recognise that they are challenging to sustain. They recognise that schools are dynamic places: that experience changes with personnel shifts; that legislation and priorities changes; and that there may be a difference between what schools say they want and in their practice. In addition, because of other pressing demands and needs, schools may not be able to fully commit to the ITE partnership. Partnership development work is also extremely time-consuming but does not sit well within university governance and reward structures. Partnership development work is not accounted for in academic promotion criteria, it does not contribute to academic standing or module evaluations and can detract from other work that academics are expected to do. If partnership work is not part of the quality/standards criteria of a university, then it often goes unnoticed and unrewarded.

In response to this, some institutions have introduced specialist partnership workers. These (often non-academic) teacher educators can focus specifically on partnership development. But unless they are fully integrated into the other aspects of the programme, it can create a gap in programme provision, where partnership is seen as outside of the learning experience rather than central to it. OISE has worked hard to ensure that this doesn't happen through their investment and integration of casualised staff. Other places like the IOE have created structures to ensure that partnership work is incorporated into the academic work of the teacher educators. But none of these are ideal solutions.

Accountability and oversight

An increasing part of the ITE landscape is the prevalence of accountability and oversight. Every site I visited was responding to changes in accountability either at a university or teacher education level, and sometimes both. This is not to suggest that all accountability measures are the same. Often introduced as part of a rhetoric of driving up standards (Ingvarson, 2019; Ingvarson et al., 2014), accreditation and validation requirements are a policy technology (Ball, 2003) that may seem benign but that can affect a change to practices. The Foucauldian concepts of performativity and subjectivity are important here, as accreditation often requires the laying out of certain practices for judgement: teacher educators described ensuring the visibility of certain aspects of their programme as a process of performativity, inviting judgement against a set of indicators, particularly when preparing documentation for scrutiny for programme accreditation or validation. Whether accountability comes from professional bodies or government agencies, the requirement to fulfil certain obligations necessitates a narrative of compliance. This narrative foregrounds those practices which are deemed desirable and renders others invisible. As such, the technologies of accountability and oversight affect what and how teacher education is enacted: they limit and constrain practices.

As part of the Education Complex, teacher education is also part of a landscape of accountability practices, including those pertaining to universities and to schools. This makes up what Ling (2017) has called a landscape of supercomplexity with multiple stakeholders, beholden to different accountability regimes. The role of accountability within the practice architecture is significant: the influence is predominantly in the social-political arrangements as accountability regimes hold the power of accreditation, validation and, in the case of inspections, can award prestige in the field. Within universities, accountability can also affect the material-economic arrangements as funds are made available or withheld for certain developments. But more pervasively, accountability regimes may also affect the cultural-discursive arrangements through dominating the professional language that dominates teacher education and that holds and retains power within the "elite" (see, for example, the term "authentic partnerships" outlined in Chapter 6 and the discussion in Chapter 4). When accountability is introduced, there is an assumption that it then becomes the benchmark: it becomes what teacher education is seeking to achieve and so closes down discussion, innovation, debate and alternative viewpoints. As Sleeter (2019) argues, it sustains the status quo of who holds power and who is able to define quality.

In this sense, accountability has the effect of instrumentalising practice: to parse it down so that it can be rebuilt in the novice incrementally and ticked off once it has been achieved. This is not the language or practice of transformation. But it is the reality of teacher education today in many countries. It is not the case that accountability takes away criticality, but reduces the opportunity for it to occur productively, and so could have the effect of reducing teacher education to replication rather than transformation.

Teacher educators

In Chapter 5, I discussed how changes to the teacher education provision can affect the roles and responsibilities of teacher educators. The challenges outlined by Ellis and McNicholl (2015) about the constitution of teacher education as academic work were echoed in each location, albeit with a slightly different expression. Ultimately the challenge is for a teacher educator to be (regarded as) a productive member of the academic community as well as having credibility in the professional (i.e., school-based) community. This is reflected in Yuan and Yang's (2020) research, which notes that teacher educators need to cross both horizontal and hierarchical boundaries. Horizontal boundaries were those with relatively equal power, enabling an exchange between equal partners (university and school-based teacher educators for instance). Hierarchical boundaries were more structured, such as within the university itself with different affordances given to research and teaching.

In nearly all the sites visited, teacher educator roles were differentiated into specialist areas of expertise, and those that undertake partnership or supervisory roles with schools. In other words, there were hierarchical arrangements put in place between university-based teacher educators. Those teacher educators with less power tended to focus on the partnership arrangement, undertaking the horizontal boundary crossing. For example, at both the IOE and OISE, teacher educators were expected to undertake the full range of duties (teaching, site visits etc.) alongside undertaking research. In both cases, however, this was not always possible. At OISE, faculty members who have taken up leadership positions had a lower teaching load, leaving course and site visits to sessional staff. At IOE, some teacher educators were being offered teaching-only contracts, removing the research expectation within their roles. At QUT, university partners were introduced to support partnership work, and in both QUT and University of Auckland, there were examples of teacher educators letting their certification slide, making them ineligible to undertake school visits.

Changes to the work of teacher educators have to be reflected in other parts of the system: where responsibilities are taken away from one group, they need to be picked up by another. For example, Chapter 5 outlined how the changing roles of the site leads and lead teachers were being negotiated under the new teaming model of teaching practice at ASU. In QUT, there was a growing sense of increasing the responsibility of schools across the partnership, accompanied by a shift to Professional Learning Conversations as a way of linking this school experience to the overall programme approach around reflection on practice. The role of a teacher educator is dynamic.

Central to all of this is an erosion of the status proffered to teacher educators. This is replicated in the responsibilities and titles they were given. At ASU, the site and regional leads were "clinical faculty". The taught courses around specialist content were taught predominantly by tenured faculty (clinical faculty were required to teach one or two taught courses). Several teacher educators highlighted to me the casualised nature of clinical faculty contracts, and how tenured faculty were less easily incorporated into reform initiatives. The contractual status of teacher educators is important for their continuity, development and the desirability of the role, but also for their status both within and without the university. The status of teacher educators can also affect the practice of teacher education: their capacity to act, adapt, change and ultimately to take action to ensure that transformation in their student teachers can occur.

The division between academic and supervisory work on teacher education programmes exacerbates the theory/practice divide across ITE. It divides the accountability responsibility for the assessment of practical teaching to a lower hierarchy of staff, allowing more experienced tenured academic staff to focus on research and administrative duties. However, many university-based teacher educators are keen to do this, questioning the value of undertaking school visits for their own career trajectory. Undertaking school visits is time-consuming. Cultivating school partnerships is time-consuming. The benefit of these activities are for the student teachers but not necessarily for the university or the teacher educators, unless this is recognised through accountability, governance and promotion criteria – and it often isn't. However, having been away from schools as a practicing teacher can also mean that teacher educators can easily become out-of-date with the practices in schools. This was particularly commented on by both student teachers and school-based staff in some of the sites I visited. This is not to say that the specific expertise of university-based teacher educators was not valued, but that there was a disconnect between how their expertise was developing and whether they undertook school visits.

However, it was also widely recognised that if teacher educators did not visit their student teachers on practicum, this could generate a gap between theory and practice, both in the experience of student teachers but also in the way that programmes were configured. At QUT, the teacher educators recognised that not being able to observe their student teachers teach affected how well they knew their students and also affected how well they could assess the impact of their own teaching. In terms of transformation, these practice arrangements made it difficult for them to fully understand how transformation was taking place – or indeed if it was.

Creating the conditions for transformation

Across and between these different practice arrangements, a number of themes are pertinent. One significant challenge is the power afforded by accountability structures. These do not just have the power to change practice arrangements, as programmes seek to comply with what is required, but also to obscure practice arrangements. The rhetoric of a programme may be adapted to match key words within a framework, whilst the practice itself may not be adapted. This was the case with one programme, where it was commented to me that following re-accreditation, some teacher educators where "slipping back" into previous ways of doing things. In addition, there can often be a tension between the stated visions and values of a programme with the infrastructure it has to adopt. This can be the case with issues around parsing the programme into modules or timetabling constraints which prevent teacher educators from making the connections they wish (particularly between theory and practice). These infrastructural constraints can lead to a lack of authenticity in some programmes: for example, deliberate practice conducted in artificial environments with peers role-playing at being students; assessment that orientates itself to a scheme of work for a fictional class; or taught lessons discussing the implementation of an approach with a fictional school/class. These activities were described by teacher educators as being less-than-satisfactory for the learning experience, but a necessary modification when faced with constraints in the practice arrangements of the programme (particularly within the material economic sphere).

There are similar concerns when practices need to be adapted due to challenges presented by the large scale of a programme. For example, the lack of availability for suitable placements, or the reassurances given to students about maximum travel times can affect the provision of suitable practicum experiences. Teacher educators also discussed modules which spanned different programmes (such as combining early years, primary and secondary student teachers) that had to compromise on both content and specificity in order to cater for the expanded audience, or that pedagogical approaches, particularly when teaching about anti-racist approaches, needed to be compromised through class sizes and the lack of small group interactions. These developments were often attributed to constraints imposed through limitations in the material-economic arrangements which had then a knock-on effect in how the programme was taught.

Finally, with the number of partners involved in teacher education, a significant concern was in the variety of values held. It was not always possible to develop coherence across the programme in relation to what they were seeking to achieve – particularly if, for example, schools privileged practice over research or downplayed the university contribution to the programme. The teacher educators suggested that this dissonance in the cultural-discursive arrangements had a knock-on effect in the overall effectiveness of the programme.

In most of these examples, we see a tension between the philosophical and the operational: a challenge between what teacher educators wanted to achieve and what was possible within the resource and legislative constraints operating in their context. The process of being involved in teacher education appeared to be a continual process of compromise between these elements to seek to ameliorate negative influences and maximise the experiences available.

In Edwards-Groves and Grootenboer's (2015) research, they note that practices are often connected directly to site-based concerns, which can result in tensions between how decisions are derived as compromises are made between what is desirable and what is possible. In other words, these tensions are not unique to teacher education, but are, I would argue, exacerbated in teacher education due to the complexity of the activity and the number of stakeholders and partners involved. Across a range of partners, there can be tensions between the moral and technical dimensions of practices and different interpretations of what the practice is seeking to achieve. To use Hordern's terminology, practices have to be *educational* in their intent as well as in the content. Therefore, for the execution of the practice of teacher education to be considered educational, it has to be more than technical but also connected to site- and situation-specific judgements. As Edwards-Groves and Grootenboer (2015) argue:

> many practice situations demand moral-ethical judgment and creative problem solving, rendering reliance on prescribed procedures or rule-following action inappropriate or deprofessionalising by succumbing to regimes of performativity and managerialism.

It is the responsibility of teacher educators to ensure that their practice lives up to this challenge, particularly as they adapt to changing accountability structures and requirements as well as traditions and expectations. Having an understanding of these localised influences are key, as we shall see in the next chapter.

References

Ball, S. J. (2003). The teacher's soul and the terrors of performativity. *Journal of Education Policy*, 18(2), 215–228. doi:10.1080/0268093022000043065

Ball, S. J., Maguire, M., & Braun, A. (2012). *How schools do policy: Policy enactments in secondary schools*. London: Routledge.

Biesta, G. (2019). Reclaiming teaching for teacher education: Towards a spiral curriculum. *Beijing International Review of Education*, 1(2–3), 259–272. doi:10.1163/25902539-00102015

Bullough Jr., R. V. (2014). Toward reconstructing the narrative of teacher education. *Journal of Teacher Education*, 65(3), 185–194. doi:10.1177/0022487113519131

Cochran-Smith, M. (2003). The unforgiving complexity of teaching. *Journal of Teacher Education*, 54(1), 3–5. doi:10.1177/0022487102238653

Cochran-Smith, M., Ell, F., Grudnoff, L., Haigh, M., Hill, M., & Ludlow, L. (2016). Initial teacher education: What does it take to put equity at the center? *Teaching and Teacher Education*, 57, 67–78. doi:10.1016/j.tate.2016.03.006

Edwards-Groves, C. (2018). The practice architectures of pedagogy: Conceptualising the convergences between sociality, dialogue, ontology and temporality in teaching practices. In O. B. Cavero & N. Llevot-Calvet (Eds.), *New pedagogical challenges in the 21st century – contributions of research in education*. London: IntechOpen.

Edwards-Groves, C., & Grootenboer, P. (2015). Praxis and the theory of practice architectures: Resources for re-envisioning English education. *Australian Journal of Language and Literacy*, 38(3), 150–161.

Ellis, V., & McNicholl, J. (2015). *Transforming teacher education: Reconfiguring the academic work*. London: Bloomsbury Publishing.

Grudnoff, L., Haigh, M., Hill, M., Cochran-Smith, M., Ell, F., & Ludlow, L. (2017). Teaching for equity: Insights from international evidence with implications for a teacher education curriculum. *The Curriculum Journal*, 28(3), 305–326. doi:10.1080/09585176.2017.1292934

Habermas, J. (1987). *The philosophical discourse of modernity* (trans. Lawrence, F.). Cambridge, MA: MIT Press.

Harvey, L. (2007). The epistemology of quality. *Perspectives in Education*, 25(3), 1–13.

Hordern, J. (2020). Why close to practice is not enough: Neglecting practice in educational research. *British Educational Research Journal*. doi:10.1002/berj.3622

Ingvarson, L. (2019). Teaching standards and the promotion of quality teaching. *European Journal of Education, 54*(3), 337–355. doi:10.1111/ejed.12353

Ingvarson, L., Reid, K., Buckley, S., Kleinhenz, E., Masters, G., & Rowley, G. (2014). *Best practice teacher education programs and Australia's own programs*. Canberra: Department of Education.

Kemmis, S., & Mahon, K. (2017). Coming to 'practice architectures': A genealogy of the theory. In *Exploring Education and Professional Practice* (pp. 219–238). Singapore: Springer.

Kemmis, S., Wilkinson, J., Edwards-Groves, C., Hardy, I., Grootenboer, P., & Bristol, L. (2014). *Changing practices, changing education*. Bristol: Springer Science & Business Media.

Kennedy, M. (2015). Parsing the practice of teaching. *Journal of Teacher Education, 67*(1), 6–17. doi:10.1177/0022487115614617

Labaree, D. F. (2006). *The trouble with ED schools*. New Haven, CT: Yale University Press.

Lave, J., & Wenger, E. (1991). *Situated learning: Legitimate peripheral participation*. Cambridge: Cambridge University Press.

Ling, L. M. (2017). Australian teacher education: Inside-out, outside-in, backwards and forwards? *European Journal of Teacher Education, 40*(5), 561–571. doi:10.1080/02619768.2017.1385599

Mayer, D., Allard, A., Bates, R., Dixon, M., Doecke, B., Kline, J., ... White, S. (2015). *Studying the effectiveness of teacher education*. Singapore: Springer.

Orchard, J., & Winch, C. (2015). *What training do teachers need? Why theory is necessary to good teaching*. Salisbury: PESGB.

Perryman, J. (2006). Panoptic performativity and school inspection regimes: Disciplinary mechanisms and life under special measures. *Journal of Education Policy, 21*(2), 147–161. doi:10.1080/02680930500500138

Schatzki, T.R. (2012). A primer on practices. In J. Higgs, R. Barnett, S. Billett, M. Hutchings, & F. Trede (Eds.), *Practice based education* (pp. 13–36). Rotterdam: Sense Publishers.

Sleeter, C. (2019). Considering core assumptions about what it means to teach. *Teachers College Record, 121*, 1–4.

Smith, I., Brisard, E., & Menter, I. (2007). Models of partnership developments in initial teacher education in the four components of the United Kingdom: Recent trends and current challenges. *Journal of Education for Teaching, 32*(2), 147–164. doi:10.1080/02607470600655136

Wenger, E. (1998). *Communities of practice: Learning, meaning, and identity* (Vol. 15). Cambridge: Cambridge University Press.

Wyse, D. (2020). Presidential address: The academic discipline of education. Reciprocal relationships between practical knowledge and academic knowledge. *British Educational Research Journal, 46*(1), 6–25. doi:10.1002/berj.3597

Wyse, D., Brown, C., Oliver, S., & Poblete, X. (2020). Education research and educational practice: The qualities of a close relationship. *British Educational Research Journal*. doi:10.1002/berj.3626

Yuan, R., & Yang, M. (2020). Understanding university-based teacher educators' boundary crossing experiences: voices from Hong Kong. *Teachers and Teaching*, 1–21. doi:10.1080/13540602.2020.1777961

8
THE CONTEXTS FOR TRANSFORMATION THROUGH A SPATIAL LENS

To deepen our understanding of how universities "do" teacher education, it is important to explore the significance of their locations. So far, we have seen how the practice arrangements pertaining to teacher education can enable or constrain practices, and how teacher educators negotiate site-based practice architectures as they seek to address a range of quality conundrums. In each case, unique locational factors underpin both how the quality conundrum is understood and the context in which it is being addressed. This observation ties in with the theory of practice and practice architectures which notes the significance of site-ontologies: teacher education happens, and it happens in a range of sites. But this is not to suggest that location is a determinant of practice: contexts do not necessitate how teacher education should be, but make up a range of spatial factors which can act as drivers to influence how teacher education gets played out in specific locations.

Signalling the importance of the spatial context to teacher education is not new but is often under-theorised. Many research accounts of innovation in practice will note the peculiarities of a particular context, but often refer to context in a simplistic or a-spatial way: lacking a serious engagement with how space is conceptualised and how the different conceptualisations of space can influence action, or how space can influence the production and reproduction of inequalities. Initial teacher education (ITE) is fundamentally a spatial practice: operating in different physical locations under the supervision of various organisations who are working in partnership. Context therefore involves the complexity of those specific locations, the way they interact with each other and the implied and actual hierarchies involved and the different degrees of importance and meaning they attach to the practice-based activity of ITE. The categorisation of the spatial into the triad adopted by Lefebvre (1991) and Harvey (2004) can open up the significance of these contexts so that they are seen both in relation to their physical location, their relative status within the hierarchy of other organisations, and their representational nature in how they replicate ideas of the "good" teacher and the purpose of education; in other words, to see context through the lens of spatial theory.

Taken alongside the theory of practice and practice architectures, spatial theory provides a robust theoretical lens to explore both the micro and macro dimensions of ITE practice within universities, attending to their specific contexts. Taken together, these two theoretical approaches help to open up the space and the practice of ITE, and as such provide a way of examining the contexts for transformation: how the flow of ideas can be enabled or constrained through teacher education pedagogy.

Spatial dimensions

An emphasis on the spatial is particularly important for teacher education as it takes place in a variety of settings, such as universities and schools, each with different spatial reach. Individual settings do not exist in isolation but are situated within national policies contexts and global debates. They have their own networks and internal structures. In addition, they affect individuals at a local scale: through their personal experience. As the production and reproduction of inequalities occurs in space, it is important to understand the spatial dimensions of the various scales at which teacher education occurs.

The public debates and quality conundrums facing university-based teacher education are situated within these scalar perspectives: they are enacted locally but can be influenced by what happens nationally and globally through policies and trends. To analyse these relationships, spatial theory offers a way of understanding the relationship between space and scale and the practice of teacher education through:

- Understanding teacher education as a scaled activity which enables an exploration of how the size (or volume) of the practice can affect its (perceived) quality, and how the practice and perspectives on practice of teacher education in one location is related to that of other locations, including the personal (the scale of the body), the local, the national and the global; and
- Seeing teacher education as a practice that produces and reproduces space through the messages it communicates about education and the role of education in society and for the individual; these messages occur in both epistemological and ontological space through sites of practice and dominant discourses about teachers.

Teacher education and the production of space

Lefebvre (1991) argues that space matters: spatial practice mediates between production and reproduction, revealing both the conceptual and the representational, and in doing so perpetuates the flow of capital. Lefebvre acknowledges that education is not directly controlled by capital but is needed (and provided by governments) to support the flow of capital. Therefore, education, conceptualised as the flow of social, cultural and intellectual capital, can perpetuate uneven development, as more affluent communities have access to higher-quality education and disadvantaged communities are left with less-qualified teachers (Allen & Sims, 2018). Put in practical terms, the concerns of teacher education in, say, Auckland (the supply of teachers particularly to "low decile" schools) is as spatially and socially relevant as the concern to provide teachers to rural and remote schools across Queensland, or to the distribution of good teachers in high-performing systems in Ontario and London; the challenges in doing so however can be quite different. The spatial context influences how the "problems" for teacher education are defined and how the practice of teacher education needs to adapt accordingly. This is one of the reasons that quality in teacher education is such an elusive concept. A spatial practice like teacher education is influenced by several factors, including the socio-economic and academic background of the group of people who aspire to become teachers, the needs of the communities they serve and the priorities and policies of the governments and regulatory bodies that oversee the provision.

This is not the same argument as the popular position adopted in many national systems that teacher quality matters as the most significant variable in student achievement and in terms of global competitiveness. But it does acknowledge the significance of teacher education as part of the overall education infrastructure (the Education Complex to use Kemmis et al.'s, 2014, term). Teacher education is a practice that can produce and reproduce space and spatial inequalities through the messages it communicates about education and the role of education (both in society and for the individual). In this sense, teacher education happens in both epistemological and ontological space.

Adopting a Marxist analysis, Lefebvre (1991) and Harvey (2004) contend that space, how it is experienced, conceptualised and enacted, is key in how activities and inequalities (or to use Smith's (2010) phrase "uneven development") get produced, evolve and are sustained. Lefebvre draws upon a conceptual triad to support his critical examination of space. The three fundamental pillars of this triad are:

1 Spatial Practice – which embraces production and reproduction and the particular locations and spatial sets characteristics of each social formation. Spatial practice ensures continuity and to some degree cohesion. In terms of social space, and each member of a given society's relationship to space, this cohesion implies a guaranteed level of competence and specific level of performance;
2 Representations of space - which are tied to the relations of the production and to the 'order' which those relations impose, and hence to knowledge, to signs, to codes, and to 'frontal' relations;

3. Representational spaces - embodying complex symbolisms, sometimes coded, sometimes not, linked to the clandestine or underground of social life, as also to art (which may come eventually to be defined less as a code of space than a code of representational spaces).

(Lefebvre, 1991: 33).

The pillars are not intended to be viewed separately but as a relationship between the lived and conceived space. These pillars offer a way for the drivers that unpin the practice architectures, outlined in Chapter 7, to be understood. David Harvey has taken this further by exploring how practices move between these spaces, noting the distinction between actual space (as location), relative space (in how spaces relate to each other) and representational space (how ideas are represented spatially). Through critically exploring and seeking to understand the complexities of these spatial practices, Harvey argues we will be in a position to transform them.

There are many similarities between Harvey's and Lefebvre's conceptions of space (Harvey, 2001), and taken together they provide a useful framework for looking at spatial influences on teacher education through its:

- **Location within space**: Large-scale teacher education tends to happen in locations where there is a large demand for teachers and a large supply of potential teachers, such as in large cities. These locations have features in themselves (such as large diverse populations) which affect the nature of the teacher education provision. Teacher education must serve these local communities, as partner schools are a key part of the infrastructure of the provision.
- **Relative nature**: Large-scale teacher education is only defined as such in relation to the size of the other providers in the vicinity. A large-scale provider is proportionally bigger than others, but is also likely to have distinctive relations pertaining to its scale, such as with the individual, the local, the national, the regional and the global. Scale in this sense represents relative power or capacity to leverage, and closer access to national and global networks which are afforded to large-scale providers and may evade smaller providers. Conversely, the larger the scale of a provider, the less personal it may appear to be (the scale of the human) which can adversely affect perceptions of quality.
- **Representational nature**: Teacher education is dominated by images or conceptions of how both education and teacher education should be. All providers live within this representational space, including discourses around quality, standards and quality conundrums (as discussed in Chapter 1), but large providers are arguably more affected than most, both in their role in contributing to and shaping the discourse, and in bridging the distance between the representational and the lived experience of teacher education.

These three categories offer a way of thinking about the drivers and influences that affect how teacher education pedagogy and its capacity for transformation can produce and reproduce space and spatial inequalities.

Location matters

One could argue that as someone with a background in geography and geography education, it was inevitable that I saw location as a significant factor in each of the sites I visited. As a traveller, when faced with a new context, it is common to immediately compare what you have observed with what you are familiar with – how somewhere unfamiliar is different from home (De Botton, 2008). An outsider gaze can help to reveal implicit and tacit assumptions. In my data collection, I asked questions to understand why practices were enacted and arranged in the way they were. Sometimes this caused interviewees to reflect on their tacit practice traditions: things that were part of the legacy of a programme, the original reasons of which having got lost in the mists of time. Many of these reasons were related to the specific context of the programme and its historical legacy. In each location, there was a strong spatial narrative, which I have tried to summarise here:

- The UCL Institute of Education (IOE) has a tradition of providing teachers for London for over 100 years; there is respect and love for a dynamic, multicultural and demanding world city that permeates the service of providing teachers for that city;
- Auckland as a major urban hub takes on a leadership role for New Zealand's educational reform in both practical and representational terms: to support and actively promote equity, particularly for marginalised groups;
- Brisbane, as Queensland's major urban centre, has a responsibility to support rural and remote communities, a responsibility that goes to the heart of Queensland University of Technology's (QUT) teacher education and education-related research;
- As one of the US's fastest growing cities, Phoenix has to radically rethink how to supply teachers for its growing and diverse population; Arizona State University (ASU) is an innovative university: providing innovative teacher workforce solutions is part of ASU's DNA; and
- Ontario Institute for Studies in Education (OISE) is committed to research and teacher professionalism grounded in research within a context of diversity, high standards and deregulation; it is OISE's responsibility to ensure that teachers adopt a scholarly stance as they teach in Ontario and elsewhere.

These narratives incorporate how the institution seeks to respond to the challenges facing teacher education, particularly around recruitment, partnership, accountability and issues pertaining to curriculum, pedagogy and assessment, which can be found in all locations although variously expressed and experienced. The narratives influence how the teacher educators perceive the importance of the flow of ideas: which ideas need to be foregrounded and which are given high levels of visibility and are tied to the local problems of their specific location.

The differences between these locations are underpinned by a complex web of geographical/socio-economic factors: changing population demographics, economic developments, cultural traditions and changing social dynamics. These factors will continue to change as the cities and their regions change but also as the cities morph and populations change through time. No doubt the differential ways in which communities have been affected by the COVID-19 pandemic will also influence not just the cities where these universities are based, but also the education and teacher education landscapes that surround them.

However, the differences and similarities between these locations are more than the geographical factors. The localised demand for teachers will influence the teacher education programmes, particularly in terms of their ability to attract applicants that meet their entry requirements and who are able to devote sufficient time out of their lives for training. Several of the programmes I visited had lowered their entry requirements in order to attract more students; this was often in the face of a buoyant employment market, which either meant that suitable graduates had more career options or where increased opportunities through the so-called gig economy had meant that applicants that were looking for a flexible working environment had greater choice. Some universities had adapted their programme to cater for part-time students, or career changers who had other work or family-related commitments. The demand for teachers was also related to the perception of the value of academic award of these programmes. Where teachers were in high demand, there was less perceived need for a prestigious academic award, as certification would be sufficient to secure employment. Universities are also finding themselves operating within a competitive market: sometimes in competition for a limited pool of prospective students, and navigating more sophisticated marketing strategies from competitors. This notion of competition could also be applied to a lesser extent to securing school placements for student teachers. These factors were all determined by local conditions.

However, in each location, there were also a range of practice traditions which were influential. In some cases, these practice traditions were formalised through organisational structures; a good example would be the funding of Normal Schools in New Zealand, as a complementary partner to the university teacher education programmes. Partnership traditions, including expectations around payment, roles and responsibilities, are influential in how a university could structure its programme. However, there were also more implicit practice traditions, which also influenced who sought to become a teacher educator, their expectations of the role and how they perceived the relationship between their academic roles and duties and still being connected to the school community. Practice traditions were also strongly linked to a programme's local reputation and values, in which aspects of teacher education were privileged.

These practice traditions were influential in shaping the teacher education programmes: they made up a cultural and material environment that was difficult to change, as it was embedded in perceptions and expectations of all of the stakeholders. These traditions were useful in many ways, as they set a baseline of understandings from which partnerships could work together and detailed problems could be worked through across the partnership. However, they could also be restrictive: blocking out alternative or innovative approaches, particularly when these require changes to the teacher education infrastructure which were beyond the control of the university.

Location then does not just set the spatial context for practice, but also is key in the temporal context, as teacher education programmes generate practice traditions which are location-specific and can be enduring. However, cities are dynamic, and the services they require need to be similarly dynamic in order to continue to cater for their changing needs. Teacher educators need to be attuned to what those changing needs are: how the city and its catchment area is changing, how those changes will affect education and what teacher education needs to do to respond. They also need to consider how those changes will align with their practice traditions and the problems this may cause.

Relative space

Whilst the local context is important, teacher education is also influenced by what happens at a number of other scales. The previous section commented on the changing demographics of student teachers. The smallest spatial scale is that of the individual. How a programme is experienced by individuals is particularly significant for those individuals and can make up part of a programme's reputation. As the student profile changes, so programmes need to take into account how this might change the way the programme is experienced. There are, of course, a number of other scales that will affect practices. Teacher educators are beholden to national and regional accountability regimes and governance structures, which, in turn, are often influenced by global trends and the prevalence of policy borrowing or policy lending. Mayer (2017) has argued that the Global Education Reform Movement (as termed by Sahlberg, 2010) has resulted in a limited range of policies which have dominated national teacher education policies. Advisory reports provided for governments often survey the policy context of other nations/region in order to make recommendations for future teacher education policy directions. For example, Ingvarson (2014) and colleagues (2019) specifically advises that increasing the role of Teacher Standards is an international benchmark of quality. A common problem with policy borrowing is that it fails to take into account the locational complexity and the influential practice traditions outlined in the section above. However, there is substantial power and authority afforded to an approach that cites international standards as it denotes a form of benchmarking, creating a discourse of comparability that creates a demand for action and replication. It is no surprise then that construction of ITE as a policy problem and the policies designed to resolve that problem are similar in many contexts.

However, the policy context is not the only place where relative space can be seen. Universities are also part of a global industry, with their own ranking, league tables and forms of prestige. Highly ranked universities often use this status as part of their marketing and public image. As indicated in Chapter 1, the quality of an institution (according to its ranking) was included in the selection criteria of this research. Different ranking systems draw upon different criteria, and many of the ranking systems around university quality do not relate directly to the quality of the teaching or to teacher education. For example, the US News ranking methodology includes assessments from peers and educational professionals as well as the qualities of enrolled students, the faculty resources and the research activity. The QS World Rankings focuses on both academic and employer reputation, numbers of international faculty and students as well as the faculty to student ratio and citations ration. In other words, there are no metrics directly related to the transformative effect of teaching. However, universities are concerned with maintaining status and ensuring their reputation for quality continues, and this does influence how a university may value teacher education. Teacher education is not a high-status field in most universities (Labaree, 2006), and in some contexts, teacher educators have been subjected to changes in contracts limiting their opportunity for secure employment and to undertake research. There is also a growing divide between teacher educators who research and those who teach and undertake school visits. This does not just affect the relative status of teacher educators within their own institutions but across the intellectual field. Vanassche and Kelchtermans (2015) have noted the growth of research identified as self-study as a way of addressing these issues, but also recognise that this is also a lower status of research engagement.

Teacher education also crosses boundaries of research space. ITE is sometimes considered a practice field, where scholarly inquiry can be inspired or rooted in practice and can yield insights which inform and deepen our understanding of that practice. Within such a scenario, there would appear to be an opportunity for practitioner research to make a contribution to the wider field. However, it is rarely able to make this contribution, and when practice-orientated fields lack prestige through their claim to philosophical and or theoretical knowledge, so practitioner research is likely to be regarded as even less able to make a contribution.

Relative space, then, is not just about the scale and reach of different policy contexts, but also to do with status and prestige. When a field experiences a reduction in status, so other professions can seek to replace its function (Abbott, 1988). Grossman (2008) warned of this happening to teacher education, and it can be seen with the rise of new Graduate Schools of Education (Cochran-Smith et al., 2020) and alternative programmes such as Teach First and Teach for America and other parts of the Teach for All movement.

Another symptom of this loss of status is the restriction to professional autonomy. As ITE providers continue to adapt and acquis to accountability measures, such measures increasingly dominate the landscape and erode teacher educators' abilities to determine their own curriculum, pedagogy and assessment. For example, in England, teacher education is already a highly regulated context with a complex set of regulations, and a detailed and punitive inspection framework. In 2020, the government Department for Education introduced the Initial Teacher Training Core Content Framework which prescriptively defines both the curriculum and pedagogy of teacher education programmes. It is based on a narrow and limited range of research and a focus on teacher behaviours over knowledge and understanding. The policy rhetoric around this framework is about raising standards and providing a baseline of entitlement, but Mills (2020) has argued that it demonstrates a fundamental lack of respect for teachers. However, I would argue that it is more damaging than that, as it undermines the capacity for teacher educators to draw upon their own expertise in how they adapt their work. As some teacher educators enable and in some cases even welcome such approaches, they diminish their own ability to self-determine how teacher professionalism is defined and the contribution that teacher education can make to that.

However, universities also have an opportunity aligned with relative space: that of their capacity to leverage. As large-scale and networked institutions, which perform an important role in society (the education of teachers), teacher educators can leverage their position more broadly. I offer three short examples:

- The IOE is also a large-scale provider of teacher education, playing a significant role in providing teachers for London schools. During a funding crisis under the Directorship of Geoff Whitty, the IOE threatened to pull out of teacher education unless it received additional specialist funding. In more recent times, the move to school-led teacher education has not produced sufficient capacity to supply the required number of teachers, leaving the IOE still in a strong but under-utilised position in relation to teacher education.
- ASU has also used its scale and position in Arizona as a way of promoting their approach under the Next Education Workforce initiative. Through advocacy and media representations, the initiative was able to move from two pilot school districts to 14 in only one year. Such considerable growth and reach across the State is only possible through the leverage capacity of ASU.
- Teach First is a large-scale provider in England, linked to an influential global network brand Teach for All. Teach First has a lot of influence over politics, policymakers and the public discourse around education and teacher education in the UK. They have consistently grown in size, with the support of all political parties, and leverage their scale through their large ambassador network to infiltrate a number of influential corporate and social organisations.

Universities have wide social reach within the localised communities, and potentially through their alumni networks. These are often underused for promotional purposes but are significant in terms of the influence of educational ideas, and how they can permeate and influence practice in schools. Many long-term teacher educators reflect on how they have seen the education in an area transform as a new idea, promoted by the university, has taken hold, facilitated through the influx of new teachers, the practice tradition becomes embedded in the local school network. These spheres of influence, however, are often informal, with little evidence generated or presented as to their impact and reach. A key dimension of their significance is how scale is enacted, a theme we shall return to at the end of this chapter.

Representational space

Chapter 1 argued discourses about quality and what makes a good teacher dominate both the public and private spaces of education. In that sense, teacher education can be seen as a representational space: representing images of what education is for, what is a good teacher and what teachers are expected to do. Biesta (2019) argues for a turn away from the current emphasis on outcome and attainment, which he describes as the age of measurement, towards realigning with the challenging and complex questions about educational purpose. Biesta argues that focusing on educational purpose should be at the centre of teacher education from the outset, as teaching is a moral endeavour – one where the educational purpose is embedded in every action and decision, and that teacher education should foreground these challenges and questions for teachers to use as part of their understanding of their role and responsibilities.

The representational space of being a teacher, and of education, is however shot through with competing notions of what it means to be a good teacher. Recognition and status for teachers varies globally (Dolton and Marcenaro-Gutierrez, 2013). Connell (2009) has argued that new discourses of the good teacher focus on the auditability of teachers' work that can demonstrate impact within a narrow set of indicators. Here the discourses of standards, quality indicators and quality assurance are paramount in defining what it means to teach. These acts of governance make teacher education the subject of reform, which when aligned with a culture of performativity, "makes people up".

However, the representational space also applies to the other teacher education stakeholders too: universities occupy a representational space, particularly around prestige and institutional vision made visible through international university league tables and ranking statistics. Performance here is paramount to success in the global marketplace. But also representational space is important in the local context, in a university's ability to attract new students and to develop relationships with partners. This is often highlighted as being aligned with a university's reputation. In each of my site visits, I asked about what made the institution so "good", and answers often referred to the university's reputation. Reputations were built on perceptions that included their student teachers being better prepared for placements, were more attractive to employ and had more attentive teacher educators. These reputations were significant locally as they affected how the university ranked in relation to local competition, a factor that appeared to be becoming more and more significant.

For universities having a key brand or identifier that taps into their reputation, but also that reflects local discourses about quality teaching, is an important strategy. For example, the IOE focussed on specialisation, Auckland on equity, ASU on innovation, OISE on research and QUT on rural and remote communities. These simplified monikers are important because they tap into the representation space as to what the university and the teacher education programmes stand for and why they are needed.

Spatial influences

The spatial triad outlined above enable a deeper understanding of the significance of the location of these programmes. Examination of the location, relative and representational spaces across all five universities, reveals a network of power relationships. In location, we can see the influence of a dynamic, geographical space alongside practice traditions which are embedded in local infrastructures and ideas and which are resistant to change. Not only are hierarchies of scale important in the relative space, but also how this can affect the status of the institution and the field, which, in turn, can affect its capacity to self-determine. Influence and reputation are just as important in the representational space as universities seek to carve out their distinctiveness and what aspects of teacher education they represent. These representations are linked to the priorities and values of the communities the university serves.

Each university is uniquely situated within this complex of spatial influences. In order to be successful, the teacher education programme has to be able to be effective within these competing influences and opportunities: searching out where adaptations can be made, how those adaptations relate to reputations, values and practice traditions and how they can be represented internally and externally. To undertake this complex task requires teacher educators to have a detailed understanding of their local contexts, the hierarchies which influence them and the priorities of their stakeholders as well as the pedagogy of teacher education and what is needed in order to enable transformation to occur. This is the work of the university teacher educator.

In addition, the university has a further complication: that of scale. Universities tend to be large teacher education providers (particularly in relation to school-based programmes or some alternative providers). The larger they are, the more partners are involved and the greater the complexity of the partnership. Successful university-based teacher education programmes have to be able to navigate the complex spatial landscape outlined above, at a large scale. How they do that is explored in the next section.

Quality at scale

Enacting teacher education at scale spans location, relative and representational space. For example, when we discuss how practice occurs in space, there is a tendency to use abstract categories (like local, global), and there is a danger that these categories become metaphorical conceptions of scale rather than referring to clearly defined entities. Smith (2010) notes that activities do not necessarily move in a linear way but can jump scales. As such, a phenomenon such as deliberate practice can be part of a global trend that is not represented in policy discourses, but can be influential in local programmes. However, it is also true that different things happen at different scales. For example, in Peter Taylor's analysis, he categorises that different things happen at a local scale (which he calls reality) in contrast to the ideals which are presented at a national scales and trends identified at global scale (1989). However, this does not mean that scale determines influences: for example, because something happens nationally, it does not mean it is necessarily ideological (Moore, 2008; Sayer, 1985). Noyes extends this by noting that (2013, p. 110) "scale, whether real or imagined, is not pre-existent but constructed or reconstructed over time in complex ways". And so the scale of an activity, its size relative to its neighbours, is key to understanding its social and cultural positioning (Swyngedouw, 1997): big can be powerful!

Across the five universities, approaches to handling the size of the provision varied, but between them, four strategies emerged for how they sought to accommodate (large) scale:

- *Student grouping*

    For example, increases in numbers, which either meant that numbers of groups were increased or the numbers of students in those groups increased. This strategy was also used when cost-cutting measures were required and groups were brought together to cover similar topics or to share units. At OISE, the university adopted a "cohort" approach: where groups of 30 student teachers (or teacher candidates) were brought together, working with a group of instructors (teacher educators) who taught several of their courses. At QUT, the taught component of the programme was designed around a series of units each taught by specialists. However, as the programme grew in size, it no longer became possible for the specialist teacher education to support all the students on that unit, and other faculty members were assigned to support (supervise) the students. This is an example of where class sizes were increased, often as a result of reduced choice of elective modules, or the bringing together of different cohorts with shared modules (examples of which were seen at both QUT and the University of Auckland). Whilst this approach ensured that each of the students received high-quality specialist input, some teacher educators were concerned at their ability to support students adequately. One teacher educator described how she felt that in a combined curriculum unit covering two subject specialisms, she was offering a different quality of experience to those students that shared her expertise than with the others. This suggests that such an approach can result in a variety in teacher education practices and the experience offered to individual students.

- *Specialisation*

    Where increased numbers of students brought additional revenue, providers often used this to employ specialist staff; the addition of which, it was argued, enhanced both the quality of the programme and its attractiveness to new students. Specialisation can also be seen in some extent with the chosen grouping strategy, as can be seen in the example of QUT, University of Auckland and in particular at the IOE, where a subject specialist perspective, privileged over the generic, was seen as key in the formation of a subject specialist teacher identity formation. New teachers are socialised into subject communities and networks and taught to teach through the lens of their subject, key to the deployment of specialist teachers in English secondary schools. This is reflected in the partnership arrangements which were focussed on the school subject departments and the subject specialists at the IOE. The number of different schools across London (around 700) adds to the diversity of this experience, allowing the student body to expand their understanding of different contexts.

- *Batching processes*

    Economies of scale also meant that certain processes could be batched together and overseen by a specialist team. This was often the case with the organisation of partnerships and practicums. In several cases, for example, in QUT, a department was devoted to the organisation of practicums and to developing relationships with schools. In each university, however, the extent of this batching and how it was integrated into other aspects of the ITE provision varied. For example, at QUT, the practicum had its own monitoring and quality assurance processes, including coordinating a team of university partners who oversaw practicum but some of whom were separate to other aspects of the taught provision. At ASU, regional leads and site leads also participated in the monitoring of practical experiences but did have some responsibility for course content. At the IOE, student teachers were supported by their academic team (who undertook all site visits), but a specialist group of teacher educators, identified as partnership managers or Institute Partnership Managers, oversaw specialist partnership work. For example, within the Secondary Post Graduate Certificate of Education (PGCE), a mentoring coordinator role was established to develop mentoring across the partnership and different subjects, working with key ITE representatives within schools, school-based mentors and the IOE subject teams. Such an approach enables a degree of specialisation in processes (such as mentor training) and represents an economy of scale across the partnership. A former lead of the Secondary PGCE noted how development of the Institute Partnership Manager role had significantly reduced issues with partnership schools and mentors and therefore had enhanced the quality of the programme provision overall.

Within Teach First, the batching of processes was a deliberate strategy promoted through the growth of the programme and the corresponding expanded complexity:

> When the numbers grow you try to be more efficient: you try to batch processes. So we started having a school relationship team producing both materials and data but also we developed backroom processes [around administration and data collection] so that the team could be out there supporting schools.
>
> *(Interview with member of Teach First leadership team, 2019)*

This was also aligned with other economies of scale, which were used when purchasing marketing materials or negotiating accommodation rates for the national Summer Institute (an intensive block of campus-based teaching).

The decision of how and which process to batch reflects how aspects of the programme are considered to contribute to the overall learning experience. Batching purchasing, for example, is unlikely to result in any changes in the quality of the teacher education, unlike the decision to batch the authoring of the module content. OISE teacher educators described the balance they sought to reach through making resources available for sessional instructors, whilst giving them scope to adapt and personalise. This was made possible through faculty meetings and professional development events where the programme expectations were discussed in detail, and space offered for instructors to consider how their version of the course content contributed to those programme expectations individually and as part of the whole programme experience.

- *Monitoring and oversight*

One of the threats to quality, particularly for large-scale programmes, is the concern over coherence. The three strategies outlined above are all orientated around the teaching arrangements of the programme. However, the final category is more aligned with accountability and how programme leadership and management can ensure that adherence to the programme design is consistent, particularly on a large and varied programme.

Specific references to in-programme monitoring were only made by IOE, Teach First and OISE. However, all programmes had some form of internal accountability and quality assurance measures – mostly in the form of module or instructor evaluations – and a periodic quality review process. The internal evaluations appeared to be tied to the perceived quality of the student experience rather than coherence to the overall programme design. At OISE, monitoring and coherence were presented as an area for discussion and development, as the monitoring policies mostly consisted of the regular cycles of internal and external quality review. Both the IOE and Teach First operate within a high accountability culture and are beholden to external government inspection (by Ofsted, the Office for Standards in Education, Children's Services and Skills) which requires evidence of monitoring and oversight of the quality of provision. For example, in order to gain a judgement of Outstanding (under the 2019 inspection framework), providers need to demonstrate performance against 11 grade descriptions around leadership and management of the partnership (these are detailed in Figure 8.1).

This high accountability framework goes some way to explaining the approach adopted by both institutions. For example, the Institute Partnership Managers on the IOE's PGCE programme have a role in ensuring the monitoring of trainees' progress, the work of the partnership and that data is made available for the necessary improvement planning and "rigorous, accurate and systematic analysis". Whilst this is constructed at the IOE as a supportive, developmental process, the monitoring dimension is important for overall programme management.

- *The pursuit of excellence in all of the ITE partnership's activities is demonstrated by an uncompromising and highly successful drive to strongly improve, or sustain, the highest quality of provision and outcomes over a sustained period of time. Leaders and managers base their actions on a deep and accurate understanding of local, regional and national needs and the ITE partnership's performance and strengths.*
- *Rigorous and well-embedded quality assurance systems are used extremely effectively to sustain high-quality outcomes and to continuously improve the quality of provision across the ITE partnership.*
- *Improvement planning is based on the rigorous, accurate and systematic analysis of internal and externally validated data, thorough self-evaluation and is extremely responsive to satisfaction surveys from employers, trainees and former trainees, including the newly qualified teacher (NQT) survey (where appropriate), who attest to the high quality of the training.*
- *All leaders and managers focus relentlessly on continually improving the quality of provision and outcomes for trainees.*
- *Mentors and trainers are of the highest quality and benefit from high-quality and well-focused professional development. As a result, the quality of training across the partnership is likely to be outstanding or at least consistently good and improving.*
- *Schools, colleges and/or other settings are influential in shaping the provision and are heavily involved in recruitment and selection, and the strategic leadership and management of the ITE partnership.*
- *The partnership must include schools in challenging socio-economic circumstances and those judged as requires improvement; these schools are strongly engaged with the partnership.*
- *Rigorous selection procedures ensure that the best possible trainees are recruited to meet specific local, regional and national needs. Trainees selected demonstrate relevant subject and curriculum knowledge, or a clear potential to develop this during their course, and have the potential to meet the required professional standards by the end of their training.*
- *The performance of trainees and groups of trainees is monitored extremely rigorously from the point of selection to final assessment to ensure that all who are awarded qualified teacher status (QTS) or early years teacher status (EYTS) become good or better teachers, with excellent subject knowledge, by the end of their training and are well prepared for employment.*
- *Engagement and liaison with employers ensures an effective continuum from initial teacher training to induction and continuing professional development for NQTs/former trainees.*
- *Leaders and managers oversee and take responsibility for trainees' safe use of technology and social media. (Ofsted, 2019)*

FIGURE 8.1 Ofsted outstanding grade descriptors for leadership and management of the partnership.

Teach First is beholden to the same Ofsted criteria, but they work at a national scale, with eight university partners (at the time of data collection). Their response has been to centralise programme planning on a design and delivery model. The Teach First Leadership Development Programme is designed by a central unit of Curriculum Designers. Whilst shared with university partners (IOE were sent 60 documents specifying the content and script of each taught session), Teach First Participant Development Lead (PDL) staff were trained in the delivery of these contents as part of their induction. The language is important here: the distinction between design and delivery indicates not just a delineation of labour, but also a conception of the roles and responsibilities of different practitioners and how those contribute to the overall experience of learning to teach. Focusing a centralised design team on curriculum construction is intended to allow space for delivery teams to spend time on individual support, reflecting the concerns expressed by Teach First about parity and consistency, and the need to ensure that the student experience is commensurate. However, it does raise a question about the role of the teacher education curriculum: PDLs were inducted into a process of scripted contents and close monitoring (alongside other induction and development activities). The relationship between the "deliverers" and the "designers" of the curriculum was initially quite wide. In this approach, the Teach First staff are seen as variables in the provision of curriculum delivery, which speaks to a distinction in how specialisation can be viewed in teacher education provision, and the role of the teacher educator. In addition, the different approaches between Teach First and the IOE programmes reflect the differences between the relative expertise of their teacher educators. The high levels of centralised control and oversight in the English system makes teacher education adaptation a high-risk activity. The prescriptive inspection regime discourages innovation and adaptation.

The question as to whether a provider seeks to "control" scale through monitoring and oversight or to use scale to innovate and improve quality depends largely on the contexts in which the teacher educators find themselves, which may include those present at the university or through the wider accountability regime. The accounts above about how providers deal with scale shows their individual capacity to adapt and shift teacher education practices in the light of their particular contexts. Whilst there may be some similarity in the strategies they use, the actions they take and the approaches vary.

No doubt scale adds complexity, but it also signals opportunity: increased revenue, wider sphere of influence and capacity to leverage. What this chapter has sought to demonstrate is the complexity of the landscape within which such strategies occur. The interplay of factors around space is shot through with different types of power to influence change and the capacity to respond. All of these are situated within unique contexts. In the next chapter, these different influences are represented in a model of ITE practice which seeks to offer a framework of how teacher education can enact quality at scale.

References

Abbott, A. (1988). *The system of professions: An essay on the expert division of labor.* Chicago, IL: Chicago University Press.

Allen, R., & Sims, S. (2018). Do pupils from low-income families get low-quality teachers? Indirect evidence from English schools. *Oxford Review of Education, 44*(4), 441–458. doi:10.1080/03054985.2017.1421152

Biesta, G. (2019). Reclaiming teaching for teacher education: Towards a spiral curriculum. *Beijing International Review of Education, 1*(2–3), 259–272. doi:10.1163/25902539-00102015

Cochran-Smith, M., Keefe, E. S., Carney, M. C., Sanchez, J. G., Olivo, M., & Smith, R. J. (2020). Teacher preparation at New Graduate Schools of Education; studying a controversial innovation. *Teacher Education Quarterly, 47*(2), 8–37.

Connell, R. (2009). Good teachers on dangerous ground: Towards a new view of teacher quality and professionalism. *Critical Studies in Education, 50*(3), 213–229. doi:10.1080/17508480902998421

De Botton, A. (2008). *The art of travel.* London: Vintage.

Grossman, P. (2008). Responding to our critics: From crisis to opportunity in research on teacher education. *Journal of Teacher Education, 59*(1), 10–23. doi:10.1177/0022487107310748

Harvey, D. (2004). *Space as a key word.* Paper presented at the Marx and Philosophy Conference, Institute of Education, London. http://frontdeskapparatus.com/files/harvey2004.pdf

Ingvarson, L. (2019). Teaching standards and the promotion of quality teaching. *European Journal of Education, 54*(3), 337–355. doi:10.1111/ejed.12353

Ingvarson, L., Reid, K., Buckley, S., Kleinhenz, E., Masters, G., & Rowley, G. (2014). *Best practice teacher education programs and Australia's own programs.* Canberra: Department of Education.

Kemmis, S., Wilkinson, J., Edwards-Groves, C., Hardy, I., Grootenboer, P., & Bristol, L. (2014). *Changing practices, changing education.* Bristol: Springer Science & Business Media.

Labaree, D. F. (2006). *The trouble with ed schools.* New Haven, CT: Yale University Press.

Lefebvre, H. (1991). *The production of space* (D. Nicholson-Smith, Trans. Vol. 142). Oxford: Oxford Blackwell.

Mayer, D. (2017). Professionalizing teacher education. In *Oxford Research Encyclopedia of Education* (Vol. 1). Oxford: Oxford University Press. http://doi.org/10.1093/acrefore/9780190264093.013.96

Mills, M. (2020). *Inaugural lecture: Teachers and teaching: The politics of respect.* London: UCL Institute of Education.

Moore, A. (2008). Rethinking scale as a geographical category: From analysis to practice. *Progress in Human Geography, 32*(2), 203–225. doi:10.1177/0309132507087647

Noyes, A. (2013). Scale in education research: Towards a multi-scale methodology. *International Journal of Research & Method in Education, 36*(2), 101–116. doi:10.1080/1743727x.2012.683648

Sahlberg, P. (2010). Educational change in Finland. In *Second international handbook of educational change* (pp. 323–348). Dordrecht: Springer.

Sayer, A. (1985). The difference that space makes. In D. Gregory & J. Urry (Eds.), *Social relations and spatial structures* (pp. 49–66). London: Macmillan Education UK.

Smith, N. (2010). *Uneven development: Nature, capital, and the production of space*. Georgia: University of Georgia Press.
Swyngedouw, E. (1997). *Excluding the other: The production of scale and scaled politics*. London: Arnold.
Taylor, P. J. (1989). *Political geography* (2nd ed.). Harlow: Longman.
Vanassche, E., & Kelchtermans, G. (2015). The state of the art in self-study of teacher education practices: A systematic literature review. *Journal of Curriculum Studies, 47*(4), 508–528. doi:10.1080/00220272.2014.995712

9
MODELLING ITE PRACTICE

The global pandemic COVID-19 and the Black Lives Matter protests following the killing of George Floyd were both events that became defining features on society and culture as I was writing this book, and which have enormous implications for education. Never has being a teacher been more important as we ask fundamental questions about teaching and education as part of the fabric of our society. Locally, education systems continue to restructure, change and introduce accountability measures, particularly in and around teacher education. Teacher educators have to continually respond assessing what these changes are, the impact on education and the corresponding changes that are necessary. What do we expect of our teacher educators in this context, and how can they respond?

David Harvey has argued that inequalities get produced and reproduced in space (2010). Education and teacher education are both profoundly spatial activities happening in specific locations, beholden to influences from a variety of scales. The examples of initial teacher education (ITE) practices explored in this book have shown that university-based teacher educators have to interpret a range of changing discourses interpreted through the specific conditions of their local context. By focusing on these discourses as quality conundrums, new light has been cast on how they get manifest and affect the work of teacher educators. Teacher education, with its complexity of stakeholders and interested parties, may be difficult to change, but teacher educators are adept at doing so, often navigating contradictory influences in order to provide the best possible educational experience for new teachers. So, what can we learn from these experiences to help understand teacher education more and that will support teacher educators as they prepare to address new quality conundrums as they arise?

Teacher education can be viewed as a fundamentally practical activity. It is an activity that takes place in universities, school classrooms, cafes and virtual spaces. It involves thousands of interactions between individuals, and requires new teachers to make sense of all these experiences in a coherent way so that they are prepared, in the "white heat" of action (to coin Donald Schön's term), to make a range of decisions in the best interests of their students. To become a teacher requires transformation through a teacher education pedagogy which allows a flow of knowledges and ideas. However, theory, knowledge and what is widely concerned to be university-based learning can seem far removed from the practice of teaching. But nevertheless, teachers need more than just practical experience in order to make good decisions. The complexity of this task is further compounded by the accountability infrastructure around schools, teacher education and universities, and the different ways in which quality in these contexts is expressed and understood. This book has sought to lay out those practices, so that we can understand more how universities "do" teacher education.

It was not the original intention of the research to present a defence of university-based teacher education. The focus of the research was to undertake an empirical account of how universities were able to enact high-quality, large-scale teacher education. This was based on a recognition that most countries around the world were experiencing a teacher shortage, and most countries were reliant upon universities for the majority of their teacher education provision. It was also mindful of the trend for alternative routes into teaching, and that some of these routes were experimenting with a "footloose" approach: using online and distance learning tools so that new teachers did not need to be located in the regions where the university was based. I wanted to know if it was possible to undertake such programmes with the same quality, the same depth and rigour in both understanding and practice as the more traditional university-based routes. I surmised that this question was only possible to answer if we knew what universities did in large-scale programmes: how they enacted teacher education.

The recognition that teacher education is a spatial practice is key. However, this recognition does not mean that teacher education should only be rooted in specific locations; indeed, I would argue that a spatial lens helps to both understand the spatial nature of teacher education and to release us from it. Exploring, for example, how a university in Brisbane is able to support teachers in rural and remote communities can challenge thinking in other locations about teacher education in other communities. The paradox is that this emphasises the importance of place whilst releasing us from the confinements of location. At the centre is an understanding of situated knowledge, how it is useful and what role it plays in the education of teachers.

Additionally, there are two distinguishing features of university-based teacher education: scale and a view of teacher education which centres on transformation. Universities, in their varied social, political and governance contexts, are able to enact effective teacher education, often across a large scale and with multiple partners and across various governance contexts. Universities also navigate a range of competing notions of quality (hence the quality conundrums) and the different ways they are expressed and made real (such as through standards, accountability structures and dominant discourses). Looking at university practices in different countries has revealed that many of these quality conundrums are common, but are handled differently depending on the local context. This is a paradox of simultaneously being both universal and unique.

The idea of transformation within education has its roots in higher education (Harvey & Knight, 1996). Transformation in teacher education occurs through teacher education pedagogy. The model of ITE practice is an attempt to represent diagrammatically how universities navigate this complexity in order to enable transformation to occur at scale. This approach goes beyond the idea that you can understand teacher education through a set of metrics or indicators that respond to an accountability agenda or a governance regime, but that it is based on a set of values and understandings about what high-quality teaching looks like, the societal needs it serves and the role communities expect it to play. This vision of quality is profoundly moral, and as such acts as a powerful reminder as to why universities, as part of civic society, are fundamental to teacher education.

Bringing these different practices together also has something important to say about teacher education expertise. There is a growing body of research on teacher educators: research, which highlights the complexity of the role, and that teacher educators are rarely inducted well or experience professional development. Often teacher educators based in universities have the challenge of having been career changers who navigate a complex set of rules about what is valued in academia, whilst still seeking to maintain their understanding of the changes happening in schools. This research highlights the need for teacher education expertise to be highly adaptive. This adaption needs to take place both at the scale of the individual teacher educator and at the scale of the university programme leadership, as all aspects of the landscape of teacher education are in constant change and development. Such an observation flies in the face of critics who argue that university-based teacher education is out of date, incumbent, overly traditional and abstract. As the practices outlined here have shown, adaptation is not always conducted at a grand and public scale, but through the artistry of the individual teacher educator as they support new teachers' transformation, whilst remaining committed to offering their student teachers a wide range of ideas and knowledges which they understand to be important in learning to be a teacher. However, we still need a way of articulating those changes, representing their value and distinguishing them from practices which may indeed be out of date and reluctant to change.

The model of ITE practice

How and why each university responded to the challenge of maintaining quality at scale was contingent on their individual circumstances, even though these experiences and the challenges they faced were shared internationally. This is represented in the model of ITE practice (see Figure 9.1), which was developed iteratively through the empirical data analysis. The model of ITE practice highlights three spatial knowledges which are pertinent to teacher education. The

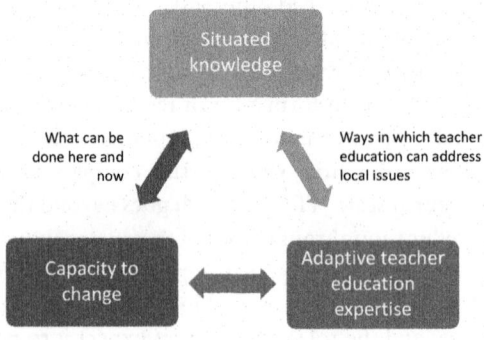

204 Modelling ITE practice

FIGURE 9.1 Model of ITE practice.

layout of the model illustrates how these three spatial knowledges are related and interconnected through the teacher education practice. These relationships are bidirectional: spatial influences will affect practices and pedagogy, and in turn, these may shape ways of knowing about teacher education. The framework is designed as a way of laying these elements out, showing how they intersect and interrelate. The model has been verified and critiqued with key actors, participants and stakeholders in each of the locations to ensure rigour and validity.

Whilst discourses around quality, practices and spatial influences varied in each location, there was some similarity in the factors which influenced how each university responded. The model attempts to capture these opportunities and influences through bringing to the fore the three spatial knowledges, and suggesting these knowledges interact in the unravelling of the practice of teacher education. Each knowledge is related to the specific location of the practice and how it is situated within the relevant relative and representational spaces of ITE. The spatial knowledges are therefore contingent upon the location of the practice, the degree of control and influence the university can exert and the dominant representations of being a "good teacher" in this context.

- **Situated knowledge**: Teacher educators have an in-depth knowledge of education in both a broad and localised sense: they draw upon a detailed understanding of the catchment area of the university, its unique features and key issues/priorities. This understanding is situated within national and global discourses: for example, what are the specific demands for new teachers in this local area? This knowledge also needs to be mindful of the scale of the individual: how do these debates/issues affect pupils, students, and teachers? The localised knowledge is highly situational: it includes educational debates and issues that matter at a range of scales, but specifically how they affect the local context. One would anticipate that within universities this knowledge would also be informed by the educational research literature. The knowledge is dynamic and will be affected by trends in education that affect schools as well as new research findings.

- **Adaptive teacher education expertise**: University-based teacher education navigates complex accountability structures and multiple stakeholders within teacher education, universities and schools, and situates them within the field, particularly in relation to pedagogy and practice. To do this requires teacher education expertise stemming from a range of sources, including theories of professional learning, the experience of working with student teachers in a range of contexts and knowledges of learning and teaching from other fields and from research. This specialist teacher education expertise is grown from, but distinct to, the experience of teaching, and has to be highly adaptive to local and dynamic contexts. This knowledge base enables teacher educators to make informed decisions about how to structure, teach and assess their programmes.
- **Capacity to change**: The ability to make the decisions outlined above are often limited and constrained by context such as university governance systems, local funding or accountability arrangements or practice traditions around partnership. Universities and schools are necessarily designed for other activities (such as research, teaching and education of students or pupils), and so their systems may not be optimum for ITE. Therefore, any adaptations need to be adjusted with these constraints (and opportunities) in mind.

The three factors identified are spatially situated, interdependent and contingent upon each other. For example, in a place where there is a strong situated knowledge, like the dominant and shared discourse around the need for more equity in education in New Zealand (Cochran-Smith et al., 2016), this discourse will influence ITE practice, which is itself contingent upon the degree of autonomy and agency afforded to teacher educators. The situated knowledge may not directly change practice itself but will be highly influential, as it will drive not only what changes are needed (for example, in response to a change in the local teacher demand, in the governance or accreditation requirements), but also how teacher education programme can respond to such changes. The programme therefore needs to listen to all school partners, and to develop an understanding of the challenges they face, and pertinent infrastructural factors such as local governance (school autonomy or oversight from local school boards, school districts or chains of schools such as Multiple Academy Trusts) which can influence how partnerships are negotiated.

Similarly, a limited capacity for change, for example, in a highly regulated context with a prescriptive curriculum, will likely restrict opportunities for innovation or adaptations due to a change in circumstances. Capacity to change may be outside the scope of the teacher educators, or indeed the university's Education department or faculty. It may be controlled externally by professional associations or government bodies. It is however also scaled, contingent on individual institutions through the autonomy and agency afforded to individual teacher educators or programme leaders.

Central to the maintenance of high-quality ITE practice at scale is the adaptive expertise of teacher educators, which will also vary across different locations and roles (particularly between university, schools and other partners). It is necessary in both leaders and individual teacher educators. Approaches which are too fixed or dogmatic are unlikely to respond to a changing local context. Teacher educators themselves often fail to recognise this expertise, or to appreciate its adaptive nature, is key when responding to dynamic definitions of quality. Adaptive teacher education expertise is particularly important in a context where many university-based teacher educators are employed on temporary, casual and teaching-only contracts.

Universities have a wide sphere of influence, both geographically and within their specialist communities. They can develop the infrastructure to facilitate large-scale provision and can generate robust situated knowledge, although their size and bureaucratic nature may make it difficult for them to respond to changes and needs. University regulations however are often not designed specifically for ITE and can limit what adaptations are possible. This can be seen when teacher educators have sought to be innovative (such as the introduction of whole cohort school-based Mahi Tahi days at the University of Auckland, an initiative challenged by the timetabling constraints of the university). Scale brings complexity as the number of partners, students and stakeholders increase. Centralising key functions and overzealous control mechanisms can help universities to ensure consistency, but needs to be balanced against reducing teacher educators' ability to adapt their practice. Universities also have a role in informing these debates: shaping the way in which local concerns are identified and problematised, what is known about the best way to educate new teachers and the impact of accountability regimes. Universities do this through research, through dissemination and using their expertise to influence policy and practice.

The three spatial knowledges therefore are interrelated. As change occurs in one area of the model such as in the local context, or through new regulations, or new research, so other areas of the model need to adapt. Navigating this complex landscape requires leadership at a variety of levels of ITE practice: through influencing the direction of policy, considering the alignment with university systems, developing the pitch and dynamic of each programme, formulating and sustaining stakeholder partnerships as well as considering the capacity and development of each teacher educator. The model offers a way of conceptualising or informing that leadership. By extension, it suggests that universities have a range of specific actions they can take to improve the quality of their ITE, through:

- Ensuring that teacher educators are fully conversant in situated scaled knowledges around education and consider their potential impacts on teacher education;

- Considering the capacity to change afforded to teacher educators and how university governance structures enable or constrain high-quality ITE; and
- Ensuring that teacher education expertise within the university is suitably adaptive – dogmatic ideologies need to be challenged.

These three priorities suggest three areas of development and a specific research agenda for teacher education that would be practical, quality enhancing and that would make substantial contributions to the field.

Doing ITE at scale

Universities have a wide sphere of influence, both geographically and within the research fields they serve. Even in cases such as England, where the IOE was involved in a range of school-led provisions as well as its own programmes, the scale and scope offered by the core Post Graduate Certificate in Education programme dwarfs the scale of other programmes and other non-university providers. Universities have the infrastructure and social networks to facilitate large-scale provision. However, the model of ITE practice also points to other areas where universities can make a distinctive contribution to ITE.

Scale creates an opportunity for leverage. Whilst their size and bureaucratic nature may make it difficult for universities to appear to respond quickly to changes in education, universities also have distinctive advantages. Centralising key functions and mediating against overzealous control mechanisms can help universities to harmonise processes and limit variance in practice. This needs to be offset against university regulations, often not designed specifically for ITE, which can limit what adaptations are possible, but can also be informed by the university's capacity of generating robust situated knowledge informing how to respond. High-quality teacher education is a valuable reputation builder for universities, particularly within local communities. It is one of the few points of contact that the public can have directly with the working of university faculty. Arizona State University has been able to use their scale and influence to leverage their approach to teacher education with a range of local school districts, and so have been able to bring innovation to areas beyond teacher education. Scale can be an opportunity to raise some interesting questions:

- Can large scale offer possibilities of different approaches to addressing local concerns?
- Can large scale enable the introduction of a wider range of strategies and approaches?
- How can adaptive teacher education expertise be encouraged and developed and in what ways can our collective adaptive teacher education expertise be enhanced through adding new specialist understandings?
- Can large scale open up greater capacity to change through leveraging, or through economies of scale, or through adding specialist support?

Universities can fulfil this "promise of scale" if they maintain their ability for transformation. The accountability measures adopted in many jurisdictions reflect a preoccupation with input or output measures (see Chapter 1), a focus on standards rather than transformation. In many ways, this is to be expected and is a recognised outcome of "deliverology" accountability regimes. But quality is not an entity in itself but an expression of what is considered to be of value. The model of ITE practice reflects that quality is more than a series of metrics or indicators that respond to an accountability agenda or a governance regime, but is based on an understanding of education as transformation: built on a set of values and understandings about teaching, the societal needs it serves and the role communities expect it to play; in other words, it sees teacher education as being profoundly *educational*.

The model, therefore, does not promote uniformity but recognises that quality can be enacted in a variety of ways. Quality is a highly contested concept. One person's interpretation of what needs to be done and what is possible will depend on what they consider quality education to be, what a quality teacher looks like, what sort of teacher education they are referring to and what they consider good practice in teacher education to be. This model reflects this nuanced approach to understanding quality: by recognising that transformational pedagogy is possible even when some aspects of the practice architecture make transformation challenging. In other words, the model is applicable to the different circumstances in most teacher education contexts, and even for teacher education providers not located in universities. Barriers to ideal practice will always be in place, but that need not prevent teacher education from striving for transformation.

The model also recognises that some aspects of high-quality provision, such as the availability of "ideal" candidates or particular types of partnership, may be outside the immediate remit of the teacher educator. A high-quality programme will be one that addresses that problem specifically and in an informed way, such as through either considering how to support new teachers to be the best teachers they can be or by seeking alternative ways to attract and accommodate different types of applicants. Teacher education provision will always need to adapt to reflect changing social and educational contexts.

The case for university-based ITE

The model of ITE practice does not speak directly to the processes of teacher education or suggest that these are unique to universities. The model also does not invite commentary on different policy practices on what Ellis and Spendlove have called the political economy of teacher education (2020). Political influence on teacher education will continue but will likely change (particularly as the world recovers from the COVID-19 pandemic): more quality conundrums will appear as others subside. Teacher education will need to adapt to these changing circumstances, and to do so will require detailed knowledge of the site and situation (situated knowledge), opportunities and developments in the field itself and how they might be gainfully deployed (adaptive teacher education expertise) and what possibilities there are for affective change (capacity to change). Moreover, high-quality teacher education will need to consider how these elements are interdependent and contingent upon each other.

One area of teacher education provision however that is unique to universities and that add useful insights into the dynamic context outlined above is the purpose with which it conducts research. Both Menter (2017) and Furlong (2013) have identified that one of the key roles of a university involved in teacher education is its close and tight relationship to research. However, it would be wrong to assume this is the unique purview of universities; the changing landscape of research means that many organisations consider themselves to make valuable and relevant contributions to educational research. Also, it does not necessarily follow that having a strong research reputation makes for high-quality teacher education. Several of the universities in this research are known for their high-quality research output, often used as a marketing tool to attract students. However, many of the teacher educators in those universities have highlighted the specific challenges this creates for teacher education. Those who undertake high-quality research may make "guest" contributions to teacher education programmes but are unlikely to be full-time supervisors on them. Being a research-intensive institution in and of itself does not make a university a good teacher education institution.

What is more significant, I would argue, is how being part of a research organisation changes how teacher education is conceptualised, lifting it beyond the notion of technical training, and placing greater emphasis on the educational dimension outlined here as transformation. Teacher "training", as a form of professional training, is distinctively different to teacher education: the role of research is not just to inform about "best practices" or "what works" but to contribute to a body of knowledge that may inform decision-making and to support critical situational judgement. In the "white heat" of action, teachers may not realise they are drawing on research-based knowledge, but will be drawing on their understanding of a situation: why a pupil has acted out in a particular way, why an activity fell short of the expected learning gains. To be prepared to make these situational judgements requires knowledge, and during ITE, new teachers need access to a variety of ideas and knowledges in order to develop that knowledge base. It is not that research-based knowledge is better or more relevant than that gained from experience, but that new teachers need a variety of ideas and knowledges so they can develop their understanding of teacher professional practice.

Universities do not have the monopoly on relevant research-driven or theoretical knowledge. But the civic remit of a university uniquely situates them, as being beholden to and part of civic society. Universities have a duty to evaluate, assess, verify and hold knowledge to account. In other words, universities should be more resistant to fads, trends and educational "snake oil". Universities are accountable to the societies they serve: not through governance or inspection structures but because their role in civic society requires them to be.

Whilst the idea of being accountable to societies may seem a little detached, the other key and important aspect of universities is their close connection to the communities they serve. This is particularly the case in professional "training", where part of the educational experience takes place in professional settings. Here the partnership between the university and the professional settings are not just fundamental to the experience of "training", but also within this context, the university remains connected to the fields of practice. Moreover, universities should be key in communicating their expertise with a range of stakeholders: professional associations, unions, policymakers, publishers and accountability organisations. This presents an opportunity not just to be informed but to influence. This is possibly an untapped and underappreciated dimension of university provision, and one in which, if fully realised and carefully deployed, could reassert the value and contribution of universities to teacher education and other aspects of education generally.

Quality at scale – the next steps

The majority of this research was conducted before the COVID-19 pandemic in 2020. Much of the social media and education press are speculating on what the impact of COVID-19 and the coronavirus is likely to be, including the impact on universities. Within England specifically, the status of teachers appears to be on the rise (as parents realise that educating their children at home is not as easy as they suspected), and the demand for teacher education places is likely to grow as the effects on the wider economy are more broadly felt. Under these circumstances, questions of both quality and scale are likely to become more prominent.

Optimists suggest that the shift in societies may bring an end to accountability and overly rigid governance structures. I suspect this may be more of a wish than a reality. Any changes following this period will require teacher educators to respond. The model presented here offers an insight into what needs should be considered. Scale is a unique way for universities to make a valuable contribution in ITE, one which raises some interesting questions:

- Can university-based teacher education offer possibilities of different approaches to addressing local problems with and for a range of partners?
- Can university-based teacher education enable teacher educators to try out a wider range of strategies and approaches? How can adaptive teacher education expertise be encouraged and developed and in what ways can our collective adaptive teacher education expertise be enhanced through adding new specialist understandings?
- Can university-based teacher education open up greater capacity to change through leveraging, or through economies of scale or through adding specialist support?

Large-scale ITE is an opportunity not just to increase the supply of high-quality teachers but to change the way universities engage in and promote ITE. However, in order to do this, universities must be clear on why they are involved in teacher education and be confident of their distinctive contribution to it. Claims about the importance of theory and research are not enough. However, the practice of universities which educate new teachers at scale shows the incredible flexibility of what they can achieve. An understanding of quality in teacher education orientated around the concept of transformation (rather than standards) and an appreciation of the significance of the spatial context in which teacher education takes place is central to the work of "high quality" university-based teacher educators.

References

Cochran-Smith, M., Ell, F., Grudnoff, L., Haigh, M., Hill, M., & Ludlow, L. (2016). Initial teacher education: What does it take to put equity at the center? *Teaching and Teacher Education*, 57, 67–78. doi:10.1016/j.tate.2016.03.006

Ellis, V., & Spendlove, D. (2020). Mediating 'School Direct': The enactment of a reform policy by university-based teacher educators in England. *British Educational Research Journal*. doi:10.1002/berj.3607

Furlong, J. (2013). *Education – An anatomy of the discipline: Rescuing the university project*. Abingdon: Routledge.

Harvey, D. (2010). *The Enigma of capital and the crises of capitalism*. Oxford: Oxford University Press.

Harvey, L., & Knight, P. T. (1996). *Transforming higher education*. Bristol: Open University Press.

Menter, I. (2017). *The role and contribution of higher education in contemporary teacher education*. Retrieved from http://www.scde.ac.uk/wp-content/uploads/2017/05/Report-Ian-Menter-2017-05-25.pdf

INDEX

Note: **Bold** page numbers refer to **tables** and *italic* page numbers refer to *figures*.

accountability: "era of accountability" 13–14, 141; and governance 1–2; instrumentalising practice 177; in ITE 140–141; local and national mechanisms 106; and oversight 176–177; policy problem 140; practice architecture 177; quality conundrum 24; university-based initial teacher education 9
accreditation process: authentic partnerships 147–149; in diverse communities 107; documentation 147, 148; engagement of community groups 149; governance quality conundrum 147; local community involvement 147–149
Adams, P. 15, 51
American Educational Research Association 14
Arizona: teacher education in 121; teacher shortages in 119–120
Arizona State University (ASU) 113
assessment: Bachelors or Masters level 171; class-based formative assessment techniques 133; documentation 129; idea of transformation 12; parsing of practice 172–174; from peers and educational professionals 22, 190; primary PGCE 43; Research Excellence Framework (REF) 38, 142, 144; secondary PGCE 44–45; teacher education programme 105, 147; teacher educators 172–173; UCL Institute of Education 38

Auckland University of Technology University (AUT) 156
Australian Catholic University 93
Australian Institute for Teaching and School Leadership (AITSL) report 95
Australian Institute of Health and Welfare 93
Australian Professional Standards for Teachers (APST) 97, 104
authenticity: definition 147; lack of 180; partnership, secondary PGCE 47

Bailey, P. L. J. 63
Ball, S. J. 7, 54, 83, 107, 174
batching processes 195–196
Berry, W. 116
Beutel, D. 94
Biesta, G. 173, 192; critique of "learnification" 2
Black Lives Matter movement 85, 91
Bologna Agreement 43
Brekelmans, M. 116
Brisard, E. 174
Brunner, M. 15

Canterbury Christ Church University 48
Carney, M. C. 35, 119
Carter Andrews, D. J. 32
Carter Review 38
categorisation 16, 22, 139
cinematic pedagogies 32

classroom-readiness 37
clinical or academic faculty 129
clinical practice: adoption of 65–66; apprenticeship model of teacher education 66; criticisms 66–67; Oxford Internship Scheme (OIS) 66; practical theorising 66
Cochran-Smith, M. 13, 35, 86, 119, 140
community-based teacher educators 135
Connell, R. 1, 7, 13, 141, 192
contexts for transformation: accountability and oversight 176–177; conditions for transformation, creating 179–181; cultural-discursive arrangements 180; curriculum, pedagogy and assessment 170–174; ecologies of practices 163–164; lack of authenticity 180; partnerships 174–176; philosophical and operational 180; practice of teacher education 164–168; practice theory and architectures 162–163; quality conundrums within practice architecture 168–170; to site- and situation-specific judgements 180–181; spatial lens (*see* spatial contexts for transformation); teacher educators 177–179
Coombs, L. 67
Cordingley, P. 13
coronavirus pandemic *see* COVID-19 pandemic
Council for the Accreditation of Educator Preparation standards 125
COVID-19 pandemic 1; impact on universities 202, 210; online and distance learning 202; research on educators 203; scale and transformation 202–203; space, production and reproduction of 188, 201; teacher education 201–202
cultural-discursive (the sayings of a practice) 17, 23
curriculum: class-based formative assessment techniques 133; clinical practice 132; content-rich approach 133; curriculum-based faculty 131–132; importance of practice 132; leadership team 131; logistical concerns 172–173; practice-turn tradition 131; situational judgements 173; specialist at MLFTC 130; "taught" curriculum 130–131

Darling-Hammond, L. 40
deliberate practice 36–37; pedagogy 34, 50, 51, 54; practice quality conundrum 33–34; Teach First Leadership Development Programme 49, 50

diverse communities, teachers for: KGTECE and QUT programme 105, 106, 107; local and national accountability mechanisms 106; pedagogical approach 106; processes and procedures at QUT 105; programme accreditation 107

Early Career Framework 36
Early Years Initial Teacher Training (EYITT) 42
Education Complex 5
educators: academic and supervisory work 179; and adaptations 128–130; call-outs and call-backs 129; changing roles 178; clinical faculty 178; clone-teachers or "widgets" 129; continuum of educator roles **126**; horizontal and hierarchical boundaries 178; IOE and OISE 178; judgmentoring 128; lead teacher 128–129; members of leadership of programme 125–126; Next Education Workforce initiative 125; practicum experience 130; professional (school-based) community 178; roles and responsibilities 177; site lead, role of 130; teaming approach 126, 128; team member 129; workforce and teacher professionalism 127
Edwards-Groves, C. 180, 181
effective teacher education 35, 65
Ellis, V. 19, 32, 33, 34, 66, 118, 177
employment-based programmes 35
English teacher education system 38, 54
enquiring teacher 65
Eraut, M. 87
Exley, S. 54

faculty: clinical or academic 129; curriculum-based faculty 131–132; Masters of Teaching (MT) programme 76–77; "taught" curriculum 130; university 117–119
Faculty or Department of Education 8
Farley-Ripple, E. 65
Freidson, E. 62
"funds of knowledge" 90
Furlong, J. 7, 64, 67, 142, 209

Gaertner, H. 15
gig-economy 95, 188
Gladwell, M.: 2008 *Outliers* 33
Global Education Reform Movement (GERM) 7, 189
Goldhaber, D. 6

"good teacher" 13, 86
Gore, J. M. 102
governance quality conundrum: different interpretations of quality 155–158; growing accountability in ITE 140–141; local community involvement 147–149; pedagogical initiatives: Mahi Tahi days 151–152; role of normal schools 152–154; specific to New Zealand (*see* New Zealand); teacher education programme accreditation 147; university considerations 154–155; university pressures 141–144
Grace, G. 67
Griffith University 100
Grootenboer, P. 180, 181
Grossman, P. 7, 88, 190
Groundwater-Smith, S. 101

Hammerness, K. 16, 88
Harvey, D. 23, 183, 185, 201; categorisation 16, 22
higher education (HE): in modern world 142; partnership between schools and universities 142; policy technologies 140; standards, quality assurance and quality 139–140
Higher Education Institutions (HEIs) 97
high performing systems 63
high-quality teachers: primary PGCE 43; quality conundrums 4–5; QUT 102; in rural and remote communities 98; university-based teacher educators 211
Holme, R. 116
Hordern, J. 66; critique of British Educational Research Association's close-to-practice research 166–167
Human Rights and Equal Opportunity Commission 94

Ingvarson, L. 189
initial teacher education (ITE) 25, 37
Initial Teacher Training (ITT) 25, 36, 38
Institute of Education (IOE) *see* UCL Institute of Education (IOE)

Jones, J. 19, 32, 33, 34
judgmentoring 128

Karpyn, A. 65
Kelchtermans, G. 190
Kelvin Grove State College 97
Kelvin Grove Teacher Education Centre of Excellence (KGTECE) 97–98; Brisbane-based universities 100; complementary programme 98, 99, 100; mentoring 99; pedagogical features 99; in rural and remote communities 98; targeted feedback 99; teachers teaching teachers 98
Kemmis, S. 17, 23, 163, 164
Kennedy, A. 15, 51, 87
Kennedy, M. 170
Klette, K. 16
Knowledge Exchange Framework 144
knowledge quality conundrum 24; community knowledge 90; contextualized or ecological knowledge 90; core practices and culturally relevant pedagogies 88–92; cultural identity 92; diverse communities, preparing teachers for 105–107; equity and justice issues 89; "funds of knowledge" 90; good teaching and expectations 86; hierarchies and representation 86; inquiry-based approaches 89; knowledge and skills 87; Masters-level ITE programme 91; new teachers 95–96; for new teachers 87–88; parsing the practice of teaching 87; pedagogical practices 91–92; processing change 102–103; Queensland teacher recruitment problem 93–95; Queensland University of Technology (QUT) 92, 100–102; racism and inequalities, issues of 85; research-based and effective practices 89; rural and remote communities, teachers for 93–95, 97–100; social justice and equity 88; subject-based investigations 88; supervising "prac" 103–105; teacher education providers, issues 90–91; theory and practice 86, 88
Korthagen, F. 116
Koster, B. 116

Labaree, D. F. 6, 32, 61, 143
lead teachers *see* school-based mentors
Lefebvre, H. 23, 183, 184, 185
Lemov, D. 32; *Teach like a Champion* 32
Lim, L. 90
Ling, L. M. 7, 177
Linklater, H. 17
London: demand for teachers 40–41; "London factor" 41; Teach First for 40
Loughran, J. 16

Mahi Tahi days 151–152
Mary Lou Fulton Teachers College (MLFTC) 113, 125, 133–134

Masters of Teaching (MT) programme: Academic Program and Practice Teaching 70; construction of teacher identity 76; data collection 75; Educational Research, courses on 70–71; faculty teaching 76–77; form of apprenticeship 75; issues 73–74; job protection and instability 72–73; MT Research Conference 78; OISE 68, 69, 78; practitioner research 74; programme documentation 71; programme leadership 73–74; research driven process 70–71; staffing of the programme 72; teacher educator 74–75; "teaching stream" 72; vision of 76; website Graduate Research 69
material-economic (the doings) 17, 23
Mayer, D. 1, 189
May, H. 65
McDonald, M. 88
McDonough, K. 65
McDougall, D. 68
McNicholl, J. 118, 177
Meizrow, J. 12; ideas of transformational learning 12
Menter, I. 65, 87, 142, 174, 209
mentors, university-based 127
Mills, M. 191
Mitchell, J. 101
Mockler, N. 101
modelling ITE practice *204*; adaptive teacher education expertise 205; capacity to change 205; case for university-based ITE 208–210; doing ITE at scale 207–208; quality at scale 210–211; situated knowledge 204–205
modules 171
Moore, A. 13
Māori Education ("Ka Hikitia") 145
"move to online" learning 96
Muller, J. 61
Mullin, S.: *What they didn't teach me on my PGCE* 65
Multiple Academy Trusts 52
Murray, J. 86

NAMSA website 152
National Foundation for Educational Research (NFER) 40
neoliberal education policies 7
Netolicky, D. M. 12; conception of transformational professional learning 12
Next Education Workforce 125, 133–134
new Graduate Schools Education 7

Newman, J. H. 142
New Policy Management 143
New Zealand: bi-language expression 147; early years' curriculum *Te Whāriki* 149–150; educational tradition 149; establishment of self-managing schools 150; high-quality education 144; inclusion of Māori language 146–147; inquiry pedagogical model 150; ITE concerns 144–146; Masters of Teaching (MTchg) programme 145; Ministry of Education 145; Organisation for Economic Co-operation and Development (OECD) countries 145; pedagogical approach 149–151; practice for Māori and Pasifika students 146; quality and equity 151; Research Teaching for Equity (RITE) 145; teacher standards and code of responsibility 146–147; University of Auckland 145
Normal and Model Schools 153–154
Normal schools or teacher training colleges 141
Nuffield Foundation 40

Oancea, A. 67
occupational professionalisation 3
Olmedo, A. 63
Ontario: context of teacher education in 68–69; population profile 69; teacher supply shortage 68–69
Ontario Institute for Studies in Education (OISE) 20, 68, 187
Orchard, J. 67, 173
Organisation for Economic Co-operation and Development (OECD) 3; countries 145; "high-achievement, local equity" nation 13

parsing of practice 170
partnerships: accreditation process 147–149; aspects of arrangements 175; authentic 175; collaborative partnerships 174; development work 176; hierarchical partnership arrangement 174; with higher education institution 7; professionalism 134; between schools and universities 142; social-political arrangements 175–176; specialist 176; Teach First 20; transformational contexts 174–176; universities and 175; working or teaming 123
part-time staff 104
Pasifika Education Plan 145

Payne, K. A. 90
pedagogy: apprenticeship type pedagogical model 115; approach in New Zealand (*see* New Zealand); best practice 167; binaries and politics 35–37; cinematic 32; classroom behaviours 54; as collective social practice 164; content knowledge 46; culturally appropriate or culturally sensitive 89; culturally relevant 88–92; culturally responsive 89–90, 92, 105; deliberate practice 34, 50, 51, 54; Mahi Tahi days 151–152; Māori language 147; phase-specific 172; professional formation 47, 67–68; reflective practice 34, 66, 105; research as 63, 65, 67–68, 76–77; subject-specific 45–46, 172; teacher education 16–18, 24, 31, 33, 34, 43, 45, 60, 66, 86, 88, 101–102, 124, 127, 140, 161, 184, 186, 203; transformational 208
Perspectival data 15
Philip, T. M. 33
place: employment-place programme 168; of Māori culture and language in New Zealand society 150; practicum placements 94; prescriptive practices 33; professional settings 210; quality assurance processes and procedures 47; on schooling 5; school partnerships 107, 140; sites of practice 167; teacher education practice 5, 141, 147, 211; teaching and learning 17; year cohorts and specialisms 103
policy borrowing or policy lending 189
political economy of teacher education 208
Ponte, P. 101
Popkewitz, T. S. 33
PostGraduate Certificate of Education (PGCE) 37; 60 Masters credits 42; Masters-level programme 43; primary PGCE 41–44; Qualified Teacher Status 42; secondary PGCE 41–43, 44–47
practice: being classroom-ready 53, 54; best practices 167; categories 161–162; "close to practice" 167; communities of 162; definition 166; deliberate practice 33–34, 36–37, 49, 50, 51, 54; discursive and political dimensions 166; ecologies of 163–164; elements of 166; is political 53–54; range of stakeholders 163–164; of teacher education 164–168; teacher education ecosystem 164; theory and architectures 162–166, 168; theory of education *165*; value of 36

practice architectures 24, 162, 163, 165; high-quality programme 170; idea of research 168–169; practices of individual teacher educators 169; quality assurance measures 169; quality conundrums 168–170; research and alternative knowledges 169; role of student teachers' practical experience 168; time and space relationship 170
practice arrangements 24, 162, 163, 165; cultural-discursive arrangements 167; material-economic arrangements 167; social-political arrangements 167–168; of teacher education programme at QUT 169
practice quality conundrum 24; "cinematic pedagogies" 32; Core Practice Consortium 33; core practices 32; deliberate practice 33–34; demand for teachers in London 40–41; diverging approaches to teacher education 41–43; effective teacher behaviours 32; English context 38; note on insider research 37; pedagogical binaries and politics 35–37; pedagogy of teacher education 33; practical experiences 31; practice is political 53–54; practice turn 31–32; prescriptive practices 33; primary PGCE 43–44; professional training or apprenticeship 32; reflective practice 34; secondary PGCE 44–47; teachers' knowledge and understanding, importance of 32; Teach First 39–40; Teach First Leadership Development Programme 48–50; UCL Institute of Education 38–39
"practice turn" in teacher education 31
practicum (prac) 103–104
primary PGCE 41–42; assessment and expectations 43; Professional Studies 43; recruiting high-quality tutors 43; Reflective, Teaching and Learning cycle 43; Teaching and Learning 43; theory and practice 44
Pring, R. 7, 62
Professional Experience (PEx) 103
professionalisation narrative 3–4
professionalism: community-based teacher educators 134; issue of recruiting 134; Next Education Workforce initiative 133–134; notion of relative status 134; occupational professionalisation 3; partnership arrangement 134; peers and educational professionals 22, 190;

professional formation 47, 67–68; professional settings 210; professional training or apprenticeship 32; and quality discourses 133–135; reflective professional 45; site-based professional learning conversations 104–105; teacher professionalism 65, 79, 133; universities and teacher education 62, 63; workforce and teacher professionalism 127; work of teacher educators 134
Professional Learning Conversation 104
professional teacher, definition of 67
Professional Tutors 48
programmes and modules 26
Puustinen, M. 66

qualification: Australian Qualifications frameworks 101; graduate-level qualification 78; importing qualified teachers from Philippines 120; for individual teacher candidates 8; less-qualified teachers 185; metric of qualifications 14; post-qualification options 64; qualified mentors for STEM teachers 121; Qualified Teacher Status 38, 42, 197
Qualified Teacher Status 38
quality: AUT, marketing efforts of 156; context of governance regimes 157; data collection and analysis 22; definitions of **10**, 12, 23, 139; different interpretations of 155–158; "era of accountability" 13–14; global pandemic coronavirus in 2020, incidence of 20; high-quality teachers 4–5, 98, 156, 157; infrastructure, university-based 155–156; input measures 14–15; measures, categories of **14**; measures of quality 20, **21**; output measures 15; partners and stakeholders 157–158; perspectival data 15–16; practice theory and architectures 23; programme features or processes 16; research project 20; spatial theory 23–24; teacher or teaching, notion of 15; Teaching for Equity 157; university ranking systems 22
quality conundrums in ITE 18; accountability and governance 1–2; cause and effect relationship 11; core practices 12; critical-dialectic epistemology 12; description 19; educational context 4; "good teacher" 13; high-quality teachers 4–5; idea of transformation 12–13; inspections and regulations 1; locational factors 5; movement of capital 4; poor teacher education 161; professionalisation narrative 3–4; quality and standards, definitions of 10, **10–11**; quality assurance 9, 11, 12; research project, quality at scale 19–24; spatial importance of context 4–5; teacher training, notion of 2; transformation and pedagogy 16–18; university-based initial teacher education 2–3, 6–9
Queensland College of Teachers (QCT) accreditation system 100
Queensland College of Teachers Excellent Leadership in Teaching and Learning TEACHX Award 97
Queensland Professional experience framework 104
Queensland teacher recruitment problem: rural and remote communities 93–95; in urban centres 93
Queensland University of Technology (QUT) 92, 93–94; accreditation process 100–101; high-quality relationships 102; knowledge quality conundrum 105; Korthagen cycle of reflection 102–103; "move to online" 96; notion of praxis 101; online learning 101–102; policy advisory documents 95; QUT Real World 2020 Vision 101; reimagining process of teacher education provision 100–101; role of reflection and continuing research 102; teacher education at 100–102; theory and practice 101, 103

Rauschenberger, E. 15, 39, 51
recruiting high-quality tutors 43
reflective practice 34
reflective teacher 65
relative space 23; accountability measures 190–191; ASU 191; IOE 191; policy borrowing or policy lending 189; practice-orientated fields 190; ranking systems 190; status and prestige 190; Teach First 191; universities 189–192
representational space 185, 186; of being teacher 192; universities 192–193
research: "acceptable" research, definition of 36; Carter Review 64–65; certification and accreditation requirements 67; challenging assumptions 65; as content 63; curation of research 64; effective teacher 65; enquiring teacher 65; and field 77–78; form of academic

engagement 63–64; "guest lectures" 64; high performing systems 63; as pedagogy for professionals 63, 67–68; practical experience and teaching expertise 64; programme design 68; qualitative data methods 67; reflective teacher 65; teacher professionalism 65; theory and practice 67; transformative teacher 65
Research Excellence Framework (REF) 38, 142, 144
Research in Teaching for Equity 162
research quality conundrum 24; career-enhancing form of professional development 80; clinical practice 65–67; context of teacher education in Ontario 68–69; institute and university 79–80; MT programme 69–77; OISE 68, 78, 79; practice-orientated fields 80; resolving research quality conundrum 78–80; teacher professionalism 79; universities and teacher education 60–63; validity of research outputs 79
Richmond, G. 32
Robb, A. 116
Ronnerman, K. 101
rural and remote communities: KGTECE 97–100; preparing teachers for 97–100
Russell Group of universities 52

Sachs, J. 1, 7, 12, 67
Sahlberg, P. 13
Saito, E. 90
Salisbury, J. 67
Schatzki, T.R. 163; notion of "site-ontologies" 18
school-based mentors 127
school-led teacher education system 41–42, 61
"science of learning" 35–36
secondary PGCE 41–43; aspects of course 44–45; authentic partnership 47; concept of pedagogical content knowledge 46; context of London 47; provision of "thinking frameworks" 45; "reflective professional" 45; subject specialisms 45–47; trust and autonomy 47
second order 116
Shulman, L.: concept of pedagogical content knowledge 46
site-based professional learning conversations 104–105
site leads *see* university-based mentors
situational judgements 173
Sleeter, C. 12, 86, 89, 92, 177

Smith, A. 142
Smith, I. 174
Smith, K. 116
Smith, N. 194
social-political arrangements (the relatings) 17, 23
Souto-Manning, M. 89
space: actual, relative and representational space 186; COVID-19 pandemic 188; geographical/socio-economic factors 188; gig economy 188; influences on teacher education 186; lived and conceived space 186; location within 186, 187–189; partnership traditions 188–189; practice traditions 188–189; production of 184–186; relative (*see* relative space); representational (*see* representational space); and scale, relationship between 184; social, cultural and intellectual capital 185; spatial practice 185; teacher quality 185
spatial contexts for transformation: batching processes 195–196; importance of 183–184; leadership and management of partnership **197**; location matters 187–189; monitoring and oversight 196–198; quality at scale 193–198; relative space 189–192; representational space 192–193; spatial dimensions 184; spatial influences 193; specialisation 195; student grouping 194; teacher education and the production of space 184–186
standards 13–16; definitions of **10**; New Zealand teacher standards 146–147
Stringer Keefe, E. 35, 119
student grouping 194
"student teachers" 26
Studying Effectiveness in Teacher Education (SETE) 162
Syed, M.: 2010 *Bounce* 33

Tan, M. 90
Tatto, M.T. 32, 66, 114
Teacher Education Centre of Excellence (TECE) program 97
teacher educator quality conundrum 24; academic teacher educator 115; and adaptations 128–130; Arizona, teacher shortages in 119–120, 121; changing teacher education practices 127–128; changing teachers to educators 125–127; classrooms activities 114; close-to-practice experience and expertise 115; community-based teacher educators

116; experienced veteran classroom practitioner 115; as members of university faculty 117–119; MLFTC 121–123; next education workforce initiative 121–123; new teaming approach 114; opportunity to learn 114; partnership working or teaming 123; phase or subject specialism 116; practice turn or practicum turn 116; professionalism and quality discourses 133–135; roles and responsibilities of university- and school-based teacher educators 117; second order 116; student teacher (or teacher candidate) 114–115; supervision and teaching 115; teacher-directed activities 113–114; teacher education curriculum 130–133; teaming approach 123–125; in times of change 119; "unforgivingly complex" 161; workforce design problem 122; worksheet-based tasks 113

teacher professionalism 4; effective teacher 65, 87; enquiring teacher 65, 87; reflective teacher 65, 87; transformative teacher 65, 87

"teacher quality" 3

Teachers Colleges and Normal Schools 6

Teach First 5, 35; control scale 198; criticism 40; distinctive features of 40; educational disadvantage 51; English education policymaking 53; in-service or employment-based route into teaching 25–26; IOE 39; for London region 40; long-term career-orientated approach 51; origins of 39; Participant Development Lead (PDL) staff 198; partnership 20; policy on recruitment 52; positive reviews 40; practice-based orientation 53; practice conundrum 51–52; problem of teacher education 51; provision 38; relative space 52; "Tier One" towards "Regional" universities 52

Teach First Leadership Development Programme 48–50; challenges 48; Curriculum Designers 198; deliberate practice 49, 50; design, different approaches 50–51; goal of effectiveness 49; "horses for courses" argument 51; leadership and training 49–50; Participant Development Leads (PDLs) 48; PGDip (Post Graduate Diploma) 48; principles 33, 37; programme principles 48–49; Recruitment Centre(s) 48

Teach for All movement 7, 39–41, 190

Teach For All network 52, 63

Teach For America (TFA) 35; adaptation of TFA 40; criticism 40

"teaching stream" 72

Teach like a Champion (Lemov) 32

teaming approach: cultural discursive arrangements 124–125; educators 126, 128; in elementary and middle schools 123–124; responses to problems 124; school-based lead teachers 124; site leads 124; student teachers 124; wider vision of 124

technical or skill-based training 25

Tilley, K. 65

Times Higher Education ranking 68

Toom, A. 65

transformation: contexts for (*see* contexts for transformation); intellectual capital 18; learning and teaching, relationship between 17; movement of ideas 17; practice architecture 17; quality conundrums 18; site-ontologies, notion of 18; teacher education pedagogy 17–18

transformative teacher 65

Treaty of Waitangi, 1840 144–145

Turvey, K. 62

tutors, university-based 127

UCL Institute of Education (IOE) 19, 37; education establishment 53–54; England's largest teacher education provider 39; "outstanding" grades, 2014 38; PGCE programme 41; position of 51; Qualified Teacher Status 42; recruitment strategy for teacher educators 42; research power 38; School Direct Salaried programme 42; specialist expertise 51; Strategy for ITE 42; and Teach First 39, 41; vision of "IOE teacher" 42

UK Government's Department for Education (DfE) 38

university-based initial teacher education: accountability frameworks 9; Advice Paper 143; Carter Review, 2015 6; current trends affecting 6–9; "discourse of derision" 7; Education Endowment Foundation (EEF) 62; education provision 2–3, 6; educators' practices 24–25; Global Education Reform Movement 7; Hillage Report, 1998 6; Holmes Group report 6; idea of transformative learning 144; issues of teacher formation 143; neoliberal education policies 7; networks of social

enterprises 63; New Policy Management 143; new teachers and partners 143; Normal schools or teacher training colleges 141; partnerships with higher education institution 7; philosophy, psychology, history and sociology, disciplines of 61; policy interventions 7; practice turn in education 62–63; professional education or training 141; professionalisation 62, 63; provision for new teachers 60–61; recruitment practices 142; research-assessment exercises 62; socialisation and gatekeeping 62; status of teachers 61; supercomplexity 8; teacher standards and accreditation processes 8; theory-building or empirical research 61; university's reputation 192
university-based mentors 127
university-based programmes 35
university-based teacher education 202
University of Auckland 156
University of the Sunshine Coast 100
"university partners" 104

value-added metrics 15
Vanassche, E. 190

What they didn't teach me on my PGCE (Mullin) 65
White, S. 116, 135
Whitty, G. 3
Wieser, C. 66
Winch, C. 36, 67, 87, 173
Wubbels, T. 116

Yang, M. 178
Yuan, R. 178

Zeichner, K. M. 6, 88, 90

Taylor & Francis eBooks

www.taylorfrancis.com

A single destination for eBooks from Taylor & Francis with increased functionality and an improved user experience to meet the needs of our customers.

90,000+ eBooks of award-winning academic content in Humanities, Social Science, Science, Technology, Engineering, and Medical written by a global network of editors and authors.

TAYLOR & FRANCIS EBOOKS OFFERS:

- A streamlined experience for our library customers
- A single point of discovery for all of our eBook content
- Improved search and discovery of content at both book and chapter level

REQUEST A FREE TRIAL
support@taylorfrancis.com

Routledge
Taylor & Francis Group

CRC Press
Taylor & Francis Group